House and Home in Georgian Ireland

Spaces and cultures of domestic life

Conor Lucey

EDITOR

FOUR COURTS PRESS

Typeset in 10.5 pt on 13 pt EhrhardtPro by
Carrigboy Typesetting Services for
FOUR COURTS PRESS LTD
7 Malpas Street, Dublin 8, Ireland
www.fourcourtspress.ie
and in North America for
FOUR COURTS PRESS
c/o IPG, 814 N Franklin St, Chicago, IL 60610.

© The various authors and Four Courts Press 2022

A catalogue record for this title is available
from the British Library.

ISBN 978–1–80151–026–4

All rights reserved. Without limiting the rights under copyright reserved alone, no part of this publication may be reproduced, stored in or introduced into a retrieval system, or transmitted, in any form or by any means (electronic, mechanical, photocopying, recording or otherwise), without the prior written permission of both the copyright owner and publisher of this book.

SPECIAL ACKNOWLEDGMENT

This publication was made possible through the financial assistance provided by the Apollo Foundation and the Esmé Mitchell Trust, and a Publications Grant from the Paul Mellon Centre for Studies in British Art.

PAUL MELLON CENTRE
for Studies in British Art

Printed in Spain by Castuera.

For my friend and guru,
Christine Casey

Contents

	LIST OF ILLUSTRATIONS	8
	LIST OF ABBREVIATIONS	11
	NOTES ON CONTRIBUTORS	12
	ACKNOWLEDGMENTS	14
	INTRODUCTION: species of domestic spaces *Conor Lucey*	15
1	Brought to bed: the spaces and material culture of the lying-in *Emma O'Toole*	29
2	A male domain? The dining room reconsidered *Patricia McCarthy*	49
3	Fashioning, fitting-out and functionality in the aristocratic town house: private convenience and public concerns *Melanie Hayes*	65
4	The merchant house in eighteenth-century Drogheda *Aisling Durkan*	85
5	'Baubles for boudoirs' or 'an article of such universal consumption': ceramics in the Irish home, 1730–1840 *Toby Barnard*	104
6	Communality and privacy in one- or two-roomed homes before 1830 *Claudia Kinmonth*	125
7	Entertaining royalty after the Union: space, decoration and performance in Charleville Castle, Co. Offaly, 1809 *Judith Hill*	145
8	'A taste for building': domestic space in elite female correspondence *Priscilla Sonnier*	166
9	Single lives, single houses *Conor Lucey*	185
	INDEX	207

Illustrations

Introduction
I.1 21 Merrion Street Upper, Dublin, 1756. 17
I.2 George Mullins, *John, Mary Anne and Francis Wyse*, c.1786. 24
I.3 Sir Edward Lovett Pearce, section of unidentified house, c.1730. 25

Emma O'Toole
1.1 I. Cruikshank, *A male midwife*, 1793. 30
1.2 Anon., A mother in bed after giving birth, c.1800. 36
1.3 Folding adjustable birthing chair, eighteenth–nineteenth century. 37
1.4 Marguerite Gérard, *The nourishing mother*, 1804. 42
1.5 Furniture bill listing a mahogany nurse's chair, 1805. 43
1.6 Female bedgown in silk and taffeta, c.1740 to c.1760. 45
1.7 Caudle cup, cover and stand, Derby porcelain factory, c.1785. 47

Patricia McCarthy
2.1 Robert Adam, eating parlour at Headfort House, Co. Meath, 1771. 51
2.2 *Aesop* ceiling, Phoenix Lodge, Phoenix Park, Dublin, 1754. 52
2.3 Chinese export porcelain plate with arms of the Roche family, c.1750. 54
2.4 Silver épergne by Thomas Pitts, London, 1761. 56
2.5 George Wickes, the Leinster dining service, marked for 1745–56. 57
2.6 Benjamin Pyne, monteith bowl, silver-gilt, 1715–16. 58
2.7 Wine bottle stamped 'AL' and '1688'. 59
2.8 Claret or drinking table attributed to Gillows of Lancaster and London. 62
2.9 *L'après-dinée des Anglais*, France, 1814. 63

Melanie Hayes
3.1 Façade of 10 Henrietta Street, Dublin. 66
3.2 10 Henrietta Street, Dublin, conjectural reconstruction of facade, c.1730. 66
3.3 Former entrance hall ceiling, 10 Henrietta Street, Dublin. 67
3.4 Upper stair hall, 10 Henrietta Street, Dublin. 68
3.5 John Brooks after Charles Jervas, *Luke Gardiner, M.P. (d.1755)*. 71
3.6 'List of goods at Henrietta Street house'; inventory taken in 1772. 73
3.7 Luke Gardiner, Dublin, to Nathaniel Clements, London, 19 March 1744/45. 77
3.8 10 Henrietta Street, Dublin, reconstructed floor plan. 79
3.9 Breakfast Parlour at 10 Henrietta Street, Dublin. 80
3.10 'Mountjoy House', *Dublin Penny Journal*, 13 February 1836. 82

Aisling Durkan

4.1	Gabriele Ricciardelli, *View of Drogheda from Ball's Grove*, c.1755.	86-7
4.2	Ground-floor plans of two Dutch Billy gable houses.	88
4.3	Façade of 21 and 22 Fair Street, Drogheda.	89
4.4	Ground-floor plans of 21 and 22 Fair Street, Drogheda.	92
4.5	Façade of 33 St Laurence Street, Drogheda.	93
4.6	Ground-floor plan of 33 St Laurence Street, Drogheda.	93
4.7	Façade of 15 and 16 Fair Street, Drogheda.	95
4.8	Ground-floor plans of 15 and 16 Fair Street, Drogheda.	95
4.9	Façade of 17 Fair Street, Drogheda.	99
4.10	Ground-floor plan of 17 Fair Street, Drogheda.	99

Toby Barnard

5.1	Irish delft small platter, chinoiserie, mid-eighteenth century.	111
5.2	Irish delft small platter, chrysanthemum, mid-eighteenth century.	111
5.3	Rouen faience wall-fountain, mid-eighteenth century.	113
5.4	Higginbotham invoice for utilitarian wares, 13 May 1843.	115
5.5	Irish delft shaped sweetmeat or pickle dishes, mid-eighteenth century.	117
5.6	Mason's ironstone shaped dish for Monaghan grand jury, c.1835.	118
5.7	Minton, Staffordshire dish, marked for 'Donovan', c.1800.	121
5.8	Staffodshire platter with view of General Post Office, Dublin, c.1830.	122
5.9	Trade card for Higginbotham, Dublin, c.1810.	123

Claudia Kinmonth

6.1	'Bed & Floor Matts' from *The cries of Dublin*, 1760.	127
6.2	'Sleeping in stradogue' from James Connery, *The reformer*, c.1830.	130
6.3	'An Irish Cabbin' from Arthur Young, *A tour in Ireland* (1780).	131
6.4	Charlotte Edgeworth, sketch of communal potato dinner, c.1806.	136
6.5	Charlotte Edgeworth, 'Peggy Tuite and Her Family', c.1806.	137
6.6	Charlotte Edgeworth, 'Old Mrs Tuite', 'Old W. Tuite', c.1806.	138
6.7	Charlotte Edgeworth, sketch of communal meal, c.1806.	139
6.8	Bronze Age platter or table/tray.	141
6.9	Communal eating platter.	143

Judith Hill

7.1	Charleville Castle, Co. Offaly, from the northwest.	146
7.2	Charleville Castle, Co. Offaly, plan of principal floor.	151
7.3	Lady Beaujolois Bury, dining room at Charleville Castle, c.1843.	152
7.4	C.M. Bury, entrance hall and gallery, Charleville Castle, 1801–4.	153
7.5	Grand staircase, Windsor Castle, by James Wyatt, 1800–4.	154
7.6	Photograph of Charleville Castle, Co. Offaly, 5 June 1873.	155
7.7	Stair from outside the gallery, Charleville Castle (after 1809).	156

7.8	Charleville Castle from the Ordnance Survey, 1838–40.	162
7.9	Lady Beaujolois Bury, Charleville Castle from the southeast, 1848.	163

Priscilla Sonnier

8.1	Donadea Castle, Co. Kildare, 1900.	167
8.2	Castle Caldwell, Co. Fermanagh, *c.*1865–1914.	168
8.3	Donadea Castle, Co. Kildare, 1958.	168
8.4	Donadea Castle, Co. Kildare, 2020.	170
8.5	Cantilevered staircase, Florence Court, Co. Fermanagh, *c.*1760–70.	172
8.6	Lady Elizabeth Aylmer to Lady Elizabeth Caldwell, 5 May 1773.	173
8.7	Strickland Lowry, *Interior with members of a family*, 1770s.	176
8.8	George or Hill Darley, design for a chimneypiece, *c.*1770.	179
8.9	Lady Arbella Denny to Lady Elizabeth Caldwell, 28 March 1770.	183

Conor Lucey

9.1	George Hepplewhite, designs for shaving tables, 1794.	187
9.2	Carington Bowles, 'Frederick elegantly furnishing a large house', 1787.	190
9.3	Carington Bowles, 'Charles at breakfast in a genteel private family', 1787.	191
9.4	Anon., 'A pair of exquisites regaling', *c.*1818.	193
9.5	12 Gardiner Place, Dublin, 1790–2.	197
9.6	Ground- and first-floor plans of 12 Gardiner Place, built 1790–2.	199
9.7	Ordnance Survey, City of Dublin, sheet 8 (detail), 1847.	200
9.8	Advertisement for 1 Harcourt Street, 1789.	202
9.9	1 Fitzwilliam Street Upper and 11 Fitzwilliam Street Lower, Dublin.	203
9.10	Mountpleasant Square, Dublin, *c.*1808–10.	204

Abbreviations

BL	British Library
FHL	Friends Historical Library Dublin
GSR	*The Georgian Society records of eighteenth century domestic architecture and decoration in Dublin*, 4 vols (Dublin, 1909–12; reprint Shannon, 1969)
IAA	Irish Architectural Archive
IADS	*Irish Architectural and Decorative Studies*
IAM	Irish Agricultural Museum
NAI	National Archives of Ireland
NLI	National Library of Ireland
NLW	National Library of Wales
NMI	National Museum, Ireland
NMNI	National Museums, Northern Ireland
OED	*Oxford English dictionary*
PRIA	*Proceedings of the Royal Irish Academy*
PRONI	Public Record Office of Northern Ireland
RD	Registry of Deeds, Dublin
TCD	Trinity College, Dublin
UCD	University College Dublin
VAM	Victoria & Albert Museum
WCL	Westmeath County Library and Archives

Contributors

TOBY BARNARD has been a Fellow of Hertford College, Oxford, since 1976 (emeritus from 2012). His first book, *Cromwellian Ireland*, appeared in 1976, and has been followed by, among others, *A new anatomy of Ireland* (London, 2003), *Making the grand figure: lives and possessions in Ireland, 1641–1770* (London, 2004), *Irish Protestant ascents and descents* (Dublin, 2004), *Guide to the sources for the history of material culture in Ireland, 1500–2000* (Dublin, 2005), *Improving Ireland? Projectors, prophets and profiteers, 1641–1786* (Dublin, 2008) and *Brought to book: print in Ireland, 1680–1784* (Dublin, 2017).

AISLING DURKAN is a recent PhD graduate of the Department of the History of Art and Architecture in Trinity College, Dublin. Her thesis, entitled 'Regional splendour and mercantile ambition: the Drogheda town house in the eighteenth century', focused on the predominantly mercantile domestic architecture of Drogheda, placing it in the wider context of eighteenth-century Ireland and Britain. Forthcoming publications include an essay on this topic in *Louth: history and society – interdisciplinary essays on the history of an Irish county* (2022).

MELANIE HAYES is an architectural historian, specializing in Ireland's eighteenth-century architectural and social history. Her recent book, *The best address in town: Henrietta Street, Dublin and its first residents, 1720–1780* (Dublin, 2020), explores the rich architectural and social history of Dublin's first great Georgian street, during its first sixty years of existence. She is currently a post-doctoral Research Fellow on an Irish Research Council advanced laureate project, CRAFTVALUE, at Trinity College, Dublin, exploring a new skills-based perspective on the architecture of Britain and Ireland, 1680–1780.

JUDITH HILL is a Visiting Research Fellow at Trinity College, Dublin. An architectural historian and author, her publications include: *Irish public sculpture: a history* (1998); *Lady Gregory: an Irish life* (2005); 'Architecture in the aftermath of Union: building the Viceregal Chapel in Dublin Castle, 1801–1815', *Architectural History*, 60 (2017); and 'Catherine Maria Bury of Charleville Castle, Co. Offaly, and the design of the country house, 1800–1812' in T. Dooley, M. O'Riordan & C. Ridgway (eds), *Women and the country house in Ireland and Britain* (2018). She is currently writing a book on Gothic revival architecture, investigating its use as a vehicle to assert political and social status in post-Union Ireland.

CLAUDIA KINMONTH is an art and furniture historian and author of *Irish rural interiors in art* (New Haven & London, 2006), and *Irish country furniture and furnishings 1700–2000*

(Cork, 2020). In London she worked at the Victoria and Albert Museum, before moving to County Cork. She was the recipient of the 2018 Royal Dublin Society's Library and Archives Bursary. She is Visiting Research Fellow at the Moore Institute, National University of Ireland Galway and also Research Curator (Domestic Life) at the Ulster Folk Museum. In 2018 she was elected as a member of the Royal Irish Academy.

CONOR LUCEY is Associate Professor of architectural history in the School of Art History and Cultural Policy at University College Dublin. His recent book, *Building reputations: architecture and the artisan, 1750–1830* (Manchester, 2018), was awarded the prestigious Alice Davis Hitchcock medallion of the Society of Architectural Historians of Great Britain. Forthcoming publications include an investigation into the roles of women in the eighteenth-century construction industry, and a thematic essay on design as a profession and a trade in Enlightenment Europe for the pioneering *Cultural Histories* series published by Bloomsbury Academic.

PATRICIA McCARTHY is an architectural historian and author of *Life in the country house in Georgian Ireland* (2016) published by Yale University Press, and *'A favourite study': building the King's Inns* (2006). She has published widely on eighteenth- and early nineteenth-century Irish architecture in a number of books and in publications such as the *Irish Arts Review*, *Country Life* and *Irish Architectural and Decorative Studies*, and has contributed to two volumes of the Royal Irish Academy's *Art and Architecture of Ireland* (2014). Her new book, *Enjoying claret in Georgian Ireland: a history of amiable excess* (2022), looks at the vast quantities of wine consumed by the well heeled in Georgian Ireland.

EMMA O'TOOLE obtained her PhD in 2018 from the National College of Art & Design. Her thesis, entitled 'Objects, spaces and rituals: a social and material history of maternity and infancy in Ireland, *c.*1730 to *c.*1830', focused on the retailing, consumption and use of maternity and infant goods from the perspectives of retailers and families living in Ireland. She currently works as the Collections and Interpretation Manager at the Irish Heritage Trust, where she is responsible for the care, conservation and interpretation of the collections held at Fota House & Gardens, Strokestown Park & the National Famine Museum, Johnstown Castle, and the Irish Agricultural Museum.

PRISCILLA SONNIER is a PhD candidate in the School of Art History and Cultural Policy at UCD. Her thesis, entitled 'Celebrated beauties: dialogues, duty and display in Georgian Ireland, 1730–1790', focuses on the evolution of elite female portraiture in Ireland throughout the eighteenth century. She has presented her research at conferences and symposia hosted by the Paul Mellon Centre for Studies in British Art, the Historians of Eighteenth Century Art and Architecture, the Eighteenth Century Irish Society, Penn State University, and the American University. She was the 2020 recipient of the Desmond Guinness Scholarship awarded by the Irish Georgian Society.

Acknowledgments

The conceptual framework for this book emerged from ideas that were trialled and developed over many years in undergraduate and postgraduate programmes in the School of Art History at University College Dublin and the Faculty of Visual Culture at the National College of Art and Design. The present collection of essays originated in an online conference entitled 'Species of domestic spaces: house and home in eighteenth-century Ireland', convened at the Humanities Institute, UCD, in June 2021. I am grateful to Professor Anne Fuchs for providing this platform for the event, and to Valerie Norton for administration and technical support. Sarah Foster and Rachel Wilson presented papers on the day not included in the present volume: I wish to thank them for their valued participation in the conference.

I gratefully acknowledge the financial support provided by the Apollo Foundation and the Esmé Mitchell Trust in underwriting the production costs of the present volume, with additional thanks to Donough Cahill and the Irish Georgian Society for assistance with grant administration. The costs associated with image rights and reproduction was supported by a Publications Grant from the Paul Mellon Centre for Studies in British Art.

This project would not have been possible without the individual contributors. I am grateful to them for their commitment and collegiality, which has served to underline the value of working in collaboration. Martin Fanning and the team at Four Courts Press have been exemplary in seeing the book through all the stages of its production.

On a personal level, the contribution, assistance and advice of the following individuals is greatly appreciated: Toby Barnard, Carla Briggs, Christine Casey, Alison FitzGerald, Aideen Ireland, William Laffan, Anna Moran, Robert O'Byrne, Finola O'Kane Crimmins, Priscilla Sonnier, and the staff of the Irish Architectural Archive.

Introduction: species of domestic spaces

CONOR LUCEY

A house that has been experienced is not an inert box. Inhabited space transcends geometrical space.[1]

In a series of letters written over the course of four years, between 1752 and 1756, William Fitzwilliam, younger brother of Richard, 6th Viscount Fitzwilliam, set forth his attempt to secure a suitable family home in Dublin. Acting as overseer for development of the extensive family estate on behalf of his absentee brother (then habitually based at St James's, London), William's regular dispatches to Richard reveal much about his personal desires and concerns, as well as the wider conditions and perils associated with the acquisition of a town house.

The correspondence begins in November 1752, when William had 'at last' acquired a new house in Suffolk Street. As a contemporary description of urban domestic accommodation in a respectable part of the city it merits quoting in its entirety:

> It is not over Large but has greater conveniences than any I have yet seen. There is under Ground a Good fore Kitchen with Stoves & a Scullery adjoining supply'd with Water three Days in the Week, a Good back Kitchen with boilers fix'd & other necessarys. A good Larder, a Wine Cellar, a Small Beer Cellar, & Vaults for I believe 50 or Sixty Tons of Coal. The Ground Floor has a fore Parlour & Back Parlour with a large Saloon, & on the Side of the Staircase, a large Closet with a Sash Window to it, which range of Closets run up three Stories high. Two good Garrets to it, In one of which is a Chimney. My Rent ready furnished Seventy Pounds pr. Annum neither subject to Repairs or Taxes. I have [taken it?] for three years certain; for twenty years afterwards; a Power to Quit on giving Six Months Notice so that if any thing bad in the house, God be thanked I am not married.[2]

By November 1754, after two years' tenancy, the limitations of this particular house were clear and a new build in the same street had attracted his attention:

---

1 G. Bachelard, *The poetics of space* ([1958] New York, 1964), p. 67. 2 NAI, Pembroke Estate papers, 97/46/1/2/7/1, William Fitzwilliam, Dublin to his brother the Rt Hon. Viscount Fitzwilliam, Jermyn Street, St James, 9 July 1752. I am grateful to Aideen Ireland for her professional advice on this collection.

> I have some thoughts of getting another house when my Time in this is out. It is too old & crazy to venture continuing in it … The place I have in my Eye, is a new house Two Door above where I now live. My wife has look'd at it & likes it … if we can agree about the Price, we shall move about Midsummer next.[3]

This particular property was evidently unavailable at the required time and some weeks later Fitzwilliam had resorted instead to take 'a New built House' in 'a Vile Street, (Frederick Street) but my Circumstances will not allow me to [be] over nice'. With a lease agreed for the following March, he described himself as being 'fully employed in getting & preparing Furniture of all sorts for it, which will employ Madams fingers & thoughts, & Sweat my Purse into an absolute Consumption'.[4] This deal, however, ultimately fell through: the deed was bound up with multiple mortgages on the property and no 'clear title' could be adduced. Forlorn, Fitzwilliam found himself 'on the Pavement agen, & nothing is so hard to get as a house. I am really in great distress, & don't know how to help myself'.[5] All was not lost. In October 1755, William had his sights on the present 21 Merrion Street Upper on the Fitzwilliam Estate – which he reckoned 'as Good a [house] as any in Dublin'[6] – and hoped 'to be favour'd in the Ground Rent', not least for his role in helping his brother to realize 'a Neighbourhood to promote your Designs' (fig. I.1).[7] Although troubled by the high cost (£1,200) demanded by the builder, William acquiesced and purchased the as yet unfinished house in April 1756.[8] By the following September, plans were afoot to finally quit Suffolk Street:

> I shall at that time, Remove my Goods & Servants, & go to Gormanstown for a Month or So, during which Time, They may be burning fires in all the Rooms, & leave Us no fear of going to a Damp House, Especially since for these three months past, I have had Braiseurs with Charcoal burning constantly in all the Rooms.[9]

The accommodation and situation evidently satisfied on all fronts: the house in Merrion Street remained the family address until 1764, when it was sold in anticipation of their relocation to England.[10]

Aside from the vivid (and familiar) account of the priorities and anxieties predicated on choosing a home, what immediately strikes the modern reader is the clear delineation of Fitzwilliam's expectations: at the outset, his description of the

---

3 Pembroke papers, 97/46/1/2/7/42 (26 Nov. 1754). **4** Pembroke papers, 97/46/1/2/7/43 (19 Dec. 1754). **5** Pembroke papers, 97/46/1/2/7/44 (11 Jan. 1755). **6** Pembroke papers, 97/46/1/2/7/71 (29 Jan. 1756). **7** Pembroke papers, 97/46/1/2/7/73 (24 Feb. 1756). **8** Pembroke papers, 97/46/1/2/7/77 (13 Apr. 1756). **9** Pembroke papers, 97/46/1/2/7/87 (7 Sept. 1756). **10** This was one of two houses (now 21 and 22 Merrion Street Upper) built in 1755–6 by Murtagh Lacy, a bricklayer and builder, and adjoining a lot originally leased to a Mr Johnson, bricklayer, who went bankrupt; that ground (together with a new house) was surrendered to Bryan Fagan (agent to Richard, 6th Viscount Fitzwilliam) in 1756, and subsequently leased by Lord Fitzwilliam to Charles Monck (RD, 182/595/123197). Monck acquired the house next door to William Fitzwilliam (number 22) for his own

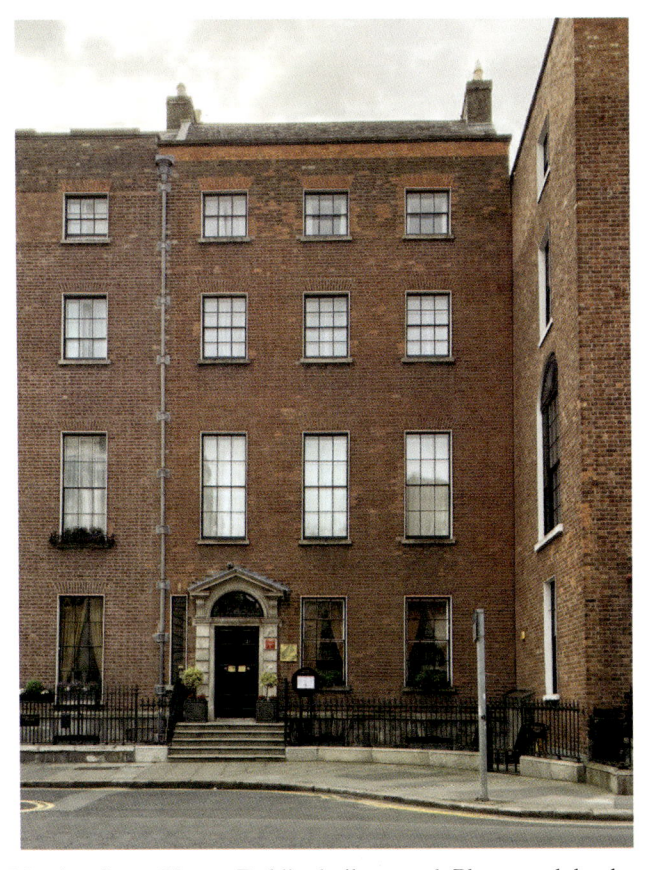

I.1 21 Merrion Street Upper, Dublin, built 1755–6. Photograph by the author.

Suffolk Street premises emphasizes domestic functions and services (boilers, cellars, water supply and goods storage), followed by polite rooms of both public and private character (in the form of parlours and closets), and concluding with the agreeableness of the accommodation in the property's uppermost spaces (the garret heated by a chimney). Everyday convenience and comfort clearly trumped social performativity in the selection of this Georgian dwelling. Later, in advance of moving to the newly built house in Merrion Street Upper, he made provision to have the individual rooms fully dried to avoid dampness (presumably with the related threat of respiratory and rheumatic diseases in mind). In concert with the practicality and prestige of the property's location, Fitzwilliam's descriptive correspondence unambiguously manifests the broader social and cultural concern for physical comfort and personal wellbeing in the selection of a home in eighteenth-century Ireland.

dwelling and enlarged it by 21 feet frontage to the street; he also began another house of similar proportions, the present number 23 (also built by Lacy), which was intended for sale or lease. William Fitzwilliam disposed of 21 Merrion Street in 1764, including 'several Marble Chimney Pieces Locks, Grates Goods and Utensils', to Charles Jackson, Bishop of Ferns and Leighlin (RD, 222/481/150224).

'WHAT DOES IT MEAN TO LIVE IN A ROOM?'[11]

This book presents an Irish analogue to an innovative and burgeoning scholarship on eighteenth-century British, European and American domestic life,[12] including Amanda Vickery's consideration of the 'role of house and home in power and emotion, status and choices',[13] Karen Lipsedge's pioneering research on the complex intersection between lived domestic spaces and their fictional counterparts,[14] and extending to the many edited volumes, from *Architectural space in eighteenth-century Europe: constructing identities and interiors* (2010) to *Daily lives and routines in the long eighteenth-century* (2022), that examine different aspects of identity, performance and representation.[15] Histories of furniture and furnishings too have shifted from questions of style, comfort and visual signification to social performativity and the construction of meaning through usage,[16] as well as the role of colonial hardwoods and imported luxury goods in the 'cultural display of empire'.[17] The present volume takes a further cue from Bernard L. Herman's *Town house: architecture and material life in the early American city, 1780–1830* (2005) which, aside from its exemplary interdisciplinary approach, uniquely broadens the range of social classes under consideration, with discrete chapters devoted to a range of urban accommodation from a merchant's family house and widow's dower to a shipwright's lodgings and an enslaved servant's quarters. In Herman's account of American domesticity, each dwelling represents a frame for a series of richly textured interiorized narratives.[18]

The title of this introduction is 'borrowed' from *Species of spaces* by French novelist and essayist George Perec, first published in 1974, while the shared focus on *lived* space in the chapters that follow was inspired by a specific episode in that same book entitled 'The apartment'. Here, Perec imagined a typical modern apartment in Paris and the various ways in which its rooms were inhabited (and everyday rituals were performed) over the course of a working day: at different times the protagonists of the family (mother, father, child) occupy rooms singly and collectively (respectively

---

11 G. Perec, *Species of spaces and other pieces* ([1974] London, 1997), p. 24.   12 For an overview of the topics and themes that have dominated the literature, coupled with a problematizing of the use of the term 'Georgian' in academic discourse, see H. Greig & G. Riello, 'Eighteenth-century interiors – redesigning the Georgian: introduction', *Journal of Design History*, 20:4 (2007), 273–89.   13 A. Vickery, *Behind closed doors: at home in Georgian England* (London, 2009), p. 3.   14 K. Lipsedge, *Domestic space in eighteenth-century British novels* (London, 2012). See also P. Tristram, *Living space in fact and fiction* (London, 1989); C. Wall, 'A geography of Georgian narrative space' in M. Ogborn & C. Withers (eds), *Georgian geographies: essays on space, place and landscape in the eighteenth century* (Manchester, 2004), pp 114–30.   15 D.A. Baxter & M. Martin (eds), *Architectural space in eighteenth-century Europe: constructing identities and interiors* (Burlington, VT, 2010); G. Andersson & J. Stobart (eds), *Daily lives and daily routines in the long eighteenth century* (London, 2022); J. Styles & A. Vickery (eds), *Gender, taste, and material culture in Britain and North America, 1700–1830* (New Haven, 2006).   16 M. Hellmann, 'Furniture, sociability, and the work of leisure in eighteenth-century France', *Eighteenth Century Studies*, 32:4 (1999), 415–45.   17 S. Barczewski, *Country houses and the British Empire, 1700–1930* (Manchester, 2014); M. Finn & K. Smith (eds), *The East India Company at home, 1757–1857: the British country house in an imperial and global context* (London, 2018); M. Dobie, 'Orientalism, colonialism, and furniture in eighteenth-century France' in D. Goodman & K. Norberg (eds), *Furnishing the eighteenth century: what furniture can tell us about the European and American past* (London, 2007), pp 13–36.   18 B. Herman, *Town house: architecture and material life in the early American city, 1780–1830* (Chapel Hill, NC, 2005).

bathroom and bedrooms, sitting room and dining room). Essentially a literary meditation on the mundane, the analysis of room use within this fictional apartment ('though I'm convinced of its rightness') deliberates on the adaptable functions of, and relationships between, discrete spaces in an effort to counter what he considered to be the 'very precise ideas' about the design of houses routinely imposed on potential homeowners (and tenants) by architects, builders and urban planners.[19] Prompted by Perec's short, idiosyncratic text, the purpose of this book is to explore the different uses and qualities of domestic spaces in Georgian Ireland. Indeed, while the design and decoration of the country pile and its urban equivalent are the subjects of a distinguished and growing historiography, to date there has been no sustained examination of how rooms were habitually occupied and experienced – reflecting real as opposed to ideal patterns of living – or how the needs of different social classes might have informed real estate markets.[20] Notable contributions to the spatial and cultural histories of house and home in Ireland in the long eighteenth century include essays and monographs on the design and fitting out of state apartments and ducal households,[21] the material cultures of the patrician, bourgeois and mercantile classes,[22] and the living conditions of labourers and cottiers;[23] a special issue of the *Proceedings of the Royal Irish Academy* (2011), dedicated to the theme of 'Domestic life in Ireland', addressed topics as various as room usage in formal and vernacular contexts, and the refurbishment and redecoration of interiors to reflect modern tastes and sensibilities.[24] This is complemented by a more focused if dispersed literature on the material culture of fine dining,[25] on music and dancing in elite homes,[26] and the

---

19 Perec, *Species of spaces*, p. 28. **20** Recent titles include: P. McCarthy, *Life in the country house in Georgian Ireland* (London, 2016); C. Casey (ed.), *The eighteenth-century Dublin town house* (Dublin, 2010); C. Casey, *Making magnificence: architects, stuccatori and the eighteenth-century interior* (London, 2017); M. Hayes, *The best address in town: Henrietta Street, Dublin and its first residents, 1720–80* (Dublin, 2020). **21** J. Fenlon, 'The Ormonde inventories 1675–1717: a state apartment at Kilkenny Castle' in A. Bernelle (ed.), *Decantations* (Dublin, 1992), pp 29–37; F. O'Dwyer, 'Dublin Castle and its state apartments, 1660–1922', *The Court Historian*, 2:1 (1997), 2–8; R. Wilson, 'The vicereines of Ireland and the transformation of the Dublin court, c.1703–1737', *The Court Historian*, 19:1 (2014), 3–28. **22** T. Barnard, *Making the grand figure: lives and possessions in Ireland, 1641–1770* (London, 2004); J. Fenlon, *Goods & chattels: a survey of early household inventories in Ireland* (Kilkenny, 2003); Knight of Glin & J. Peill, *Irish furniture* (London, 2007); A. FitzGerald, *Silver in Georgian Dublin: making, selling, consuming* (Abingdon, 2017); A. Moran, 'Merchants and material culture in early nineteenth-century Dublin: a consumer case study', *IADS*, 11 (2008), 140–65. **23** C. Kinmonth, *Irish country furniture and furnishings, 1700–2000* (Cork, 2020). **24** This volume considered 'the time-line of human experience in Ireland', ranging from Neolithic settlements to house extensions in the Celtic Tiger era. For the period under review: J. Fenlon, 'Moving towards the formal house: room usage in early modern Ireland'; C. Lucey, 'Keeping up appearances: redecorating the domestic interior in late eighteenth-century Dublin'; and B. O'Reilly, 'Hearth and home: the vernacular house in Ireland from c.1800', *PRIA*, 111C (2010), 141–68, 169–92, 193–215. **25** A. FitzGerald, 'Taste in high life: dining in the Dublin town house' in Casey (ed.), *The eighteenth-century Dublin town house*, pp 120–7; A. Moran, '"The eye as well as the appetite must be car'd for": glass and dining in Ireland about 1680–about 1830' in C.L. Maxwell (ed.), *In sparkling company: reflections on glass in the 18th-century British world* (New York, 2020), pp 195–229. On the broader issue of food and drink consumption in the period, see M. Shanahan, '"Whipt with a twig rod": Irish manuscript recipe books as sources for the study of culinary material culture, c.1660 to 1830', *PRIA*, 115C (2015), 197–218; D. Cashman, 'Sugar bakers and confectioners in Georgian Ireland', *The Canadian Journal of Irish Studies*, 41 (2018), 74–99. **26** K. Mullaney-Dignam, *Music and dancing at Castletown, County Kildare, 1759–1821* (Dublin, 2011); idem,

domestic situations of women at different ends of the social spectrum, from the widowed gentlewoman to the impoverished spinster.[27]

Forged principally in the disciplines of architectural and design history, the essays collected here also (and invariably) complement a broader scholarship on *home*, encompassing anthropology and auto-ethnography, cultural geography and literary memoir.[28] Unsurprisingly, eighteenth-century authors rehearsed similar preoccupations with sensibility and an emotional attachment to place. Conceived during a period of house arrest, Xavier de Maistre's *Voyage around my room* (1794) is a highly original meditation on the evocative and imaginative play engendered by prolonged (or in this case enforced) reflection on one's personal surroundings; from the 'sweet warmth' of his pink and white bed ('two colours given to pleasure and happiness') to the myriad associations and memories aroused by the collection of paintings and prints that line 'the road that remains to be travelled before we reach my writing desk'.[29] In a similar (albeit fictional) manner, Fanny Price, the heroine of Jane Austen's *Mansfield Park* (1814), routinely retreats to the former school room of the eponymous house, where 'she could scarcely see an object ... which had not an interesting remembrance connected with it'.[30] This kind of suggestive textual representation anticipates what cultural anthropologists refer to as 'thick description', a form of expository writing that represents 'more than a record of what a person is doing', being concerned with evoking 'emotionality and self-feelings'.[31] Aligned in recent scholarship to 'the period's descriptive impulse',[32] it further accords with what historians of early modern domesticity have identified as the growing awareness of 'the connections between spaces, objects and human activity: the mutually constitutive relationship between people and their houses'.[33]

Acknowledging that decorum moderated the quest for comfort in contemporary architectural theory, the use of 'house' and 'home' in the book's title has been chosen to reflect the perspectives of both house builders and homeowners.[34] Just as 'home' emerged in eighteenth-century discourse to reflect a new culture of domesticity – shaped by the demand for privacy and intimacy – so the proliferation of tall brick houses in regularized streets and squares posit speculative building as 'the critical

---

'"Spacious and splendid: music, dancing and social life at Glin Castle, 1781–1854', *IADS*, 14 (2011), 16–37. **27** V. Moffat, '"A map of her jurisdiction", the account books of Meliora Adlercron of Dawson Street, Dublin, 1782–94', *IADS*, 15 (2012), 128–49; J. McElligott, 'The ragged-gowned philanthropist: Miss Lamotte's post-mortem auction, 1769', *Eighteenth-Century Ireland*, 36:1 (2021), 79–92. **28** For example: I. Cieraad (ed.), *At home: an anthropology of domestic space* (New York, 1999); P. Hughes Jachimiak, *Remembering the cultural geographies of a childhood home* (London, 2014); D. Malouf, *12 Edmonstone Street* (London, 1985). **29** X. De Maistre, *Voyage around my room* ([1794] New York, 1994), pp 10, 20, 32. **30** J. Austen, *Mansfield Park* ([1814] Cambridge, 2005), p. 178; K.L. Moler, 'Miss Price all alone: metaphors of distance in "Mansfield Park"', *Studies in the Novel*, 17:2 (1985), 189–93. **31** N.K. Denzin, *Interpretive interactionism* (Newbury Park, CA, 1989), p. 3, cited in F. Gowrley, *Domestic space in Britain, 1750–1840: materiality, sociability and emotion* (London, 2022), p. 35. **32** Gowrley, *Domestic space in Britain, 1750–1840*, p. 67. On the evolution of the descriptive prose narrative and its representation of eighteenth-century domestic space, see C. Sundberg Wall, *The prose of things: transformations of description in the eighteenth century* (Chicago, 2006). **33** T. Hamling & C. Richardson, *A day at home in early modern England: material culture and domestic life, 1500–1700* (London, 2017), p. 6. **34** I. Ware, *A complete body*

activity of the age'.³⁵ The semantic meanings attached to words like 'house', 'household' and 'home' evolved in this period too: across Europe at mid-century, 'house' might refer either to the family household or to aristocratic lineage, although the latter usage became less common over time.³⁶ Naomi Tadmor's linguistic study of what she terms the 'household-family' in eighteenth-century England confirms that 'family' rarely described the simple nuclear unit and more typically referred to a 'wider canvas of social action', encompassing relationships of blood, marriage and kinship, but also more dynamic and organizational structures of 'co-residence and authority'.³⁷

While it is true that histories of eighteenth-century domestic architecture have customarily privileged the patrician house in town and country, it is there, and in the homes of the middling sorts of artisans, professionals and shopkeepers, that we can most readily discern the contemporary interest in new signifying modes of design and decoration and an increasing specialization in room function.³⁸ But if the urban bourgeois home was the venue for the 'new aspirations that in turn encouraged the demand for comfort',³⁹ so too was the use and significance of discrete domestic spaces 'determined by contingent circumstances'.⁴⁰ This speaks to the dichotomy between how houses were designed and how lives were lived – what has been characterized as 'the lack of correspondence between the clean lines of design and the blurred shades of habitation' in the typical metropolitan dwelling.⁴¹ In this volume, Aisling Durkan examines how the builders of Drogheda's brick terraced houses adapted aristocratic plan types to suit the needs and economies of the town's mercantile elite, while Melanie Hayes considers how the private residence of Luke Gardiner, the foremost property developer in early Georgian Dublin, acted simultaneously as a form of self-aggrandisement, a venue for hospitality and social display, and a comfortable family home. Given the ubiquity of the urban house and garden square in the popular

of architecture (London, 1756), p. 469.   **35** N. McCullough, *Dublin: an urban history* (Dublin, 1989), p. 32.   **36** J. Mathieu, 'Domestic terminologies: house, household, family' in J. Eibach & M. Lanzinger (eds), *The Routledge history of the domestic sphere in Europe, 16th to 19th century* (Abingdon, 2020), p. 31. **37** N. Tadmor, 'The concept of the household-family in eighteenth-century England', *Past & Present*, 151 (1996), 113.   **38** Classic accounts include: J. Cornforth, *Early Georgian interiors* (London, 2004); C. Saumarez-Smith, *Eighteenth-century decoration: design and the domestic interior in England* (London, 1993); M. Girouard, *Life in the English country house: a social and architectural history* (London, 1978); P. Thornton, *Seventeenth-century interior decoration in England, France and Holland* (London, 1978). On the middle-class home, see M. Ponsonby, *Stories from home: English domestic interiors, 1750–1850* (Aldershot, 2007); L. Weatherill, *Consumer behavior and material culture* (London, 1996); S. Nenadic, 'Middle-rank consumers and domestic culture in Edinburgh and Glasgow, 1720–1840', *Past & Present*, 145 (1994), 122–56. On women as designers/makers of interiors, see K. Sharp, 'Women's creativity and display in the eighteenth-century British domestic interior' in S. McKellar & P. Sparke (eds), *Interior design and identity* (Manchester, 1994), pp 10–26; D. Arnold, 'Defining femininity: women and the country house' in idem (ed.), *The Georgian country house: architecture, landscape and society* (Stroud, 2003), pp 79–95; S. Sloboda, 'Fashioning Bluestocking conversation: Elizabeth Montagu's Chinese room' in Baxter & Martin (eds), *Architectural space in eighteenth-century Europe*, pp 129–48. On the vernacular home, see J. Ayres, *Domestic interiors: the British tradition, 1500–1850* (New Haven, 2003).   **39** C. Edwards, *Turning houses into homes* (Aldershot, 2005), p. 91.   **40** B. Heller, 'Leisure and the use of domestic space in Georgian London', *The Historical Journal*, 53:3 (2010), 629.   **41** T. Meldrum, 'Domestic service, privacy and the

portrait of domestic architecture for this period – manifested in so many 'Georgian House' museums in cities and towns across Britain and America, if not Ireland – the final chapter peeks inside the little understood world of lodgings, apartments and rented rooms which often collapsed formal divisions between social and private domestic spaces.[42] This was even more acute for those lower down the economic scale: in her analysis of the dwellings of Ireland's rural poor, Claudia Kinmonth describes the versatile eating and sleeping arrangements necessitated by one- and two-roomed cabins or huts. As Janette Dillon has suggested, 'space is not really a fixed material feature, but is constructed by the way it is occupied. Our mental maps of physical structures stem from our understanding not only of the material elements of those spaces but of how their occupants functioned within them.'[43]

Related to considerations of room usage is the question of everyday activities. Recent histories of domesticity have focused on the spatial and temporal patterns of daily life, considering its intersection with gender, life-stage and social status.[44] In the opening chapter on the spaces and material culture of maternity, Emma O'Toole examines how the homes of the aristocracy, landed gentry and professional classes were customarily repurposed in anticipation of childbirth and the postpartum confinement or 'lying-in' period: this typically involved the refurbishment of the bedchamber and ancillary rooms (if available) and the purchase, rental or borrowing of specialist furniture (birthing and nursing chairs) and decorative wares (caudle cups). Priscilla Sonnier's analysis of the correspondence of elite women adds welcome dimension to a burgeoning scholarship on female agency in the design and supervision of building projects.[45] With reference to Gaston Bachelard and his seminal *The poetics of space* (1958), Sonnier considers the gendered and maternal contexts for important design decisions within the home: safety issues might influence the form and position of a staircase, for example, especially in a household full of boisterous children, and the furnishing of rooms often prioritized the ordinary, routine contentment and enjoyment of the resident family.[46] This amplifies what we know of women's longstanding (if idealized) association with domesticity generally and with the formal transition from house to home in this period,[47] although recent

---

eighteenth-century metropolitan household', *Urban History*, 26:1 (1999), 36. **42** For example: No. 1 Royal Crescent, Bath; The Georgian House Museum, Bristol; Fairfax House, York; The Regency Town House, Brighton; The Georgian House, Edinburgh; Powel House, Philadelphia; The Merchant's House Museum, New York. Town house museums devoted to domestic life in eighteenth-century Ireland have either been dismantled (Number Twenty Nine: Georgian House Museum, Dublin) or repurposed (The Georgian House and Garden, Limerick). **43** J. Dillon, *The language of space in court performance, 1400–1625* (Cambridge, 2010), p. 6. **44** See essays on the theme of 'domestic practice in the past' in the special issue of *Home Cultures*, 11:3 (2014); Andersson & Stobart (eds), *Daily lives and daily routines*; J. Stobart (ed.), *The comforts of home in Western Europe, 1700–1900* (London, 2020). **45** For example: J. Hill, 'Catherine Maria Bury of Charleville Castle, Co. Offaly, and the design of the country house, 1800–1812' in T. Dooley, M. O'Riordan & C. Ridgway (eds), *Women and the country house in Ireland and Britain* (Dublin, 2018), pp 116–38; R. Thorpe, *Women, architecture and building in the east of Ireland, c.1790–1840* (Dublin, 2013); F. O'Kane, '"Obliges me to dip my hands in mortar": Catherine O'Brien's influence at Dromoland', *IADS*, 7 (2004), 80–105. **46** Bachelard, *The poetics of space*, p. 81. **47** R. Larsen, 'Gender and home' in C. Edwards (ed.), *A cultural history of the home in the age of Enlightenment* (London, 2021),

scholarship continues to complicate the field with consideration of a broader range of homosocial, queer and other non-heteronormative 'reconfigurations and reorientations of material space'.[48]

'TO START WITH ... ALL ROOMS ARE ALIKE, MORE OR LESS'[49]

In tandem with more sophisticated ways of thinking about and making of house and home in this period, was a concomitant rise in its portrayal in text and image, facilitated by a flourishing print culture and fostered by an increasingly literate population. While genre painting and caricature depicted a wide range of habitations across the social spectrum, often with a didactic or moralizing purpose, visual representation is arguably best exemplified by the 'conversation piece', a mode of portraiture depicting groups posed primarily in domestic settings and popular with the aristocracy, gentry and bourgeoisie (fig. I.2).[50] Although problems of interpretation are legion – the spaces being often altered or idealized (or even invented) to connote an ideology of refined or respectable living – as a type they offer a visual shorthand of how social status was conveyed through the selection and display of tasteful objects in well-furnished rooms.[51] Architectural representation evolved to address similar concerns. While the primacy of orthographic projection in the period does not perforce 'imply any interest in, or awareness of, the experience of interior space',[52] and mindful of the fact that, even in very grand situations, the majority of houses 'had in-built flexibility, and there was a great deal of the ad hoc about room use',[53] the prevalence of the section and 'laid-out interior' (or 'developed surface interior') as *types* of drawing confirms the appeal for clearly defined spaces dedicated

pp 131–54; J.S. Lewis, 'When a house is not a home: elite English women and the eighteenth-century country house', *Journal of British Studies*, 48:2 (2009), 336–63; W. Rybczynski, *Home: a brief history of an idea* (London, 1986), pp 72–5, 94–5.   **48** M.A. Miller, 'Making room: queer domesticity in Jane Austen's *Emma* and the Anne Lister diaries' in S.G. Hague & K. Lipsedge (eds), *At home in the eighteenth century: interrogating domestic space* (Abingdon, 2022), p. 226. See also M.M. Reeve, 'Gothic architecture, sexuality, and license at Horace Walpole's Strawberry Hill', *The Art Bulletin*, 95:3 (2013), 411–39; N. Reynolds, 'Cottage industry: the ladies of Llangollen and the symbolic capital of the "Cottage Ornée", *The Eighteenth Century*, 51:1/2 (2010), 211–27.   **49** Perec, *Species of spaces*, p. 28.   **50** K. Retford, *The conversation piece: making modern art in eighteenth-century Britain* (London, 2017); A. Crookshank, 'The conversation piece in Irish painting in the 18th century' in A. Bernelle (ed.), *Decantations* (Dublin, 1992), pp 16–20. On the display of pictures in the Irish interior, see J. Coleman, 'Evidence for the collecting and display of paintings in mid-eighteenth-century Ireland', *Bulletin of the Irish Georgian Society*, 36 (1994), 48–62; A. O'Boyle, 'The Milltown collection: reconstructing an eighteenth-century picture-hang', *IADS*, 13 (2010), 30–59.   **51** H. Greig, 'Eighteenth-century English interiors in image and text' in J. Aynsley & C. Grant (eds), *Imagined interiors: representing the domestic interior since the Renaissance* (London, 2006), pp 102–27; C. Rice, 'Rethinking histories of the interior' in M. Taylor & J. Preston (eds), *Intimus: interior design theory reader* (Chichester, 2006), pp 284–91.   **52** L. Jacobus, 'On "Whether a man could see before him and behind him both at once": the role of drawing in the design of interior space in England *c*.1600–1800', *Architectural History*, 31 (1988), 151; R. Evans, 'The developed surface: an enquiry into the brief life of an eighteenth-century drawing technique' in idem, *Translations from drawing to building* (London, 1997), pp 195–230.   **53** P. Guillery, *The small house in eighteenth-century London* (London, 2004), p. 66.

I.2 George Mullins, *John, Mary Anne and Francis Wyse*, oil on copper, *c.*1786. Waterford Treasures Museums.

to sociability, privacy and comfort. An annotated section of an unidentified town house, attributed to architect Sir Edward Lovett Pearce (d.1733), specifies the preferred hierarchical organization of 'sellars storry', 'halle storry', 'chamber storry' and 'loging in ye ruff' – an arrangement consonant with what sociologist Erving Goffman identified as the universal mode for creating formal distinction between discrete *front* (public/social) and *back* (private/service) areas of a building (fig. I.3).[54] It also serves to illustrate what historians and design theorists have variously described as the 'axis of honour' or the 'intimacy gradient' of interconnected domestic spaces, grand or otherwise, and of the signification of their respective purposes or functions through the selection of different materials and decorative finishes.[55] As Caroline van

---

[54] E. Goffman, *The presentation of self in everyday life* (London, 1971), p. 125. The specific delineation of room and storey function also confirms the particular (if unsurprising) focus on interiors rather than exteriors in property advertising for this period. On this topic, see R. Stewart, *The town house in Georgian London* (London, 2009), pp 81–5. [55] Girouard, *Life in the English country house*, p. 145, fig. 9;

I.3 Sir Edward Lovett Pearce, section of unidentified house, ink on paper, *c.*1730.
© Victoria and Albert Museum, London.

Eck has noted, early nineteenth-century aesthetic theory recognized the 'mechanism of association' in the individual's encounter with architecture.[56] For Sir John Soane, the room-by-room progression through a building was akin to watching a dramatic narrative unfold:

> The front of a building is like the prologue of a play, it prepares us for what we are to expect. If the outside promises more than we find in the inside, we are disappointed. The plot opens itself in the first act and is carried on through the remainder, though all the mazes of character, convenience of arrangement, elegance and propriety of ornaments, and lastly produces a complete whole in distribution, decoration and construction.[57]

C. Alexander, *A pattern language: towns, buildings, construction* (New York, 1977), pp 610–13. **56** C. Van Eck, '"The splendid effects of architecture, and its power to affect the mind": the workings of picturesque association' in J. Birksted (ed.), *Landscapes of memory and experience* (London, 2000), p. 249. **57** D. Watkin, *Sir John Soane: Enlightenment thought and the Royal Academy lectures* (Cambridge, 1996), p. 187, quoted in ibid. Eck notes how Soane's famous house in Lincoln Inn's Fields, London, acts in a similar capacity, describing how 'the succeeding rooms, passages and their decoration offer a portrait of the main aspects of Soane's personality, his pursuits, his education and the cultural milieu of which he

Textual sources pose similar problems of subjective representation and interpretation. Historians of early modern domestic interiors and material cultures have traditionally relied on probate inventories for narrative breadth and texture, although the current scholarly consensus accepts that they are unreliable as unmediated documentary evidence, being 'the result of strategies, biases and representational intentions'.[58] Indeed, the 'unexpected variety of contents' recorded in many eighteenth-century inventories is a reminder of the significance attached to objects and possessions of practical, sentimental and non-monetary value.[59] In her childhood memoir, *Seven winters* (1943), Elizabeth Bowen recounts how a newly acquired house in Herbert Place in Dublin, occasioned by her father being called to the bar, precipitated the purchase of new shop-bought furniture and the carriage of older pieces from the ancestral seat in Cork. Though writing for a later period, the passage demonstrates how a room's contents – old and new, cherished and ignored – rarely represent a single historical moment:

> For this new house they had to buy carpets, curtains, a chesterfield sofa, beds. The rest of the furniture that they needed was brought up to Dublin from Bowen's Court. That house had been lavishly furnished for a large family, and much that was in it, my mother saw, could be spared. So, shapely Sheraton chairs, tables, cupboards, mirrors and sideboards that had been the work of Cork cabinet-makers in the eighteenth century now occupied Dublin rooms of, roughly, their own date. They were eked out with 'pieces' – most notably a carved cherrywood writing-table – that had been given my mother as wedding presents, also by some antiques of unknown birthplace that she had bought at low prices along the Dublin quays. The family silver, also, was divided between the winter and summer homes.[60]

The limitations of inventories aside, it is clear that the identification of named objects in named spaces can evoke the embodied practices of the eighteenth-century interior and so add dimension to the 'social life of things', Arjun Appadurai's theory that objects can evince cultures and illuminate historical modes of living.[61] An inventory of 43 North Great George's Street, recorded in 1805, itemizes a range of functional yet costly items that immediately resonate with our understanding of polite hospitality in the Georgian home: among the enumerated objects in the ground-floor dining parlour, a series of cut glass candle-stands and lustres, and lanterns with

---

made himself a part'. Van Eck, '"The splendid effects of architecture"', p. 251.   **58** G. Riello, '"Things seen and unseen": the material culture of early modern inventories and their representation of domestic interiors' in P. Findlen (ed.), *Early modern things: objects and their histories, 1500–1800* (London, 2013), p. 127.   **59** Barnard, *Making the grand figure*, p. 79. On the question of value, see S.G. Hague, '"I am now determined to inform you what I am sure will amaze you": objects, domestic space, and the economics of gentility' in Hague & Lipsedge (eds), *At home in the eighteenth century*, pp 107–25.   **60** E. Bowen, *Seven winters* (London, 1943), pp 9–10.   **61** A. Appadurai, 'Introduction: commodities and the politics of value' in idem (ed.), *The social life of things: commodities in cultural perspective* (Cambridge, 1986), pp 3–63.

reflective gilt backs, substantiates the 'flexibility demanded by nocturnal socializing', providing clues to how they might be 'carefully repositioned, depending on where the light was required, where special guests might be seated, or what the host wanted guests to see'.[62] In this volume, Toby Barnard examines the cheaper, useful ceramic wares intended for everyday dining and supping, noting the ubiquity of earthenware, stoneware and faience as opposed to the prohibitively expensive dinner and dessert services in fine porcelain beloved of art historians and connoisseurs but rare in Irish houses.

Barnard's consideration of the markets for imported goods brings us to the remaining semantic component of this book's title. Given the complexity of the relationship between Ireland and Britain in the period under review, the question of what might be considered uniquely or peculiarly 'Irish' is arguably a moot point: as Barnard has noted, the cultures and practices of domestic life in Ireland were 'strongly influenced and frequently modified by what was happening elsewhere'.[63] While Patricia McCarthy's study of Ireland's major political houses suggests that English architectural tastes were not automatically emulated and 'ideas were borrowed and then adapted to an Irish way of living',[64] more generally it seems that the question of a 'national' taste in design was focused on issues of economic protectionism rather than the creation of spaces or objects (or decorative finishes) that were visually or materially distinct from their British counterparts.[65] Nonetheless, in other circumstances, the peculiar condition of Ireland, as 'both laboratory and lab partner' in the British imperial project, invites more nuanced interpretations.[66] In her chapter on Charleville Castle in County Offaly, focused on the preparations undertaken for a visit from the viceregal court in 1809, Judith Hill explores the context of the Acts of Union of 1800 – when the United Kingdom of Great Britain and Ireland was created – pointing to the functions of architectural space and decorative style in manifesting the complex social and political identities of Ireland's Ascendancy class. Elsewhere, a marked (and at times excessive) hospitality has been recognized as an innately Irish custom: in the contributions by Claudia Kinmonth and Patricia McCarthy it is clear that generosity was a feature of house visiting at every stratum of society, from the sharing of very modest meals in the poorest cottage to the seemingly limitless supply of claret served at the aristocratic table.[67]

---

[62] Moran, '"The eye as well as the appetite must be car'd for"', pp 215–16, citing TCD, Clements papers, MS 7344/32. [63] T. Barnard, 'Introduction', *PRIA*, 111C (2011), p. xi. Barnard continues: 'There is considerable potential to try to decide whether Irish exceptionalism is a tenable interpretation of domestic living. At the moment, such a conclusion, attractive as it is to romantics and tourist boards, seems implausible.' Ibid., p. xxiii. [64] McCarthy, *Life in the country house in Georgian Ireland*, p. 2. [65] FitzGerald, *Silver in Georgian Dublin*, pp 15–17. See also C. Casey, 'Art and architecture in the long eighteenth century' in J. Kelly (ed.), *The Cambridge history of Ireland, vol. 3, 1730–1880* (Cambridge, 2018), pp 463–4; W. Laffan, 'Introduction – colonial Ireland: artistic crossroads' in W. Laffan & C. Monkhouse (eds), *Ireland: crossroads of art and design, 1690–1840* (New Haven, 2015), p. 22. [66] T.G. McMahon, M. De Nie & P. Townend (eds), *Ireland in an imperial world: citizenship, opportunism and subversion* (Cambridge, 2017), p. 1. [67] On the wider cultural issue, see J. Kelly, 'The consumption and sociable use of alcohol in eighteenth-century Ireland', *PRIA*, 115C (2015), 219–55.

'IN SUM, A ROOM IS A FAIRLY MALLEABLE SPACE'[68]

In his study of the phenomenology of place and its spatial contexts, Edward Relph suggested that 'All places ... are individually experienced, for we alone see them through the lens of our attitudes, experiences and intentions, and from our own unique circumstances.'[69] Focusing on how different species of domestic spaces were used and inhabited, from mansions and merchant houses to lodgings and rural cabins, this book introduces a broader appreciation of the diverse meanings and materialities ascribed to and associated with house and home in eighteenth-century Ireland.

Although drawn from a small pool of academics and researchers, it is encouraging to note how the major themes of the wider international scholarship are substantively addressed here, ranging from questions of politeness, leisure and lifecycle to gender, consumption and performativity. Going forward, there is potential for further consideration of, among other topics, how religious confession (including Catholic, Quaker and Presbyterian) influenced choices about decorating and furnishing the Irish home;[70] the living conditions of the urban working classes; and the character of temporary accommodation available to journeymen artisans and peripatetic labourers in town and country.[71] The brisk trade in imported commodities like tea and sugar also suggest more complex patterns of daily consumption in households across the social spectrum that might warrant investigation: the barmbrack, a loaf traditionally associated with Halloween in Ireland but baked with 'exotic' fruits and spices from overseas, has recently been characterized as 'a hybrid product of empire, made by Irish hands and hearts with materials from home and abroad'.[72]

Taken together, the individual lives examined here – among them city grandees, provincial merchants, pregnant women, bachelors and farm labourers – demonstrate how diverse needs and motivations shaped personal, cultural and social identities in and through domestic space. Just as 'An Englishman's home is his castle' was 'already a hoary cliché' at the beginning of the Georgian era,[73] and the word 'home' was understood to represent 'an identifiable and distinct architectural structure that provided the family with a private place of retreat, comfort and succour',[74] so the chapters that follow unequivocally imbricate eighteenth-century Irishmen's (and Irishwomen's) houses and homes with the narratives of their everyday lives.

68 Perec, *Species of spaces*, p. 28.   **69** E. Relph, *Place and placelessness* (London, 1976), p. 36, citing D. Lowenthal, 'Geography experience and imagination: towards a geographical epistemology', *Annals*, 51 (1961), 241–60.   **70** On religious confession and its intersection with taste and consumption in this period, see Barnard, *Making the grand figure*, pp 114–21, 180–1; J. Fenlon, 'French influence in late seventeenth-century portraits', *Irish Arts Review Yearbook*, 6 (1989–90), 156–68.   **71** On the social topography of Georgian Dublin, see E. Sheridan, 'Living in the capital city' in J. Brady & A. Simms (eds), *Dublin through space and time* (Dublin, 2001), pp 136–58. For a glimpse of the living conditions of the urban poor in this period, see J. Prunty, 'The town house as tenement in nineteenth- and early twentieth-century Dublin' in Casey (ed.), *The eighteenth-century Dublin town house*, pp 153–5.   **72** McMahon, De Nie & Townend (eds), *Ireland in an imperial world*, p. 4. On the question of luxury consumption and the lower orders, see H. O'Connell, '"A raking pot of tea": consumption and excess in early nineteenth-century Ireland', *Literature & History*, 21:2 (2012), 32–47.   **73** A. Vickery, 'An Englishman's home is his castle? Thresholds, boundaries and privacies in the eighteenth-century London house', *Past & Present*, 199 (2008), 147–73.   **74** K. Lipsedge, 'The meaning of home' in Edwards (ed.), *A cultural history of the home*, p. 19.

Brought to bed: the spaces and material culture of the lying-in

EMMA O'TOOLE

In the eighteenth century, the term 'brought to bed' was used to refer to the physical act a pregnant woman undertook as she was literally brought to her bed for the delivery of a newborn infant. It also referred to the period that followed childbirth when she was confined to bed and recuperated. 'Brought to bed', also commonly called the 'lying-in', 'confinement' or 'in the family way', was a key moment in motherhood marked by a number of clearly defined stages in the recovery process.[1] Generally the stages lasted from four to six weeks and involved long stays in bed; from there the mother moved to an outer room or dressing room; downstairs, possibly to dine with the family, and finally to take her leave of the premises. While there were few financial constraints on aristocratic women, for women of the lower classes, lying-in for a month would have been impractical. Work, childcare and domestic chores typically curtailed the period of recuperation.

This chapter negotiates a significant period in the history of childbirth. Until the eighteenth century, women were firmly and collectively in control of the series of events and rituals that surrounded the lying-in.[2] Philomena Gorey argues that until the eighteenth century in Ireland, 'a woman's confinement was bound by culture, tradition and superstition'.[3] Female friends, neighbours and relatives dominated the delivery room and female midwives controlled the birth. Men's access to the birth and lying-in chamber was denied, as birth was considered a uniquely female experience. Medical men were only called upon when an emergency arose during a difficult labour, when the labour was well advanced and obstructed. In such cases the male practitioner, normally a surgeon, intervened using instruments such as forceps, hooks and crotchets.[4] By the 1730s, male practitioners gradually began to deliver infants, not just in cases of emergency. By the 1770s, the man midwife was firmly established as a new type of male practitioner, who posed a threat to the female

---

[1] See for example, C. Tait, 'Safely delivered: childbirth, wet-nursing, gossip-feasts and churching in Ireland, c.1530–1690', *Irish Economic and Social History*, 30 (2003), 1–23; P. Gorey, 'Managing midwifery in Dublin: practice and practitioners, 1700–1800' in M.H. Preston & M. Ó Hógarthaigh (eds), *Gender and medicine in Ireland, 1700–1950* (New York, 2012), p. 123; A. Wilson, *The making of man-midwifery: childbirth in England, 1660–1770* (London, 1995); A. Wilson, *Ritual and conflict: the social relations of childbirth in early modern England* (Aldershot, 2013), p. 86; L. Pollock, 'Embarking on a rough passage: the experience of pregnancy in early modern society' in V. Fildes (ed.), *Women as mothers in pre-industrial England* (London, 1990), pp 39–67. [2] Gorey, 'Managing midwifery in Dublin', p. 123. [3] Ibid. [4] Ibid.

1.1 A man-midwife represented by a figure divided in half, one half representing a man and the other a woman. Coloured etching by I. Cruikshank, 1793. Wellcome Collection. Public Domain Mark.

midwife and to traditional practices of the lying-in period, which included darkening the lying-in chamber so that every crevice was kept shut (fig. 1.1).[5]

Despite a wealth of material on maternity and childbirth in eighteenth-century England, the subject of the lying-in in aristocratic and middling class homes in Ireland has garnered far less attention. In Ireland, histories of institutional childbirth have taken precedence over examining the domestic practices and social rituals of childbirth.[6] In recent years a number of edited collections have shone a light on several neglected aspects of eighteenth- and nineteenth-century motherhood, including chapters on infanticide, medicinal care and women's reactions to the joys and sorrows of motherhood.[7] However, the social and cultural relevance of the domestic spaces, objects, and the social rituals surrounding maternity in Georgian Ireland have yet to receive significant attention.

The study of being 'brought to bed' is central to our understanding of the domestic space and the material culture of maternity in the eighteenth century. Erving Goffman's concepts surrounding the use of household spaces and the performance of objects in public and private areas of the household, what he terms as the front and back stage, are utilized in this chapter.[8] For the duration of the lying-in, a bedchamber and on occasion the dressing room, normally private and personal domestic spaces where the more concealed aspects of family life were carried out, were transformed into the lying-in chamber. Reconstituted, the lying-in chamber became an area where guests, including physicians, midwives, family members and neighbours, were welcomed either during the act of childbirth itself, or in the weeks that followed during the new mother's lying-in.

DOMESTIC EVIDENCE FOR THE LYING-IN: THE SOURCES

In order to explore maternity spaces in the Irish household, this chapter focuses on the household papers from four families from the upper echelons of the middling rank and the aristocracy. While documents containing information on the lying-in are rare, the letters, diaries, and account books compiled by Richard Edgeworth, Nicholas Peacock, William Drennan and Emily FitzGerald provide a glimpse into the use of domestic spaces during the lying-in.

The FitzGerald family are the first subjects considered in this chapter. James FitzGerald, 20th earl of Kildare (later 1st duke of Leinster), married Emily (neé Lennox) in 1747. They resided between Carton House, Co. Kildare, and Kildare (now Leinster) House, their Dublin home on Coote Street (today Kildare Street). The couple had nineteen children between 1748 and 1773.[9] Surviving correspondence

---

[5] Ibid., pp 123–4. [6] A. Wilson, 'The ceremony of childbirth and its interpretation' in Fildes (ed.), *Women as mothers in pre-industrial England*, pp 68–70. [7] E. Farrell (ed.), *'She said she was in the family way': pregnancy and infancy in the Irish past* (London, 2012). [8] E. Goffman, *The presentation of the self in everyday life* (London, 1969), p. 125. [9] F. Clarke & S. Kleinman, 'Emily Fitzgerald (1731–1814)' in J. McGuire & J. Quinn (eds), *Dictionary of Irish biography*, 11 vols (Cambridge, 2009), iii, p. 840.

exchanged between Emily and James, as well as Emily's sisters, Caroline Fox and Louisa Connolly, provides details on her lying-in during the 1750s and 1760s, including the illnesses she suffered, the physicians she hired and the family that were present during childbirth. The Edgeworths were an Anglo-Irish family who owned a landed estate at Edgeworthstown in County Longford, and a Dublin residence on Grafton Street. From the 1720s to the 1760s, Richard Edgeworth kept a detailed account of his personal expenditure. In the 1730s he recorded that his wife Jane gave birth on four occasions and noted the expenses he paid for during her lying-in.

The third subjects of this paper are the Peacocks, a family from the middling Anglican gentry. Nicolas Peacock was a land agent and farmer who lived in Kilcorly, Co. Limerick.[10] Peacock's diary and the entries he made in the 1740s and early 1750s provide a glimpse into the preparations his wife, Catherine, made for her lying-in, when she gave birth to her three sons between 1748 and 1750. The final subject is the Drennan family and the letters passed between the physician and man midwife William Drennan, his wife Sarah and sister Martha McTier.[11] Living at their residence at 33 Marlborough Street in Dublin, William and Sarah had four sons and a daughter between 1801 and 1809, and their letters provide details of her lyings-in.

The letters, account books and diary at the core of this chapter are remarkable both for their preservation, scope, and the level of detail they provide on everyday domestic matters and the consumption of mundane items. At different social levels, FitzGerald, Edgeworth, Peacock and Drennan watched minutely over receipts and spending, and provided detailed descriptions of the goods and services they consumed. Referring to the information recorded by both Edgeworth and Peacock, Toby Barnard warns the historian 'against assuming that all purchases were governed by such rational calculation'.[12] However, it is precisely the minute details provided in the household papers of FitzGerald, Edgeworth, Peacock and Drennan that make them such intriguing case studies. A close examination of such household papers and everyday objects can help in drawing out aspects of everyday life relating to maternity.

THE HOUSEHOLD, ROOMS, AND THE LYING-IN

The last few weeks of pregnancy were usually occupied in effecting preparations for the lying-in. For those that had both houses in the country and the city a decision had to be made as to where they would have their lying-in. For many, their decision involved moving temporarily to the city. Many peers' families maintained homes in Dublin. Others rented dwellings specifically for the lying-in. In the 1730s, for instance, Richard Edgeworth recorded that his wife moved from their Longford home in Edgeworthstown to their Dublin residence. Likewise, throughout the late 1750s

---

[10] M.L. Legg (ed.), *The diary of Nicholas Peacock, 1740–1751* (Dublin, 2005), p. 11. [11] J. Agnew (ed.), *The Drennan–McTier letters*, 3 vols (Dublin, 1998 and 1999). [12] T. Barnard, *Making the grand figure: lives and possessions in Ireland, 1641–1770* (London, 2004), p. xix.

and early 1760s, Emily FitzGerald travelled from Carton House in County Kildare to their Dublin residence on Kildare Street in anticipation of childbirth. In a letter dated 30 April 1760, her sister Caroline Fox wrote that 'in a large airy house like Kildare House 'twas better to be in town during confinement'.[13]

For many, a city dwelling was the ideal location to have a lying-in. One of the main reasons was that male midwives and physicians were more readily available in the city, particularly with the foundation of Bartholomew Mosse's Lying-in Hospital (popularly known as the Rotunda) in 1745. Traditionally, men were only brought into childbirth to help with difficult labours, however by the mid-eighteenth century, male midwives and physicians promoted their role in regular births in publications and pamphlets. From this point, the profession began to change direction as male midwives tended to argue in favour of anatomical study and the use of instruments instead of tradition and experience.[14] Armed with a professional education and instruments, male midwives became an increasingly fashionable choice for aristocratic women in Ireland. The availability of man midwives in Dublin perhaps attracted both Jane Edgeworth and Emily FitzGerald to the city as they both obtained the services of a man midwife. On 28 August 1734, Richard Edgeworth recorded that he gave ten guineas to 'Mr Carter the man midwife for laying my wife'; this was repeated in September 1736.[15] Outside the city, many families opted for female midwives, who generally lived locally; on occasion, however, great distances had to be travelled in order to acquire the services of the local midwife. This was the case for Nicholas Peacock who, on 24 April 1748, at the onset of his wife's labour, summoned the local midwife, a Mother Handy. Peacock recorded in his journal that he 'sent for ye midwife' at Ballingarry,[16] situated about ten hours by foot from Kilronan, the townland where the Peacocks resided.

Moving to Dublin for the lying-in also made childbirth a distinctive public event. In cities like London and Dublin the lying-in was often publicized by the custom of placing straw on the street outside the home of the expectant mother. Although intended to quieten the noise from street traffic, straw also made a distinct visual testimony to passers-by that marked the birth of a child and the mother's lying-in.[17] In 1761, straw was laid outside the home of Henrietta Cantillion, Lady Farnham, on the birth of her daughter at their city residence in Mary Street, Dublin. Unfortunately, Lady Farnham died soon after childbirth due to a fever, and Emily FitzGerald recounted how 'it shocks me to see the straw lying still before the door!'[18]

In large city residences, such as Kildare House, two rooms were often occupied for the lying-in; ideally, these rooms would be interconnected. One room, the inner room or bedchamber, would be the actual location of childbirth, where the mother

---

13 C. Fox to E. FitzGerald, 30 Apr. 1760, in B. FitzGerald (ed.), *Correspondence of Emily, duchess of Leinster (1731–1814)*, 3 vols (Dublin, 1949–53), i, p. 283. **14** Gorey, 'Managing midwifery in Dublin', pp 123–7. **15** NLI, Richard Edgeworth account books, MS 1510, p. 137 and MS 1511, p. 129. **16** N. Peacock, 24 Apr. 1748, in Legg (ed.), *The diary of Nicholas Peacock*, p. 186. **17** J. Lewis, *In the family way: childbearing in the British aristocracy, 1760–1860* (Chicago, 1986), p. 157. **18** E. FitzGerald to J. FitzGerald, 1 Sept. 1761, in FitzGerald (ed.), *Correspondence*, i, p. 131.

recuperated during most of her lying-in. The dressing room would provide a gathering place for friends and relatives who could selectively enter the bedchamber. By the 1750s, bedchambers and dressing rooms were typically located upstairs, following the general shift from formality to comfort in the design of domestic spaces.[19] The bedchamber was generally regarded as the most private upstairs room but the dressing room was often larger and habitually used for reading, writing and informal entertainments.[20] Architectural drawings for Kildare House show that Emily Fitzgerald's bedchamber and a large dressing room were interconnected and positioned on the first floor.[21] Privacy was ensured by a door at the top of the main staircase that led into the bedchamber and dressing room quarters. This provided an ideal location for childbirth, where Emily could have the privacy she required during her lying-in, and facilitate visiting family and friends in the dressing room as required.

While Emily FitzGerald and Jane Edgeworth moved to their city houses for childbirth, for the Peacocks and the Drennans the onset of childbirth and the lying-in called for a considerable reordering of existing household spaces. Catherine Peacock gave birth to her three sons at their home located close to the Shannon Estuary and within an easy ride of Limerick city. Throughout the 1740s, Peacock paid for two hearths, indicating that he and his wife Catherine lived in a simple one-storey house, and his servants lodged in his farm outbuildings and offices.[22] This suggests that space may have been limited and the activities of childbirth and the lying-in were confined to one bedchamber. Similarly, William Drennan frequently grumbled to his sister, Martha McTier, about the lack of space at his terraced town house in Marlborough Street in Dublin. On 8 March 1802, one week before the birth of their second child, Drennan wrote to his sister that he had to move out of the bedchamber he shared with his wife for the duration of her lying-in.[23] According to Drennan, he slept in the 'back drawing room', where a 'second good bed' was set up.[24]

In addition to organizing space for the expectant mother and her lying-in chamber, sleeping accommodations within the house often had to be found for the midwife and nurse attendants who were expected to live at the house for the duration of the lying-in. Servants hired to aid the postpartum mother and infant might include a monthly nurse that cared for the new mother for the duration of her lying-in, a wet nurse for breastfeeding the infant, or a dry nurse for taking care of the newborn. On 16 July 1734, some weeks prior to his wife's lying-in, Edgeworth ordered extra beds and blankets for the additional servants, as evidenced from the payment for 'a feather bedstead & blankets for servants' costing 4 shillings.[25] In the Drennan household,

---

19 J. Cornforth, *Early Georgian interiors* (London, 2004), pp 209–10.   **20** K. Lipsedge, *Domestic space in eighteenth-century British novels* (London, 2012), p. 116; P. McCarthy, *Life in the country house in Georgian Ireland* (London, 2016), p. 175.   **21** For further information on the architectural drawings of Kildare House, see P. McCarthy, 'The planning and use of space in Irish houses 1730–1830' (PhD, TCD, 2009), p. 246.   **22** Legg (ed.), *The diary of Nicholas Peacock*, p. 27.   **23** W. Drennan and S. Drennan to M. McTier, 8 Mar. 1801, in Agnew (ed.), *The Drennan–McTier letters*, iii, p. 16.   **24** Ibid.   **25** NLI, Richard Edgeworth account book, MS 1,510, fos 128, 133.

where space was limited, the employment of a dry nurse meant the rearrangement of sleeping accommodations and furniture. In February 1801, Drennan wrote to his sister that he had to reorganize the servants' sleeping arrangements to accommodate the dry nurse: their two female servants were now required to share a single settle bed, and their manservant, John, was given a new bedstead.[26] Such details indicate that rearranging domestic spaces to accommodate the lying-in was both a necessary and expensive undertaking.

PREPARING THE LYING-IN CHAMBER

As a woman's pregnancy progressed there were several steps the expectant mother needed to take to transform her bedchamber into the lying-in chamber. How the lying-in chamber was furnished greatly depended on whether a female or male midwife was hired. Traditionally, female midwives insisted on the bedchamber being physically enclosed: blocking up keyholes and closing windows limited air circulation, and the room was lit solely by candlelight (fig. 1.2).[27] By the late eighteenth century much of the formal etiquette of the lying-in chamber had begun to relax. In his treatise on *The management of pregnant and lying-in women*, the English physician Dr Charles White recommended that 'windows are to be opened', 'no board or other contrivance to block up the chimney', and the curtains were 'not to be closely drawn'.[28] One of the earliest recorded examples of this new approach to confinement was that of Emily FitzGerald in the 1760s. Contrary to the common practice of darkening the lying-in chamber, she insisted that her room be lit with daylight or plenty of candles at night. She also believed in the windows being opened for the circulation of fresh air.[29]

Specific pieces of furniture were essential in preparing the bedchamber. In some instances, female midwives brought a birthing chair to the expectant mother's home. This type of chair was transportable and shaped to assist women in sitting in an upright position during childbirth (fig. 1.3). A particular-type of bed for the birthing mother was also often required. As Judith Schneid Lewis's research on childbearing in England between 1760 and 1860 has shown, childbirth did not take place in the ancestral four-poster bed.[30] Instead, for the newly arranged lying-in chamber a lightweight portable folding bed, specially designed for the occasion, was required. This type of bed was of moderate height and constructed to make linen changes easier. By using a second smaller bed, once the woman had given birth she could be cleaned and placed in her own bed to rest without the extra delay imposed by having to change the sheets. Another benefit of this smaller bed was that it allowed the

---

[26] W. Drennan to M. McTier, Feb. 1801, in Agnew (ed.), *The Drennan–McTier letters*, ii, p. 672. [27] Gorey, 'Managing midwifery in Dublin', p. 123. [28] C. White, *A treatise on the management of pregnant and lying-in women* (London, 1773), pp 130–1. [29] S. Tillyard, *Aristocrats: Caroline, Emily, Louisa and Sarah Lennox, 1740–1832* (London, 1994), p. 232. [30] Lewis, *In the family way*, p. 161.

1.2 A mother in bed after giving birth, the midwife showing the baby to the father. Coloured stipple engraving, *c*.1800. Wellcome Collection. Public Domain Mark.

midwife to easily attend to the labouring woman. On 14 and 15 August 1748, days prior to his wife's second lying-in, Nicholas Peacock recorded in his journal: 'Catty and I putting up ye bed I borrowed 2*s*. 2*d*.'[31] Peacock's reference to putting up a

---

[31] N. Peacock, 14 and 15 Aug. 1749, in Legg (ed.), *The diary of Nicholas Peacock*, p. 203.

1.3 Folding adjustable birthing chair, eighteenth–nineteenth century. Science Museum London. Attribution 4.0 international (CC by 4.0).

borrowed bed indicates that this was a temporary and portable bed that was perhaps used for childbirth or accommodating an attending servant. The fact that it was necessary for some families to borrow or rent furniture for the lying-in chamber indicates the considerable expense attached to these items that prohibited families like the Peacocks from purchasing them outright. It also suggests that enterprising businesses or families were willing to rent furniture to families for childbirth and the lying-in period.

Cradles or cribs were an essential item of furniture in the lying-in chamber. Cradles could be used for different generations of infants within the family, shared among friends and passed down through the generations. Inventories reveal that cradles were occasionally listed as stored in cupboards or in attic spaces.[32] Wills and testaments provide evidence that parents expressed their wishes to have cradles given to their daughters.[33] However, a growing market for goods specific to infants and children meant that items such as furniture, clothing and toys were becoming increasingly available and affordable over the course of the eighteenth century.[34] On 4 May 1748, Peacock purchased a cradle costing £1 7s., and on the following day he noted that he had 'fitted ye cradle'.[35] Fitting the cradle possibly referred to items such as rugs, blankets and drapery that were used to cover the frame and keep out drafts. Drennan, on the other hand, took the loan of a crib and a basket that was in the 'English fashion'.[36] The basket, as the name implies, likely referred to a Moses basket, which was either designed to be carried and sit directly on the floor or it may have been a sturdier and less portable crib made from a basket-like material.

Linens for both the birthing bed and the newborn child were regularly referenced in midwifery publications. In his publication *A treatise on the theory and practice of midwifery*, the Scottish obstetrician William Smellie gave his readers specific instructions on the type of linen expectant mothers should use to prepare the birthing bed. Smellie informed his readers that the bed should be dressed with a piece of oiled cloth or sheepskin with several layers of linen placed over it.[37] In doing so, the linen would absorb the fluids and blood lost during the delivery, and the oiled cloth or sheepskin would prevent the bed beneath them from spoiling. In addition to linen for the birthing bed, the newborn infant required an extensive amount of clothing. Layettes or lists of clothing for newborns can be sourced in Irish household papers and provide a glimpse into the variety of types and materials customarily used. In the account of items belonging to infant Daniel McMahon after his death on 1 August 1747, it listed the following layette: 'a cradle with a bed and quilt, a gown, 4 petticoats,

---

32 See, for example, inventory of Knapton House (NLI, De Vesci papers, MS 38,905) and probate inventory of Great Stoughton (NLI, MS 4,897). 33 Will of Thomas Butler, tenth earl of Ormond, in J. Fenlon, *Goods & chattels: a survey of early household inventories in Ireland* (Dublin, 2003), p. 18. 34 E. O'Toole, 'Object, spaces and rituals: a social and material history of maternity and infancy in Ireland, c.1730 to c.1830' (PhD, NCAD, 2018), pp 143–84. 35 N. Peacock, 4 May 1748, in Legg (ed.), *The diary of Nicholas Peacock*, p. 187. 36 Agnew (ed.), *The Drennan–McTier letters*, ii, p. 674. 37 W. Smellie, *A treatise on the theory and practice of midwifery* (London, 1762), p. 203.

6 binders, 4 bibbs, 3 cradle blankets, 2 pillows, 3 pairs of sheets and one pair of shoes'.[38] While families on modest incomes might opt strictly for linen, being a practical material that was easy to wash and keep clean, other materials used for infant clothing were more luxurious, such as silk. Infant clothing could be purchased readymade or made bespoke by a seamstress; in many cases, the expectant mothers or family members stitched and embroidered items of clothing themselves. For instance, in a letter to his sister dated February 1801, Drennan noted the time his pregnant wife Sarah had invested in making clothes for their future (first-born) son: 'busy at present in making clothes for the coming Hope of our House, expected to arrive in the middle of next month'.[39]

Although the male midwife had established his presence in the lying-in chamber by the late eighteenth century, the advent of male relatives visiting the lying-in chamber developed more slowly. As a practicing male midwife, William Drennan was the exception. In a letter dated 16 March 1802, Drennan recorded that during Sarah's second childbirth, the infant 'came a little awkwardly into the world, but everything passed off well'.[40] Such details of the delivery indicate that Drennan was present at his child's birth. On the other hand, writing to her father's second wife, Elizabeth Shackleton (née Carleton), in 1824, Mary Leadbeater revealed that when her daughter Lydia was giving birth to her first-born son, Lydia's husband, James Joseph Fisher, was not permitted into the birthing chamber. According to Leadbeater, James paced 'up and down' outside the birthing chamber and could be found 'listening at the door of the birthing chamber'; according to her, he 'suffered more than anyone'.[41]

In preparing for delivery, which female friends and family members would be invited to attend the childbirth was an important consideration. On 27 April 1748, as his wife prepared to deliver their firstborn son, Pryce, Nicholas Peacock fetched their neighbour, Mrs Hartstonge, and later recorded in his diary: 'Catty ill, I wrote to Mrs Hartstonge to come to her'; a second entry noted, 'I bless God Catty was delivered att a quartr aftr 6 Mrs. Hartstonge went home'.[42] In 1801, the Drennans requested the presence of Sarah Drennan's sister Mrs Mary Hutton in the lying-in chamber: 'Mrs Hutton is to be with Sarah at her confinement, and I am at hand'.[43] Having a reliable friend or family member present remained crucial for most women, as they were able to provide a level of emotional comfort that they could not expect from their paid servants.

---

[38] B. De Breffny & R. ffolliott, *The houses of Ireland: domestic architecture from the medieval castle to the Edwardian villa* (London, 1975), p. 23. [39] W. Drennan to A. Drennan, 5 Feb. 1801, in Agnew (ed.), *The Drennan–McTier letters*, ii, p. 672. [40] W. Drennan to M. McTier, 16 Mar. 1802, in Agnew (ed.), *The Drennan–McTier letters*, iii, p. 21. [41] M. Leadbeater to E. Shackleton, 1824, in A. Bourke et al. (eds), *The Field Day anthology of Irish writing*, 5 (New York, 2002), p. 596. [42] N. Peacock, 27 Apr. 1748, in Legg (ed.), *The diary of Nicholas Peacock*, p. 186. [43] W. Drennan to M. McTier, 5 Feb. 1801, in Agnew (ed.), *The Drennan–McTier letters*, ii, p. 672. [44] Wilson, *Ritual and conflict*, p. 172; Lewis, *In the family*

THE STAGES OF LYING-IN

Once childbirth was over women entered a period of recuperation. It was at this point that the male midwife left the scene of the lying-in chamber and allowed family, friends and servants to take up the charge of caring for the new mother and infant. Adrian Wilson has highlighted that in early eighteenth-century England the lying-in mother received guests at different stages over the course of the full lying-in period, but in the first few days after childbirth only those women who were present during the delivery could visit.[44] After one week, women celebrated the 'upsitting'. The 'upsitting' came when the bed was first changed. This initiated a second phase, lasting a week to ten days, during which the mother remained in her room, not confined to bed but still enjoying physical rest. The stages identified by researchers of the lying-in in England can also be identified in the Irish households under consideration.

Ill health was common during the postpartum period and could prolong the stages of recuperation. To say that a woman had been 'safely delivered' was a common phrase in family correspondence. It referred not just to the act of surviving delivery, but was an assessment that the woman was displaying promising signs of restoration. However, many women suffered from prolonged bleeding, mastitis and general fatigue. In 1755, after the birth of her sixth child, Emily FitzGerald wrote to her husband that her 'breast was bad two days, which you know always frightens me', indicating that she suffered from mastitis.[45] William Fitzwilliam's wife was particularly sick with mastitis following postpartum. On 15 December 1757, he wrote to his brother, Richard, Viscount Fitzwilliam, recording how the 'backing up of her milk' caused her severe ill health:

> By the time the physicians came, she was in strong fits, senseless & stone blind, & had almost bit her tongue asunder; They prescrib'd to her, next morning put another blister on her back; She remain'd however in this horrid condition for four days.[46]

While recuperating during the lying-in, new mothers suspended their household duties, including daily entries in diaries, correspondence and managing the household accounts. The suspension of household activities was believed to aid women in their recovery after childbirth.[47] This is exemplified by Emily FitzGerald when she described in May 1761 that she merely wrote a little each day for fear that she might make her 'head giddy by too much at a time'.[48] Richard Edgeworth employed a monthly nurse, known as Nurse Duggan, to care for his wife Jane over the course of her month-long lying-in. While employed, Nurse Duggan looked after 'the wash

way, pp 193–201. **45** E. FitzGerald to J. FitzGerald, 1755, in FitzGerald (ed.), *Correspondence*, ii, p. 9. **46** NAI, Pembroke Estate papers, 97/46/1/2/7/105, W. Fitzwilliam to Rt Hon. Viscount Fitzwilliam, 15 Dec. 1757. I am grateful to Conor Lucey for this reference. **47** For examples on the importance of suspending work during the lying-in see, Wilson, *Ritual and conflict*, pp 173–4; Wilson, *The making of man-midwifery*, p. 27. **48** E. FitzGerald to J. FitzGerald, 10 May 1761, in FitzGerald (ed.),

woman's bill', 'household expenses' and 'grocery ware'.[49] It was also the monthly nurse's responsibility to oversee that a restorative diet of gruel and broth was consumed for at least three to four days following delivery. However, as it was left to the monthly nurse to see that diet was enforced, new mothers could often eat as they wished.

Throughout these early stages of the recuperation, the women who attended the childbirth in the lying-in chamber often remained for several days caring for the new mother and providing much needed support and company. Without the support of family and friends, a lying-in, particularly one that lasted a month or more, could be a long and lonely period for women. On 30 April 1760, Caroline Fox wrote in a letter to Emily FitzGerald that the lying-in was 'when one wants company more than at any time'.[50] Ruth Larsen suggests that sisters from families of the aristocracy in late eighteenth-century England played a particularly important role in offering support during the lying-in.[51] Larsen argues that because the process of pregnancy and childbirth was a real concern in the eighteenth century, 'sisters played a central role in the management of these risks; by sharing their knowledge and experiences of childbirth, sisters provided practical advice to one another'.[52] This theory is clearly borne out in the correspondence of Emily FitzGerald. In August 1761, after the birth of her fourth son, Henry, Emily described how her sister Caroline had been with her every evening and kept her in a 'continual hurray of company'.[53] Another sister, Sarah, also kept her company, and Emily remarked that 'Sarah being with me is mighty comfortable'.[54] During this time mothers were often confined to bed or restricted to their bedchamber, and so the company of siblings and friends was both a form of comfort and relief.

Mothers who chose to nurse their infants themselves would begin breastfeeding during these initial stages of the lying-in in the privacy of their bedchambers. By the late eighteenth century, Irish household papers compiled by families from the aristocracy and the upper echelons of the middling rank indicate that an increasing number of women breastfed their infants.[55] Depictions of nursing mothers in art during the eighteenth and early nineteenth centuries are scarce. Of the few representations of breastfeeding mothers that exist, such as Marguerite Gérard's *The nourishing mother* (1804), women are shown seated in bed or on cushioned chairs beside the bedstead (fig. 1.4). While such pictorial evidence should be interpreted with caution, it likely bears some relation to real practices.

By the turn of the eighteenth century, specific chairs could be purchased to aid women in breastfeeding their infants. A surviving bill, dated to 1804, from the Grubb family of Clonmel, Co. Tipperary, records the purchase of a 'mahogany nurse's chair'

Correspondence, i, p. 99.   **49** NLI, Edgeworth papers, MS 1,510, Richard Edgeworth account book, pp 140, 142.   **50** C. Fox to E. FitzGerald, 30 Apr. 1760, in FitzGerald (ed.), *Correspondence*, i, p. 283.   **51** R. Larsen, 'Sisterly guidance: elite women, sorority and the life cycle, 1770–1860' in T. Dooley, M. O'Riordan & C. Ridgway (eds), *Women and the country house in Ireland and Britain* (Dublin, 2018), pp 157–69.   **52** Ibid., p. 167.   **53** Tillyard, *Aristocrats*, p. 233.   **54** Ibid.   **55** O'Toole, 'Object, spaces and rituals', p. 82.

1.4 Marguerite Gérard, *The nourishing mother*, oil on panel, 1804. Villa Musée Fragonard. Wikimedia Commons.

at a cost 16*s*. (fig. 1.5).[56] This was a distinct type of chair designed for the nursing mother: its key features included its low height and the absence of arm rests, which allowed a mother to easily cradle her newborn and breastfeed without being restricted. The development of chairs explicitly designed for nursing mothers was in fact part of an array of gender- and age-specific furniture items that emerged in luxury cabinetwork from the 1760s onwards. Nursing chairs appeared alongside niche products, such as bed rests and wheelchairs for invalids, children and the elderly.[57]

[56] NLI, Grubb papers, MS 8,409 (1), furniture bill.   [57] A. Vickery, 'Fashioning difference in Georgian England: furniture for him and for her' in P. Findlen (ed.), *Early modern things: objects and their histories, 1500–1800* (London, 2012), pp 342–59.

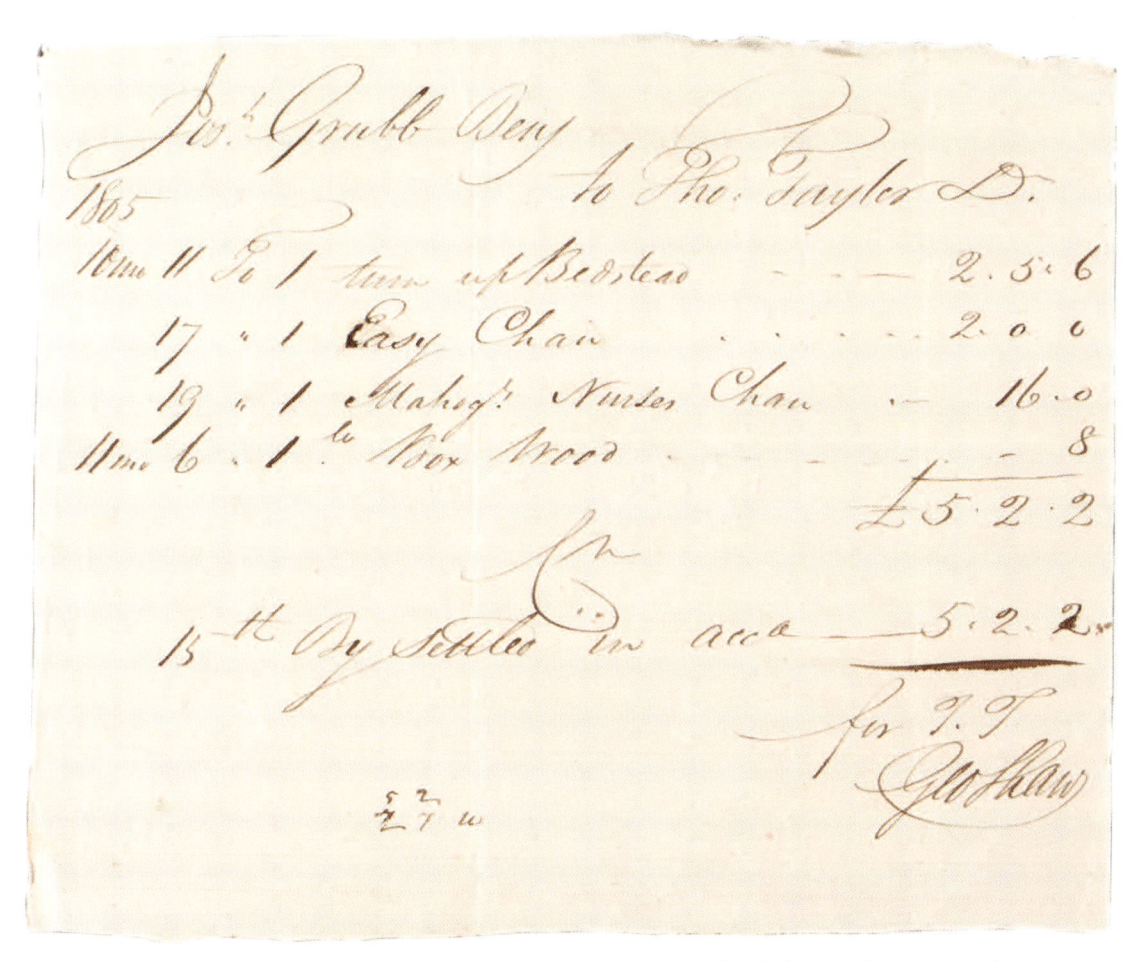

1.5 Furniture bill to Joseph Benjamin Grubb from Theo Taylor, listing a mahogany nurse's chair, costing 16 shillings, 1805. NLI, Grubb papers, MS 8,409 (1). Courtesy of the National Library of Ireland.

Following a period of rest and recuperation with the aid of servants and female family members, the next stage allowed the new mother to get out of bed but still remain within her bedchamber and its outer rooms, and receive visiting guests, both male and female.[58]

LYING-IN AND VISITING GUESTS

Family members, friends and neighbours visited mothers frequently over the course of their lying-in, but particularly once the new mother had left her bedchamber and

---

58 Wilson, *Ritual and conflict*, p. 172.

moved to either her dressing room or downstairs. On 10 May 1761, ten days after giving birth to her fourth son, Henry, Emily FitzGerald wrote to her husband, 'I have never been alone, someone or other continually dropping in'.[59] In the same month, Emily described to her sister, Louisa Connolly, the array of guests she received in her dressing room, writing that 'the boys sit with me the whole evening. Last night I had my two Viscounts, Lady Harrington and her daughter the night before, besides Lady Albemarle and her daughters'.[60]

As noted above, the advent of male relatives visiting the lying-in chamber proceeded slowly over the course of the late eighteenth and early nineteenth centuries. According to traditional ways, no man entered the chamber during the first two weeks after birth. By the third week, only male relatives could visit, and on the fourth week all were permitted. However, it is clear from the Drennan letters that these regulations had begun to relax by the early nineteenth century. On 3 April 1801, two days after the birth of his first son, Drennan wrote to his sister Martha McTier informing her that they 'had a great many visitors today, male and female'.[61]

During the lying-in period, visiting guests that called to congratulate the new mother provided families with ideal opportunities for genteel social interaction. With the anticipation that guests would be visiting and socializing at his home, Peacock consciously upgraded the interior of his household. On 1 August 1750, one day before his wife's third lying-in, Peacock recorded in his journal that he travelled to Limerick to buy '4 chairs' (16s.), 'glasses' (2s. 1d.), and a looking glass (8s. 6d.).[62] The purchase of goods such as these served the purpose of enhancing sociability within the Peacock household during the lying-in period. Sarah Drennan's bedchamber also called for some upgrading. Two weeks after she gave birth in April 1801, her sister-in-law Martha encouraged Sarah to receive guests in her bedchamber rather than downstairs as she feared it was too cold for Sarah with 'snowing days and no window curtains' in the downstairs rooms.[63] There were issues with the bedchamber too:

> Your own room, I fear would look scrub for <u>you</u> to see company in – the paper was dirty, a trifle, if John had held the brush according to the receipt I send you would have coloured it, but it had the valuable ornaments which I hope it will ever retain while the house is Drennans.[64]

Despite the poor quality of the wallpaper in the bedchamber, the 'valuable ornaments' acted as a visual and material sign of the Drennan family's polite aspirations. It also draws parallels with Erving Goffman's concept of performance, the presentation of the self with respect to front stage and backstage behaviour.[65] The ornaments were

---

[59] E. FitzGerald to J. FitzGerald, 10 May 1761, in FitzGerald (ed.), *Correspondence*, i, p. 121. [60] Tillyard, *Aristocrats*, p. 233. [61] W. Drennan to M. McTier, 3 Apr. 1801, in Agnew (ed.), *The Drennan–McTier letters*, ii, pp 694–5. [62] N. Peacock, 1 Aug. 1750, in Legg (ed.), *The diary of Nicholas Peacock*, p. 216. [63] M. McTier to S. Drennan, 14 Apr. 1801, in Agnew (ed.), *The Drennan–McTier letters*, ii, p. 696. [64] Ibid. [65] Goffman, *The presentation of the self*, pp 124–7.

1.6 Female bedgown, silk damask, lined with silk taffeta and linen, *c.*1740 to *c.*1760, England. V&A T.92-2003. © Victoria and Albert Museum, London.

perhaps displayed on a piece of furniture in the bedchamber for guests to admire when visiting Sarah; then, returned to where they were originally on show, possibly in the parlour or drawing room.

For new mothers, confinement provided a level of social informality where guests, both male and female, were permitted into the mother's bedchamber or to her private dressing room. The social informality also allowed women to receive their guests in relaxed informal attire such as loose wrapping gowns, bedjackets or bedgowns. Made from lightweight materials such as printed cotton or silk, these gowns were unrestrictive and comfortable (fig. 1.6). Jane Edgeworth perhaps wore the 'Indian satin nightgown' that her husband purchased in June 1732 for £4 9s., three days after the birth of their first child.[66] Through the letters Martha McTier sent to Sarah Drennan in 1801, we know that Anna May Chichester, Lady Donegall, during the period of her lying-in, wore a 'little light cap' and a short 'quilted white satin' bedgown that was 'trimmed in rich lace detail'.[67]

The practices of entertaining guests during the lying-in had been well entrenched in Irish society long before the eighteenth century. Clodagh Tait's research on lying-in practices in sixteenth- and seventeenth-century Ireland provides details of women hosting large banquets.[68] By the eighteenth century, an important part of the celebrations surrounding the lying-in chamber was drinking caudle, a hot drink made from a blend of wine, ale, brandy, gruel, egg, sugar, spices, citrus fruits and rice.[69] At Catherine Peacock's first lying-in held in April 1748, her husband Nicholas Peacock recorded in his diary that he sent his servant, Mick, 'to town for lemons [and] oranges'.[70] These ingredients were likely used to prepare caudle for visiting guests, when, as Peacock noted, 'some of ye neighbour[s] come to see Catty'.[71] The ingredients, particularly imported oranges and lemons, were a costly indulgence for Peacock.

Genteel social interaction during the lying-in period was greatly enhanced in the second half of the eighteenth century due to the development of accoutrements made specifically for caudle drinking. By the late eighteenth century, ceramic and porcelain manufacturers including Wedgwood, Spode, Derby, Worcester and Bow were all producing caudle cups in a variety of shapes and patterns (fig. 1.7). The eighteenth-century caudle cup was similar in style but an improvement on the design of the seventeenth-century posset pot; it was baluster-shaped with one or two handles. Unlike the posset pot, the caudle cup was designed without a spout. By the early nineteenth century, creamware caudle cups were available to buy in Dublin. For instance, at Wedgwood and Bentley's premises on Sackville Street, between 1808 and 1811, caudle cups were available for ready purchase alongside a range of creamware sick basins and physic cups designed specifically for invalids.[72]

66 NLI, Edgeworth papers, MS 1,510, Richard Edgeworth account book, p. 74.   67 M. McTier to W. Drennan, 21 Dec. 1805, in Agnew (ed.), *The Drennan–McTier letters*, iii, p. 403.   68 Tait, 'Safely delivered'.   69 For further information on caudle recipes see K. Cahill, *Mrs Delany's menus, medicines and manners* (Dublin, 2005), p. 46; Wilson, *The making of man-midwifery*, pp 26–7.   70 N. Peacock, 27 to 28 Apr. 1748, in Legg (ed.), *The diary of Nicholas Peacock*, p. 186.   71 Ibid.   72 Wedgwood Archives,

1.7 Caudle cup, cover and stand, Derby porcelain factory c.1785. V&A 7989 to B1901. © Victoria and Albert Museum, London.

The use of caudle cups is evident in the Drennan letters. In a letter dated 21 December 1805, Martha McTier wrote to Sarah to inform her of the two different types of caudle cups that Lady Donegall possessed in her lying-in chamber: 'immense large fine china cawdle cups for show' and 'smaller for use'.[73] Martha's description of the china caudle cups on show suggests that these were intended for decoration, perhaps to be used as centrepieces for a table or displayed on a shelf, where guests could admire them. The evidence suggests that hosting caudle parties created a demand for accoutrements: the introduction of creamware caudle cups and the availability of caudle recipes published in household cookery manuals from the mid eighteenth century onwards also indicates that retailers and authors were keen to capitalize on these domestic events.

Dublin Order Book, 1808–11.   73 M. McTier to W. Drennan, 21 Dec. 1805, in Agnew (ed.), *The Drennan–McTier letters*, iii, p. 403.

CONCLUSION

In May 1755, Emily Fitzgerald wrote in delight to her husband James FitzGerald, relaying that it was 'one month tomorrow since I was brought to bed' and for the first time she was able to go outside and enjoy 'the fresh air'.[74] Writing to Mary Delany in August 1771, these sentiments were echoed by Frances Boscawen, when she recounted the moment that she emerged from her bed after ten days of recuperation: 'I danced a minuet about my room in ten days, to insult my monthly and set her a scolding diversion'.[75] The lying-in was a long and arduous process for many women, and it was a relief when it finally came to an end. For many women it was a ritual that was regularly repeated throughout their fertile life.

While accepting that descriptions found in account books, diaries, letters and architectural drawings do not give a complete picture of a given room or household, the nature of the purchases made for the preparation of the lying-in chamber and the descriptions of the lying-in period indicate that Emily Fitzgerald, Jane Edgeworth, Catherine Peacock and Sarah Drennan consciously rearranged spaces in their households. On the one hand, the redecoration of their rooms increased their comfort during childbirth and the lying-in period. On the other, it appears that the interiors of the bedchamber and the outer room or dressing room were open to visiting guests during the lying-in, and that families decorated them with this in mind. This is particularly evidenced by the display of high value and new items, such as Edgeworth's purchase of new carpets, beds and clothing, or Peacock's purchase of chairs, beds, a looking glass, and new drinking glasses.

The purchase of new goods for the lying-in also overlapped with practices of borrowing furniture and furnishings from family and friends. The Peacocks and Drennans borrowed and shared items such as folding beds, cribs and cradles. The fact that families stored, kept and even inherited furniture for the lying-in indicates that these household goods were of significant monetary, emotional or social value to families. Regardless of whether the furniture and furnishings were new or borrowed, it is clear from the families examined in this chapter that they consciously changed the use of household spaces for the lying-in. For the limited time of between two to four weeks, these bedroom spaces transitioned from a very private space of the household to a public one that welcomed visiting guests.

---

[74] E. FitzGerald to J. FitzGerald, 22 May 1755, in FitzGerald (ed.), *Correspondence*, i, p. 21.
[75] F. Boscawen to M. Delany, 29 Aug. 1771, in Cahill, *Mrs Delany's menus*, p. 227.

A male domain? The dining room reconsidered

PATRICIA McCARTHY

In his book, *Life in the English country house,* published in 1978, Mark Girouard coined the terms 'male' and 'female' to describe dining rooms and drawing rooms respectively in the Georgian house, terms on which many historians have divided opinions, as one might expect. It might, with some justification, be considered unfair to refer to the dining room as a 'male space', when the onerous task of the hostess in providing the meal is ignored.[1] But research shows that in Georgian Ireland it was a space in which many men took a particular interest regarding its décor, its furniture and, especially, the accoutrements of dining and wining.

In the first half of the eighteenth century, the room in which a family ate and entertained was generally known as a 'dining parlour' or an 'eating parlour', and in town houses there was the 'front' or 'street parlour', and the 'back parlour'. By the mid-eighteenth century in Britain the term 'parlour' was no longer used in plans for new houses and, while it took another half century for the term to disappear in Ireland,[2] there was a gradual move towards the specialization of rooms, when the parlour (as an eating room) gave way to the 'dining room', the use of which term was acknowledged by the ever-alert Mrs Mary Delany who, in a letter written in 1755, referred to 'my "dining room", vulgarly so-called'.[3] The family continued to eat in a parlour, using the formal room only occasionally. By the latter decades of the century, when both roads and carriages had been greatly improved, the well off were increasingly travelling around the country, happy to accept offers of hospitality from friends and acquaintances as they did so. Dining rooms found to be too small to facilitate a greater number of visitors were extended and refurbished, as at Carton, Co. Kildare, in 1815,[4] and newly built houses, such as Rockingham, Co. Roscommon (1809), Emo Court, Co. Laois (1821), Ballyfin, Co. Laois (1822), and Lissadell, Co. Sligo (1833), were planned with more spacious rooms in which to entertain. However, as early as the mid-1760s, Lady Louisa Conolly at Castletown, Co. Kildare, undertook a major project when she created a spacious dining room out of two adjoining rooms to the left of the entrance hall. What made this such an enormous undertaking was that the dividing walls were removed through three floors of the house to roof level, and a false wall built to the west, to centre the windows, behind which two closets became serving rooms with a sink and stoves. On this point, regarding stoves, and

1 M. Girouard, *Life in the English country house: a social and architectural history* (London, 1978), p. 205; C. Saumarez-Smith, *Design and the domestic interior in eighteenth-century England* (London, 2000), p. 167.
2 P. McCarthy, *Life in the country house in Georgian Ireland* (New Haven & London, 2016), p. 84.
3 Quoted in ibid., p. 90.

keeping the dinner warm, many houses had a servery located outside the dining room, with a stove (as at Castletown), a facility that was essential particularly in a Palladian-style house where the kitchen was usually located in one of the pavilions, from where the food was carried along the colonnade and into the house by a side door. It was more straightforward and convenient in houses where the kitchen was located in the basement and had a staircase that led directly to the preparation area outside the dining room, as in John Nash's plan for Rockingham and Killeen Castle, Co. Meath (1802), with its convenient spiral stairway to the basement kitchen.

In Georgian Ireland the dining room was used fairly exclusively for the entertainment of guests, its function being to entertain family, friends and acquaintances to a meal that had been planned and supervised by the lady of the house. Apart from compiling the menu, and organizing the food and its service, she was responsible for the table setting, the seating plans, and the behaviour of the servants, in the full knowledge that the success or failure of the dinner party relied on her; any slip on her part would be noted, and with that came considerations of social standing. As for the master of the house, his main job was to provide suitable wines from his cellar. Organizing and maintaining a wine cellar was no easy task, and will not be gone into here; it is perhaps enough to say that the wine was every bit as important as the food itself, and most definitely a measure of the host's generosity and sophistication, as well as being a regular topic of conversation among men. It was the host's responsibility to ensure that the chosen wines had arrived from the cellar on time and were ready to be served when appropriate. He was well aware, too, that his social standing and taste would be judged on not just the appearance and quality of his table: as Anna Moran puts it, 'merely possessing the appropriate objects was not sufficient; one had to interact with them in the correct fashion'. It was not unknown for hosts and their wives to be laughed at in some circles for their lack of such interaction with items – indeed, some were of the opinion that a person's rank and worth could be judged on the basis of how one held one's glass.[5] The rituals attached to the consumption of food and drink, with which one should be familiar, were to be found in abundance from the beginning of the nineteenth century in written texts that described and aided those who had any doubts regarding not just the provision of food and drink, but the meal's physical and material enactment.

As a guest arriving for dinner, one was ushered into either the drawing room or the library to await the summons to dine. While in the drawing room, one could admire the rich fabrics on the windows, on the walls, and covering the soft comfortable furniture, as well as, of course, the paintings: if one waited in the library, the well-bound books lined up on shelves indicated the good taste, learning and interests of the family. However, for the owner's reputation, his standing in society, it was imperative to be known and admired also for one's generous hospitality,

---

[4] Designed by Richard Morrison, the new dining room measured 50.4 x 24 feet.   [5] A. Moran, '"The eye as well as the appetite must be car'd for": glass and dining in Ireland, about 1680 – about 1830' in C.L. Maxwell, *In sparkling company: reflections on glass in the 18th-century British world* (New York, 2020), p. 214.

2.1 Robert Adam, elevation of the eating parlour at Headfort House, Co. Meath, ink on paper, 1771. Yale Center for British Art, Paul Mellon Collection, B1975.2.793.

something that had a tradition in Ireland for centuries. Hospitality in Ireland dates back to medieval times when legal obligations to it included 'the right of a traveller to food and lodging, the right of a lord to be entertained by his vassals and the right of a king to billet his servants on the inhabitants of his kingdom'.[6] Richard Stanihurst commented in the sixteenth century that Gaelic Irish chieftains were 'the most hospitable of men, nor could you please them more in anything than by frequently visiting their houses willingly of your own accord, or claiming an invitation from them'.[7] It was said of Lord Kenmare in 1767 that 'his table was elegantly spread, his venison excellent, his wines genuine; and he gives them … like the son of an Irish king'.[8] Thomas Sheridan, father of playwright and politician Richard Brinsley Sheridan, and friend of Jonathan Swift, liked to fancy himself in the role of an ancient Irish host in his home, Quilca, in Co. Cavan. There he joyfully entertained his guests in his 'parlour' where the floor was strewn with rushes and his table spread with 'antique dishes and cuisinage obsolete'.[9]

The dining room was the stage on which the host and hostess performed. Located usually to the front of the house, the room was a showpiece, where the guests

[6] K. Simms, 'Guesting and feasting in Gaelic Ireland', *Journal of the Royal Society of Antiquaries of Ireland*, 108 (1978), 67–100. [7] D. Dickson, *Dublin: the making of a capital city* (Dublin, 2014), p. 35. [8] J. Knightley, from a draft chapter of a forthcoming study on Sir William Godfrey, kindly shared with the author. [9] McCarthy, *Life in the country house in Georgian Ireland*, p. 85.

2.2 *Aesop* ceiling at Phoenix Lodge (now Áras an Uachtaráin), Phoenix Park, Dublin, created by Bartholomew Cramillion for Nathaniel Clements in 1754. Courtesy of Dublin City Council. Photograph Paul Tierney.

could enjoy not just the food and the wine, but the décor. According to Mark Girouard, the dining room was 'always one of the best and biggest rooms in the house'.[10] Outstanding examples of purpose-built dining rooms are the original dining room at Carton, where the coved ceiling was decorated with plasterwork by the celebrated Lafranchini brothers in 1739, and the eating parlour at Headfort, Co. Meath, designed by Robert Adam (1771–5) (fig. 2.1). Ceilings, walls and chimneypieces often contained depictions and celebrations of Bacchus: examples include the *Aesop* ceiling designed and executed by Bartholomew Cramillion for the Rt Hon. Nathaniel Clements, Teller of the Exchequer and Ranger of the Phoenix Park, for his lodge in the Phoenix Park (now Áras an Uachtaráin) (fig. 2.2) and, by the same stuccodore, the ceiling in the dining room at Belvedere, Co. Westmeath, with bunches of grapes and vine leaves, also to be seen on wall lights and chimneypieces.[11] It was no surprise therefore to find the earl of Altamont engaging the architect James Wyatt to design a brand new dining room at Westport House in Co. Sligo in 1781. By the close of the eighteenth century, such attention to the decoration of dining rooms was routinely observed by Dublin's burgeoning building industry. The ceiling of the ground-floor dining parlour at 9 Harcourt Street, built and decorated by plasterer and master builder Michael Stapleton in 1785, features a decorative border of grapes and vine leaves appropriate to the function of the room.[12]

Another way of achieving architectural interest in dining rooms was with the columnar screen, found in many Irish houses. It could be used to 'frame' the sideboard on which the family silver was displayed. But there was a practical side to it too as it was often used as a service area behind which the servants operated, close to a jib door leading to the back stairs. This brings us to the question of how close was the dining room to the kitchen? It was an important consideration as a) it was not desirable for the smell of food to linger in the hall as the servant makes his way to the dining room; b) the food must be warm on arrival; and c) it was important to avoid collisions between servant and guests in the doorway.

While the drawing room was considered a female space, the dining room was a room largely planned for and provisioned by the male owner. As much time was spent there in eating (together with the ladies), and drinking (among the men, after the departure of the ladies to the drawing room), so a great deal of money, time and thought was invested in fitting it out with the accoutrements appropriate to these occasions. An important requirement for the location of the dining room was that it should be at a distance from the drawing room as the men could become quite boisterous once the ladies had departed. In 1752, George, 1st Lord Lyttleton, instructed his architect Sanderson Miller to insert 'a room of separation' between the dining room and drawing room for his design for Hagley Hall, Worcestershire, noting that 'Lady Lyttleton wishes for a room of separation between the eating room and

---

10 Girouard, *Life in the English country house*, p. 103.   **11** J. McDonnell, 'Bartholomew Cramillion and continental rococo' in C. Casey & C. Lucey (eds), *Decorative plasterwork in Ireland and Europe: ornament and the early modern interior* (Dublin, 2012), pp 160–77.   **12** Ex info. Conor Lucey.

2.3 Chinese export porcelain armorial plate, *c*.1750, decorated with the arms of the Roche family, Viscounts Fermoy. The heraldic term for the fish in the shield is 'roach', echoing the family surname. Image courtesy of Robert Morrissey Antiques and Fine Art, St Louis, MO.

the drawing room to hinder the ladies from the noise and talk of the men when left to their bottle as must sometimes happen, even at Hagley'.[13] Most if not all of the men would be familiar with each other, having formed associations through clubs, politics and sports. Thomas Conolly is one example – he frequently invited his friends back to Castletown House after a hunt, for something to eat and lots to drink. In this way, men formed ideas of how they might furnish their own dining rooms when their time came. And they did not hold back. Dinner parties restricted to men only were not uncommon, such as that in Dublin hosted by Lord Chancellor Robert Jocelyn in

---

[13] Lord Lyttleton to Sanderson Miller in C. Hussey, *English country houses*, 5 vols (London, 1955), i, p. 196.

1747, when twelve peers were treated to a rather exotic meal that included dishes of badger flambé and fricassée of frogs,[14] and a very formal dinner at Belvedere, Co. Westmeath, in 1773 where Lord Belfield, with 'four valets-de-chambre in laced clothes and seven or eight footmen', entertained just three male friends to dinner.[15]

For hosts with a distinguished lineage it was an advantage to have family portraits decorate the walls, a reminder to the guests of the weight that their invitation carried. Richard Edgeworth diligently gathered together a collection of ancestral and contemporary family portraits with that purpose in mind, and enjoyed, with his guests, the occasional replication of the expansive hospitality of his forbears.[16] Other desirable and impressive images for the dining room walls were landscapes, particularly those of the host's estate and, of course, the ubiquitous Grand Tourist image of the host among classical Roman ruins. An inventory of the dining parlour at 7 Parnell Square (formerly 10 Cavendish Row), recorded in 1763, indicates that its walls were hung with numerous paintings, including an appropriate 'Frute [sic] & Dead Game Picture' by the Dutch artist Jan Fyt.[17]

Between 1720 and 1820, more than one hundred dinner and tea services, embellished with their family coats of arms, were made in China for Irish customers, among them the duke of Leinster, the earl of Ely, and Pole Cosby of Stradbally, Co. Laois (fig. 2.3).[18] By 1755, Lord Grandison had purchased a set of china on which was his crest. Thomas Cobbe's 'magnificent' Worcester china dessert service for thirty-six people was described as showing 'his good taste and also the splendid scale of his entertainments' at Newbridge House,[19] while another purchaser of china was William Robert FitzGerald, second duke of Leinster, who in June 1775 wrote from Paris to his mother, 'I have ruin'd myself with a sett of Seve [sic] China'.[20] For his newly-built Dromoland in 1825, Edward O'Brien boasted: 'I propose buying Silver and dishes, Candlesticks, Linen, everything wanted for a Table of 18 persons to dine … I saw yesterday several very handsome sets of Coalbroke Dale China at £40'. He expected his dining room to be finished in the Spring and wanted to give some parties around the time of the Summer Assizes or the Races; moreover, he intended to spend 'about a thousand Pounds worth of goods' for the room (equivalent to approximately £92,000 in modern-day spending power).[21] While O'Brien bragged about the parties he planned and the expensive purchases for his dining room, Sir James Caldwell of Castle Caldwell, Co. Fermanagh, on a tour along the east coast of Ireland, wrote to

---

14 A. FitzGerald, 'Taste in high life: dining in the Dublin town house' in C. Casey (ed.), *The eighteenth-century Dublin town house* (Dublin, 2010), pp 120–27.   **15** Quoted in D. Guinness & W. Ryan, *Irish houses & castles* (London, 1971), p. 301.   **16** T. Barnard, *A new anatomy of Ireland: the Irish Protestants, 1649–1770* (New Haven & London, 2003), p. 47.   **17** BL, Cockburn papers, MS Add. 48314. My thanks to Conor Lucey for this reference.   **18** D.S. Howard, 'Chinese armorial porcelain for Ireland', *Bulletin of the Irish Georgian Society*, 29:3–4 (1986), 2–24.   **19** F. Power Cobbe, *Life of Frances Power Cobbe. By herself*, 2 vols (Cambridge, 1894), i, p. 19.   **20** NLI, MS 617, FitzGerald correspondence, vol. III, 1774–1790, letter 144. The duke is referring to the famous Sèvres porcelain factory, founded in 1740. Cited in C. Lucey, 'Keeping up appearances: redecorating the domestic interior in late eighteenth-century Dublin', *Proceedings of the Royal Irish Academy*, 111C (2011), 171.   **21** G. O'Brien, *These my friends and forbears: the O'Briens at Dromoland* (Whitegate, 1991), pp 111–12.

2.4 Silver épergne by Thomas Pitts I (active 1737–93), London, 1761. The Folgers Coffee Silver Collection, gift of the Procter & Gamble Co., Nelson-Atkins Museum of Art, Kansas City, MI. Wikimedia Commons.

his wife following an 'elegant dinner' in Lord Bangor's home, that the fruit served left much to be desired, but he was satisfied to note that

> Our epergne, candlesticks, service of china, variety of fruit, substantial and well-dressed dinners, and dining room far exceed anything that I have seen since I came abroad, and so it is spoken of … both Sir Patrick and Fortescue had often declared that they never had anywhere in their lives met with so much entertainment … or more elegant living than at Castle Caldwell.[22]

[22] Quoted in V. Packenham, *The big house in Ireland* (London, 2005), p. 101.

2.5 The Leinster dining service, a George II silver service with the mark of George Wickes, London, 1745–56, reputed to be the most complete surviving aristocratic dinner service. © Christie's Images.

Hosting meals certainly offered opportunities to impress not just by the quality and variety of the food and wine, but by the silver and glassware. According to Alison FitzGerald, in 1727, the nineteenth earl of Kildare purchased a silver wine cooler; Thomas Taylor of Headfort, the following year, purchased forty-two silver plates. In 1742, a silver dinner service was ordered by Joseph Leeson of Russborough, Co. Wicklow, which included a cistern, six dozen silver plates, and an *épergne* – a centrepiece for a dessert course (fig. 2.4); in 1745 the famous Leinster silver dinner service was purchased by the twentieth earl of Kildare from Wickes of London for £4,000 (it sold at Christies for just under £2m some years ago), who also that year supplied the earl with a very expensive pair of candelabra (fig. 2.5). And the clergy were not to be outdone: in the second half of the eighteenth century, the bishop of Elphin purchased a large épergne with eight branches for £100, and the archbishop

2.6 Monteith bowl, silver gilt, 1715–16, made by Benjamin Pyne, London (active 1693–1727). Courtesy of the Cleveland Museum of Art, gift of Mr and Mrs Warren H. Corning, 1965.

of Dublin ordered a dinner service costing £1000, both from London goldsmiths.[23] As the hour for dining became progressively later in the eighteenth century, a profusion of wax candles lit dining rooms from torchères, candlesticks, candelabra and sconces, the latter often fitted with a mirror to reflect light. Together with mirrors on the piers between windows, the effect of the reflections and the flickering light on the silver and glassware was calculated to impress.

Silver was frequently to be found at auctions, and was much sought-after: the armorials of original owners could easily be erased and replaced with those of the purchaser. This was done assiduously by Richard Edgeworth, who stamped all of his silver, inherited, bought at auction, or new, with the family crest and arms. Wine accessories in particular found an eager home market keen to purchase the accoutrements desired, from wine coolers to corkscrews. In the event of a shortage of servants, decanter wagons or carriages enabled wine to circulate around the table on

23 A. FitzGerald, *Silver in Georgian Dublin: making, selling, consuming* (London and New York, 2017), passim.

2.7 One of four wine bottles discovered at Rathfarnham Castle, Dublin, that have 'AL 1688' stamped on the bottoms, referring to Lord Adam Loftus, resident of the castle at the time. Photograph courtesy of Alva Mac Gowan/Archaeology Plan.

top of the tablecloth and although the servants were on hand to assist the guests if required, the latter were able to fill their own glasses if they wished. Placed on the sideboard or serving table, monteiths (fig. 2.6), with their removable notched rim, kept wineglasses hanging by the foot in water that was as cold as possible (it is notable that both red and white wines were served cold), and the silver labels suspended by a chain around the neck of the decanters ensured that every man knew what he was drinking (while simultaneously enabling the butler to recognize when a particular wine was running low). These labels became fashionable about the same time that decanters were appearing, the earliest dating to the mid-1730s. Jonathan Swift, in his will dated 1740, wrote, 'I bequeath to the Earl of Orrery the enamelled Silver Plates to distinguish Bottles of Wine by, given to me by his Excellent Lady'. This description appears to be the earliest-known reference to wine labels in an Irish context.[24] Incidentally, and on the subject of wine accessories, Laetitia Pilkington tells of Swift accusing her of stealing his gold corkscrew:

> he was sure I had stolen it: I affirmed, very seriously, 'I had not', upon which he looked for it and found it where he himself had laid it; 'tis well for you' says he, 'that I have got it, or I would have charged you with theft': 'why, pray, sir, should I be suspected more than any other person in the company?' 'For a very good reason', says he, 'because you are the poorest'.[25]

Some liked their name or initials inscribed on their own wine bottles: Adam Loftus of Rathfarnham Castle was one. During a recent archaeological excavation at the castle, remnants of bottles were discovered with '1688, AL' inscribed on them (fig. 2.7).[26] Jonathan Swift also favoured this practice: one of his bottles, now in the collection of the National Museum of Ireland, is embossed with his name and the year '1727'.[27]

At Castle Coole, Co. Fermanagh in *c*.1797, the earl of Belmont engaged the architect James Wyatt (1746–1813) to design a sideboard suite for his dining room. The elegant mahogany sideboard remains in situ and is flanked by urns on pedestals; brass rails running along the back provided for a short curtain to protect the wall from food stains or splashes; and beneath it is a fluted sarcophagus wine cooler with a lion mask: when filled with crushed ice, it kept the wine cold. An auction notice in the *Dublin Evening Post* in March 1793 includes a similar sideboard suite in the Clare Street home of the Right Revd Lord bishop of Down, described as 'an elegant side board with pedestals, vases, wine cooler, and two pier tables to match', and underlining the clergy's continued enthusiasm for such luxury goods.[28] Wine coolers could make a statement: they came in all shapes and sizes and were made of various materials. Visitors admired the quality of the mahogany used in the dining table and its chairs, which often had leather or horsehair seats that did not retain the smell of food or stain easily.[29]

For most of the eighteenth century, drinking wine during dinner occurred only when a toast was given. Glassware was important, adding to the beauty and sparkle of the table; the host would gain satisfaction from the fact that his guests would recognize not just the quality of such glasses, but that he could fill them with endless amounts of wine. Small wine glasses, sufficient for one draught and suitable for toasting, were kept on side tables, together with the wine, to be served by the footman/servant, and re-charged for the next toast. The master of the house would

---

24 C. O'Brien, 'Dean Swift's and some early Irish labels', *Journal of the Wine Label Circle*, 9:3 (1992), 54–60. 25 A.C. Elias Jr (ed.), *Memoirs of Laetitia Pilkington*, 2 vols (London, 1997), i, p. 31. 26 C. Gleeson, 'Hoard of 17th century artefacts found at Rathfarnham Castle', *Irish Times*, 30 Oct. 2014. 27 NMI, DC:1941.34. 28 *Dublin Evening Post*, 7 Mar. 1793. My thanks to Conor Lucey for this reference. 29 S. Paston-Williams, *The art of dining: a history of cooking and eating* (London, 1999), p. 247.

name a lady in the company and drink to her health, and then each of the men followed suit. In the early eighteenth century, tall, slim 'toasting glasses' were made to be broken after a single use by snapping off the stems; it was considered that, after toasting the health of a fair lady present, it devalued the toast to use it to drink to another lady.[30] As glass was expensive, this was not something that became popular, but apparently the Prince Regent (later George IV) instituted the habit of doing just that at parties to ensure that his friends drank as much as he did.[31]

For the normal dinner party, the large dining table was covered with a white linen tablecloth that extended to the floor. This protected the wood and hid any joins in the table. It also had another purpose; it was used as a napkin with which to wipe one's mouth. The removal of the cloth at the end of the meal signified a change in the nature of the occasion: before, the business was eating; afterwards, it was drinking.[32] The ladies would have a glass or two of wine and, at the end of a half hour or so, departed to their tea and chat in the drawing room.

At this point, the large wine cooler was rolled out from beneath the sideboard, laden with bottles of wine in iced water, to the delight of the gentlemen; at the same time the toasting glasses were replaced by (larger) goblets. Not all male parties remained in the dining room. At Castle Blayney, Co. Monaghan, Lord Blayney and his 'merry men', as he called them, typically adjourned to a little room which he called his 'own glory hole – and there we had such fun, such jolly stories, that it was difficult to leave our seats'.[33] Some men found that the volume of drinking expected at such occasions was at times rather alarming, every man having to drink in turn, for the bottles would go continually around the table in one direction, and the master of the house made sure that no one missed a turn – it being considered unsportsmanlike to do so. This represented a certain amount of social pressure. One guest found a way out of it at an all-male dinner: having watched his companions around the table falling victim to the power of alcohol, he slipped under the table where he lay for a while with others. Suddenly he realized that a small pair of hands were at his throat. When he asked the boy what he was up to he was told, 'Sir, I'm the lad that's to loosen the neckclothes', his job being to ensure that no guest should suffocate.[34]

The third president of the United States, Thomas Jefferson, was a great believer in the use of dumb waiters; he had a total of five, rectangular in shape, and used them at dinner in his private dining room at the White House. Jefferson disliked having servants in attendance there, believing that 'much of the domestic and even public discord is produced by the mutilated and misconstructed [*sic*] repetition of free conversation at dinner tables, by these mute but not inattentive listeners'. He brought back from France the idea of such a piece of furniture on which was arranged the

---

30 P. McCarthy, *Enjoying claret in Georgian Ireland: a history of amiable excess* (Dublin, 2022), p. 79. **31** R. Rupp, 'Cheers: celebration drinking is an ancient tradition', *National Geographic*, 26 Dec. 2014. **32** Paston-Williams, *The art of dining*, p. 249.   **33** Quoted in McCarthy, *Life in the country house in Georgian Ireland*, p. 151.   **34** A. Simon, *Bottlescrew days: wine drinking in England during the eighteenth century* (London, 1926), p. 46.

2.8 Claret or drinking table, attributed to Gillows of Lancaster and London. The demi-lune leaf is removable and the hinged flaps can be folded down as in the image. Courtesy of Ronald Phillips Ltd.

entire meal, then placed between the guests who helped themselves. Another dumb waiter of Jefferson's, and thought to be invented by him, was the pulley kind in his home at Monticello, in Virginia, hidden behind the chimneypiece where wine and other items were conveyed from the cellar to the dining room.[35] These items of furniture are to be found in few Irish inventories, possibly indicating that families living in Ireland were not perturbed by the presence of servants while they ate, or, that they simply enjoyed being waited upon.

Other items associated with hospitality included the claret table, also called a drinking or a hunting table. Recorded in a few Irish furniture inventories, it is horseshoe-shaped and designed for after dinner drinking around the fire. The flaps would be locked into position and the table wheeled to the fireplace where the master of the house and his guests would take their places around the outer edge. The bottle(s) would be placed on the coaster to slide around the inner part of the table (fig. 2.8).

35 J. Hailman, *Thomas Jefferson on wine* (Jackson, MS, 2006), pp 291–2.

2.9 *L'après-dinée des Anglais*, from *Scènes Anglaises dessinées à Londres, par un français prisonnier de guerre.* Hand-coloured etching, France, 1814. © Trustees of the British Museum.

A satirical etching entitled *L'après-dinée des Anglais,* one of a pair produced in France in 1818, mocks the idea of couples being separated after dinner in Britain, something that was simply unheard-of in France (fig. 2.9). Here, the men are quite drunk: one fumbles with the chamber pot from the sideboard – alas too late! The inebriated state of the men and the use of chamber pots in the dining room was the reality in Ireland and England at this time. One might speculate why Thomas Taylor of Headfort, Co. Meath, went to the huge expense of purchasing a silver chamber pot in 1723 that weighed 24 ounces and cost 6*s.* 10*d.* per ounce?[36] It must have been for use in the dining room, though the extent to which his guests appreciated this extravagance is another question.

---

36 FitzGerald, *Silver in Georgian Dublin*, p. 44.

Calling the dining room a male domain is not, in my opinion, wide of the mark. It is probable that many women played a part in the furnishing of the room but there was an unspoken acceptance that after dinner, when the women had departed the table, the dining room was given over to the host and his male guests for their enjoyment and their privacy. The contents of the wine cooler were too inviting to refuse and the contents of the sideboard, as mentioned above, ensured that there was no need for any of them to leave the room, thereby missing out on the stories and gossip that many might have considered the best part of the evening. On a more practical note, a well produced table, and a constant supply of claret enhanced the sociability of the occasion which in turn established and reinforced the political and fraternal bonds between them, whether they be drunk or sober.

Fashioning, fitting-out and functionality in the aristocratic town house: private convenience and public concerns

MELANIE HAYES

Every man's proper mansion-house, and home, being the theatre of his hospitality, the seate of selfe-fruition, the comfortablest part of his own life, the noblest of his sonne's inheritance, a kinde of private princedome, nay, to the possessors thereof, an epitome of the whole world.[1]

The early eighteenth-century town house fulfilled a myriad of functions both public and private, physical and conceptual, often simultaneously. These buildings formed the backdrop to every stage of life, from birth and marriage to sickness and death. They were the settings for social occasions, for political intrigues and dynastic dramas; the *loci* in which elite networks came together, in which communities were formed and where kinship and ethnographic ties were strengthened. And yet the experience of the people who occupied these spaces, of use and the user, has received intermittent attention in Irish architectural history.[2] Focusing on 10 Henrietta Street, a significant Dublin house of *c.*1730, which was home to the Gardiner family for almost a century, this essay will consider the fashioning, fit-out and functionality of the aristocratic town house in the first half of the eighteenth century. Moving beyond considerations of the layout and appearance of rooms, it seeks to draw out the quotidian experiences of these domestic spaces, both public and private. What role did the user play in the conception of these spaces and the functions they served? What meaning did these individuals attach to their material possessions and how did the fitting out of their residence assist in the art of self-fashioning? What impact – sensory, symbolic and practical – did the material finishes and fittings have on their occupants? What do these choices say about perception and taste in this period? And what, moreover, can their fashioning and fit-out tells us about the dual tensions of domestic comfort and formal display in these spaces?

10 HENRIETTA STREET: MATTERS OF EVIDENCE

Number 10 Henrietta Street, later known as Mountjoy House, has a complex building history. The house was built *c.*1730 for Luke Gardiner (*c.*1680–1755) and his wife

---

[1] H. Wotton, *Elements of architecture* ([1624] London, 1969), pp 82–3. [2] T. Barnard, *Making the grand figure: lives and possessions in Ireland, 1641–1770* (New Haven and London, 2004); P. McCarthy, 'From

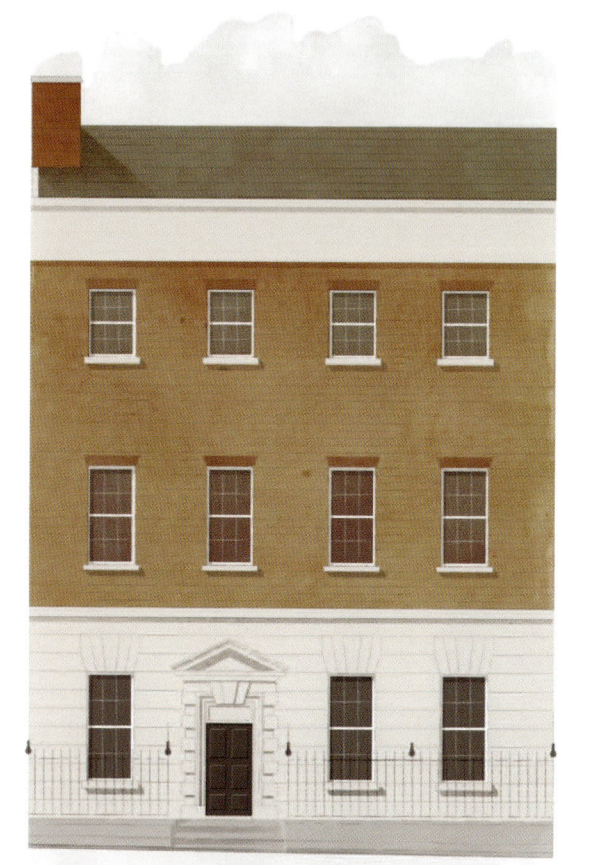

3.1 Façade of 10 Henrietta Street, Dublin. Photograph by Melanie Hayes.

3.2 10 Henrietta Street, Dublin, conjectural reconstruction of the facade, *c*.1730. © Marcus Lynam.

3.3 Former entrance hall ceiling (now first-floor anteroom ceiling), 10 Henrietta Street, Dublin. Courtesy School of Art History & Cultural Policy, University College Dublin.

Anne (*c.* 1697–1753), during the initial phase of works at Henrietta Street and served as the Gardiner family's town residence until 1854.[3] During this time the building fabric underwent a series of alterations and additions, which often seem to have coincided with a change in ownership or occupant. The original 1730s house was only half the size of the current building and comprised of the four right-hand bays of the now much enlarged structure; the external rendering has been altered, as has the window configuration, while the position of the door was moved at a certain point, but subsequently returned to its original location (figs 3.1 and 3.2). Internally, only the rear ground-floor parlour survives largely unaltered from the 1730s scheme, while the ceiling of the original stair hall (once a lofty double-height volume) is now incorporated in the first-floor anteroom (fig. 3.3). Extensive alterations to the layout

parlours to pantries' in C. Casey (ed.), *The eighteenth-century Dublin town house: form, function and finance*, pp 110–119 (Dublin, 2010); P. McCarthy, *Life in the country house in Georgian Ireland* (New Haven and London, 2019).   **3** M. Hayes, *The best address in town: Henrietta Street, Dublin, and its first residents, 1720–1780* (Dublin, 2020), pp 27, 42, 45–6.

3.4 Upper stair hall, 10 Henrietta Street, Dublin, part of the major alterations of the 1750s/1760s. Courtesy School of Art History & Cultural Policy, University College Dublin.

and decoration of the house in the 1740s, 1750s and again in the following century have compromised the architectural clarity of the space and complicated our reading of its original form and character (fig. 3.4).[4] Neither plans nor building records survive for the original scheme or later alternations, though a scaled and measured section drawing of a three-storey house, inscribed 'Mr Gardiner', preserved among architect Sir Edward Lovett Pearce's drawings in the Elton Hall albums, was until recently taken to correspond with Luke Gardiner's house at 10 Henrietta Street.[5] This

4 See Daughters of Charity, St Vincent de Paul, *Numbers 8-10 Henrietta Street, Dublin 1* (Dublin, 2003), pp 24–5, 36–46 for details of the programme of alterations, repair and refurbishment carried out at 10 Henrietta Street from 2001. 5 VAM, Vanbrugh album, E.2124:171-1992, 'Section of 10 Henrietta Street, Dublin, showing vaulted cellars and roof rafters in the Vanbrugh Album by Sir Edward Lovett

drawing, which seems closer to the dimensions of 11 Henrietta Street, does add to the circumstantial evidence connecting Gardiner – and his house – with Pearce. What is more, although stylistic similarities between surviving decorative elements at 10 Henrietta Street and autographed works elsewhere suggest that Pearce employed the same teams of highly skilled craftsmen across a range of contemporary projects, the identities of the artisans who brought this building into being are unknown.

Recovering a clear picture of use in this period can be just as challenging and documented accounts of how such urban houses functioned are thin on the ground. There are no contemporary descriptions, let alone views, of the Gardiner residence in the eighteenth century, and anecdotal evidence is fragmentary. However, several brief yet illuminating sources pertaining to 10 Henrietta Street survive, along with the physical fabric, which when woven together with a range of comparative material allows us to form a picture of how the Gardiners conceived and perceived of and experienced their urban residence. A series of letters, written by Luke Gardiner to his friend and neighbour Nathaniel Clements in the spring of 1745, offer a rare glimpse into the domestic world of Luke Gardiner and his 'girls' (likely a reference to his daughters), and charts their preoccupation with fitting out their 'new room' at 10 Henrietta Street. These missives capture with vivid immediacy the processes of acquisition and conspicuous consumption among such Georgian elites, while testamentary material highlights the value Gardiner attached to material possessions and property. An inventory of the house, which was taken in 1772, but refers to a schedule of the 'Household Goods Plate Linen and Furniture' which were in the house at the time of Luke Gardiner's death in 1755, is extremely valuable in allowing us to recreate a sense of the original arrangement of the rooms, their contents, and to an extent, how these spaces functioned. It is not, however, without limitations. It is not a complete inventory of the house contents, but rather only lists the items once owned by Luke Gardiner, that were included in the 1755 inventory, and still in place. The location of these possessions may have moved in the intervening decades, while others may have been removed entirely. Indeed, the purpose of the inventory in 1772, which was an attempt by successive generations to establish the current monetary value of household goods deemed 'heirlooms' under the terms of Luke Gardiner's will, highlights the transient nature of use and loss in historic buildings.[6] The related agreement between the late Luke Gardiner's son Sackville Gardiner and his grandson Luke Gardiner (son of the late Charles Gardiner, eldest son of Luke Gardiner, who died in 1769) noted that 'Household Goods Linen Plate and Furniture which were left by the said Charles Gardiner to be enjoyed with the said House are in their nature perishable and subject and liable to be wasted and made less valuable by the necessary use of them'.[7] Testament to their ephemeral nature, the inventory not only recorded

---

Pearce', inscribed in ink 'Mr Gardiner'. **6** For more on the processes of acquisition and loss of material goods in historic houses, see J. Stobart, 'Lost aspects of the country estate' in J. Raven (ed.), *Lost mansions: essays on the destruction of the country house* (Basingstoke, 2015), pp 23-43. **7** NLI, MS 36,617/1, Deed of indenture, 18 Oct. 1773, between Sackville Gardiner second son to the late Luke

high value items but also those which had been damaged, such as the '4 Bell lamps' in the Great Hall, 'two of them broke'.[8]

REPRESENTATION

'Housing', according to Toby Barnard, 'was increasingly conceived as something more than mere shelter. In Ireland, as elsewhere, it could be a stratagem – albeit costly and cumbersome – to contrive the grand figure'.[9] Luke Gardiner was a self-made man, acutely conscious of outward perception and position, who utilized a range of strategies to advance his position on the public and private stage. From his advantageous marriage in 1711 to Anne Stewart, niece of Viscount Mountjoy, whose aristocratic lineage opened up many doors in Georgian Ireland, to his ascent up the career ladder, from the ballast board, to the revenue commission and subsequently the treasury, where he courted high-ranking connections and amassed honours along the way, Gardiner sought to project an image of a 'thorough man of business, and of great weight in the country'.[10] The development of a high-class residential enclave at Henrietta Street and the establishment of his own residence there was a crucial arrow in his quiver of self-aggrandisement (fig. 3.5).

The social function of the elite urban house has been much rehearsed.[11] The extent and arrangement of rooms, and perhaps more so the furnishings and fit-out of Gardiner's house at 10 Henrietta Street, clearly signals the representative function of these domestic spaces and their role in the art of self-fashioning and hospitable display. From what can be gleaned, the original layout of the house was arranged on a broad four-room plan, with the principal staircase serving the ground and first floors in the front compartment and a secondary stair behind. The ground floor had parlours to the front and rear, while the first floor contained the more ceremonial drawing rooms, ante-chamber and closet. This arrangement conformed to established hierarchical conventions, whereby the ground and first-floor rooms were given over to public use and were therefore the largest in scale and proportion and received the greatest degree of elaboration in both decoration and furnishings. The servants' hall, kitchen and pantries were confined to the basement, while the family bedchambers – and those of senior retainers – were located in the upper storeys. Although these were

Gardiner and Luke Gardiner [the Younger] eldest son and heir to the late Charles Gardiner, eldest son late Luke Gardiner. Includes a schedule annexed of 'the Household Goods Plate Linen and Furniture which were in the said House wherein the said Luke Gardiner the elder Dwelt at the time of the death of him', 'taken and valued by Joseph Ellis and J. Kirchhoffer Novr 9th 1772'. 8 Ibid. 9 Barnard, *Making the grand figure*, p. 24. 10 Archbishop Hugh Boulter to the Duke of Dorset, *c.*1737 in H. Boulter & A. Phillips (eds), *Letters written by his excellency Hugh Boulter, DD, Lord Primate of All Ireland*, 2 vols (Oxford, 1770), ii, p. 223. 11 M. Girouard, *Life in the English country house: a social and architectural history* (New Haven and London, 1994), p. 145; J. Stobart & A. Owens (eds), *Urban fortunes: property and inheritance in the town, 1700–1900* (Aldershot, 2000), p. 44; Barnard, *Making the grand figure*; J. Styles & A. Vickery (eds), *Gender, taste and material culture in Britain and North America, 1700–1830* (New Haven, 2006), p. 10; A. Vickery, *Behind closed doors: at home in Georgian England* (London, 2009), pp 14–16, 34,

3.5 John Brooks after Charles Jervas, *Luke Gardiner, M.P. (d.1755)*, Mezzotint, 29.2 x 24.5 cm. NGI.10242 National Gallery of Ireland Collection. Photo © National Gallery of Ireland.

overtly private spaces, their contents suggest a blurring of functional boundaries: the array of seating in 'The Late Mr Gardiner's bed chamber' and its attendant 'Dressing room', which contained '6 Mohog.y & 2 elbow chairs' and '8 Mohog.y chairs [with] needle work seats', recalls the formal state bedchambers of aristocratic mansions and speaks to the impression Gardiner sought to create. Similarly, the 'Anty Chamber,' next to the 'Bleu Drawing room' on the floor below offers another example of the blurred line between public and private space in these houses. Alongside such showy high value items as '2 large landscapes in gilt frames' and a gilt-framed painting of a Dutch Market, this room contained a 'Mahogany dressing table'.[12] The first-floor closet contained such everyday personal items as a 'large walnut bureau,' an 'old tea kettle stand,' an 'old corner table' and a 'two leaf needle work screen.'[13]

If 'houses aptly embodied the antiquity, eminence and superiority (not just in wealth but in judgement) of owners', so too did the materials goods contained within.[14] Writing to Nathaniel Clements, who was then just arrived in London on official treasury business in March 1744/45 (O.S.), Luke Gardiner extolled his friend: 'Pray write to me every post, that I may know how the world goes. Make my Compliments to all my Friends, don't forget my room & think of a carpet for it, my good Friend Rumsey will assist you.'[15] Later, Gardiner broke off his account of political business to remark, 'I am undone if you do not get me a Chimney Piece'.[16] The rising importance of conspicuous consumption among metropolitan elites has also received considerable attention in recent decades.[17] Frequent advertisements of the sale of 'Household goods' in London and Dublin certainly attests to the range of luxury items available, as well as the currency attached to the acquisition and accumulation of material objects. These commodities infiltrated the public and private worlds of eighteenth-century elites, altering their perceived notions of self and others. While fashion certainly played a part in patterns of elite consumption, and newspaper advertisements regularly noted that 'the goods are all good and fashionable', there was a myriad of complex motivations behind such consumerism.[18] Other more practical considerations may also have influenced the choice of items purchased. For instance, one advertisement notes that all the household furniture 'was very fresh and clean', while Stobart notes an increased focus on notions of comfort as the century progressed (fig. 3.6).[19]

Gardiner's interest in procuring expensive furniture and fixtures from London, and Clements' agency in this process, was typical of Irish appetites for imported English fashions. There are numerous examples of the Irish abroad, acting as 'agents of civilisation' in purchasing goods generally unavailable at home, and importing the latest ideas and innovations in domestic building and interior design.[20] Ornate mirrors

292; H. Greig, *The beau monde: fashionable society in Georgian London* (Oxford, 2013), pp 40–4. **12** NLI, MS 36,617/1, 'Household Goods Plate Linen and Furniture'. **13** Ibid. **14** Barnard, *Making the grand figure*, p. 35. **15** TCD, MS 1741, Clements Correspondence 1743–55: Luke Gardiner, Dublin to Nathaniel Clements, London, 26 Feb. 1744. **16** TCD, MS 1741/16, Gardiner to Clements, Dublin, 22 Mar. 1744/5. **17** Barnard, *Making the grand figure;* Styles and Vickery, *Gender, taste and material culture;* Vickery, *Behind closed doors;* Greig, *The beau monde.* **18** *Daily Post,* 23 Oct. 1725; L. Weatherill, *Consumer behaviour and material culture in Britain, 1660–1760* (London, 1996), p. 155; J. Brewer & R. Porter (eds), *Consumption and the world of goods* (Oxford, 1994). **19** *Daily Post,* 23 Oct. 1725; J. Stobart (ed.), *The comforts of home in Western Europe, 1700–1900* (London, 2020), p. 3. **20** J. Black, *The British and the Grand Tour* (London, 1985); S. Foster, 'Going shopping in eighteenth-century Dublin', *Things,* 4 (1996), 32–61; D.M. Beaumont, 'An Irish gentleman in England: the travels of Pole Cosby c.1730–35', *Journal of the British Archaeological Association,* 149 (1996), 37–54; T. Barnard, '"Grand metropolis" or "The Anus of the World"? The cultural life of eighteenth-century Dublin' in P. Clark & R. Gillespie (eds), *Two*

3.6 'List of goods at Henrietta Street house which did belong to the late Luke Gardiner.' MS 36,617, Gardiner papers, Inventory of 10 Henrietta Street, taken in 1772. Courtesy of the National Library of Ireland.

or 'glasses' proved particularly popular. On 16 March 1744/45, Gardiner wrote: 'I want two Glasses for my room, I tell you every thing as it comes into my head.'[21] Three days later, following a lengthy request regarding 'the best manner the workmen use of flooring … as also, the ornamental way of Lighting rooms', Gardiner remarked: 'I had like to have forgot two Glasses, that will be wanted in the Peers between the window'.[22] Pier and chimney glasses were among the most costly items in household inventories. At the top end of the scale the Duchess of Chandos' dressing room at their house on St James's Square, London, contained 'A Large chimney glass in pannells' valued at £50, while the 'State chamber' had 'A large chimey [sic] glass in pannells, double brass armes w.th glass bells over them', worth £80.[23] The

capitals: London and Dublin 1500–1840 (Oxford and New York, 2001), pp 185–210; Barnard, Making the grand figure; R. Gillespie & R. Foster (eds), Irish provincial cultures in the long eighteenth century (Dublin, 2012); C. Bailey, Irish London: middle-class migration in the global eighteenth century (Liverpool, 2013); T. Barnard, '"The Irish in London" and "The London Irish", ca.1660–1780', Eighteenth-Century Life, 39:1 (2015), 14–40; J. Bush, Hibernia curiosa, a letter from a gentleman in Dublin (J. Bush) to his friend at Dover, giving a general view of the manners, customs, dispositions, &c. of the inhabitants of Ireland (Dublin, 1769), p. 36 (which notes that the 'dress, fashions, language and diversions' of the inhabitants of Dublin 'are all imported from London').   21 TCD, MS 1741/14, Gardiner to Clements, 'Treasury, Dublin', 16 Mar. 1744/5.   22 TCD, MS 1741/15, Gardiner to Clements, Dublin, 19 Mar. 1744/5.   23 S. Jenkins, '"An inventory of His Grace the Duke of Chandos's

> I want you to say something to me about the Duke of Bolton's Picture, and I am thinking, if I could get a good Copy of the Duke of Monmouth's picture, they would do very well of each side of my Chimney in my new room, and if the Countess of Yarmouth, or any other fine Lady has a mind to shew her face in Ireland, she may have it in her power to oblige me with a half length, to be over my Chimney; for I find that the lady that I intended to put in that room, my daughters will not suffer to be removed.[40]

Clements, it seems, was successful. Alongside full-length portraits of 'Lord Stafford and his secretary' and '2 pictures of the cartoons gilt frames', worth the considerable sum of £50, the Ballroom at 10 Henrietta Street included 'whole lengths of George the first and the Duke of Bolton' – onetime Lord Lieutenant and Luke Gardiner's patron.[41] This carefully orchestrated display of political alliance and polite learning clearly underlines the public function of such domestic spaces. Hospitality was an essential element in maintaining social standing and political power in Georgian Ireland, with little distinction between social and political engagements, both serving the same ends in terms of advancement. Gardiner certainly utilized his home, both as a place of business and the setting for prominent social occasions at which to forward his considerable political ambitions. In May 1736, it was reported that:

> Last Sunday his Grace the Duke of Dorset and his Duchess, dined with the Right Honourable Henry Boyle, Esq. our Speaker; and Yesterday his Grace paid the like Honour to Luke Gardiner, Esq., our Deputy Vice-Treasurer.[42]

The same week, Luke Gardiner and his son Charles were made 'Masters of the Revels in Ireland.'[43] In 1745, when the new Lord Lieutenant Chesterfield came to Ireland, Luke Gardiner once again played host to such distinguished guests:

> Last Wednesday his Excellency the Earl of Chesterfield and his Countess with a great Number of Nobility and Gentry dined with the Right Hon. the Lord Mayor; on Thursday with his Grace the Archbishop of Dublin; and Yesterday with the Rt. Hon. Luke Gardner, Esq.[44]

That same year Gardiner secured a most lucrative and powerful office, with a three-life grant of the surveyor generalship of customs. Other accoutrements of elite entertainment can be found in these spaces; there were two card tables in the ballroom, while the list of plate included a 'drinking horn' and 'gilt cup and cover', no doubt used in the endless rounds of toasting and heavy drinking which

---

40 TCD, MS 1741/15, Gardiner to Clements, Dublin, 19 Mar. 1744/5. 41 A.P.W. Malcomson, *Nathaniel Clements: politics, fashion and architecture in mid-eighteenth-century Ireland* (Dublin, 2015), pp 13–15. 42 *The Daily Gazetteer*, 20 May 1736. 43 *London Evening Post*, 18–20 May 1736. 44 *The Dublin Journal*, 3 Sept. 1745.

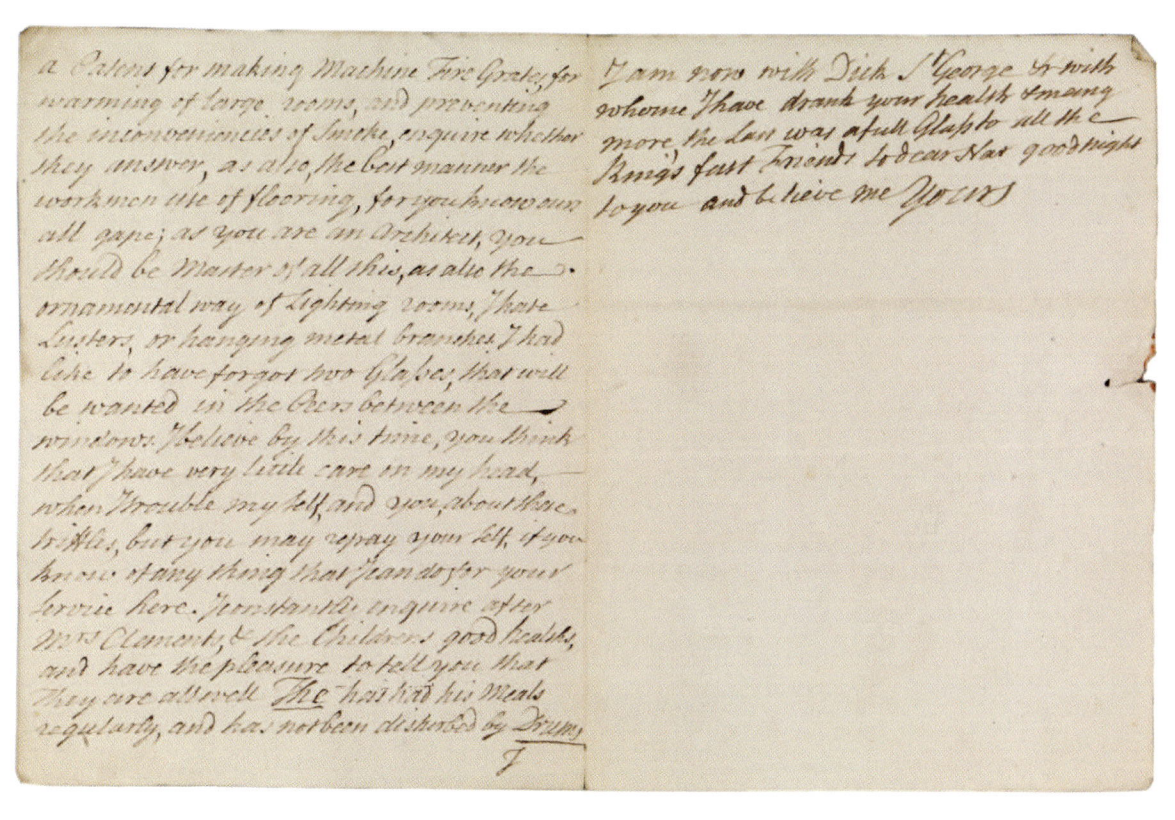

Fashioning, fitting-out and functionality in the aristocratic town house 77

3.7 Luke Gardiner, Dublin, to Nathaniel Clements, London, 19 March 1744/45, TCD MS 1741/15. © The Board of Trinity College Dublin.

accompanied such political gatherings (see chapter 2 in this volume).[45] Gardiner, who was on close terms with his neighbours, alludes to several such occasions in his correspondence, remarking on political meetings at Archbishop Boulter's palatial residence at Henrietta Street, while in closing a letter to Clements he noted: 'I am now with Dick St George [their mutual friend and neighbour] & with whom I have drank your health & many more, the last was a full glass to all the King's just Friends to dear Nat good night to you' (fig. 3.7).[46]

'Utility', as Barnard points out, 'required that houses satisfy several needs: of family; of the owner's public duties.'[47] Number 10 Henrietta Street was also a family home and it was not just Luke Gardiner who was concerned with its fit-out and functionality. The input of his daughters, Harriet and Mary, which is hinted at in the earlier comment over female portraits, becomes evident in their father's subsequent correspondence:

[45] NLI, MS 36,617/1, 'Household Goods Plate Linen and Furniture'. [46] TCD, MS 1741/15, Gardiner to Clements, Dublin, 19 Mar. 1744/5. [47] Barnard, *Making the grand figure*, p. 55.

I should be glad if possible to get a good Chimney Piece. Not one word of the Pictures ... my room is ready for furnishing and my Girls vow revenge to you, if you delay it: They bid me say Something to you of Birth day Cloaths, tho' I am too old to mind what they say, you are not.[48]

Yet despite their obvious involvement in the creation, and indeed use of these spaces, the influence of the Gardiner women, in particular Mrs Gardiner, is not readily discernable. Anne Stewart is a shadowy figure, whose life has gone largely unrecorded and for whom no known likeness survives. The items contained within 'Mrs Gardiner's Bed Chamber' and 'dressing room' offer little insight into her personal tastes – aside perhaps from a preference for Mahogany – while the notice of her death in July 1753 simply recalls 'a Lady much beloved and esteemed by all her Acquaintance for her many Virtues'.[49] However, in an earlier will written in 1736, in which he notes that his wife was then with child, Gardiner's concern for Anne's future security and his trust in her to secure his legacy is clear: he not only directed that his wife should have the use of the 'house in Henrietta Street with all the Furniture and plate therein' until their son reached his majority, but placed the 'household goods furniture plate jewels and other movables' into her 'special care', so that 'none of them be embezzled or destroyed'.[50]

CONVENIENCE

The contest between formal display and everyday convenience was a common theme in eighteenth-century writing on the domestic architecture. According to Robert Morris, 'Buildings in Town require Contrivance, more for Convenience than Grandeur', while Isaac Ware drew distinctions between the 'convenience of the inhabitant' and 'the beauty and proportion of the fabrick', noting that 'there are apartments in which dignity, others in which neatness, and others in which shew are to be consulted'.[51] Certainly there is a tension evident between formal display and domestic comfort within these spaces.[52] The parlour, in particular, represented a liminal zone, in which public 'shew' and private 'convenience' co-existed, and a taste for fine finishes vied with practical considerations and consumer economies. Although eighteenth-century conventions led to a diminished role for the parlour in the functional hierarchy of the house they were still given over to public use. In terms of the spatial organization of the typical terraced house the parlour or parlours were located on the ground floor, which was typically referred to as the 'parlour storey'.[53]

[48] TCD, MS 1741/22, Gardiner to Clements, Dublin, 2 May 1745. [49] *Belfast Newsletter*, 17 July 1753. [50] NLI, MS 36624/1, Gardiner papers, last will and testament of Luke Gardiner, 21 June 1736. [51] R. Morris, *Lectures on architecture: consisting of rules founded upon harmonick and arithmetical proportions in building* (London, 1734), pp 111–12; I. Ware, *A complete body of architecture* (London, 1756), pp 293, 469. [52] For discussion of the careful negotiation between this duality see Stobart (ed.), *The comforts of home in western Europe*, pp 5–6. [53] C. Lucey, 'Specification for a house to be built in Dominick Street', *IADS*,

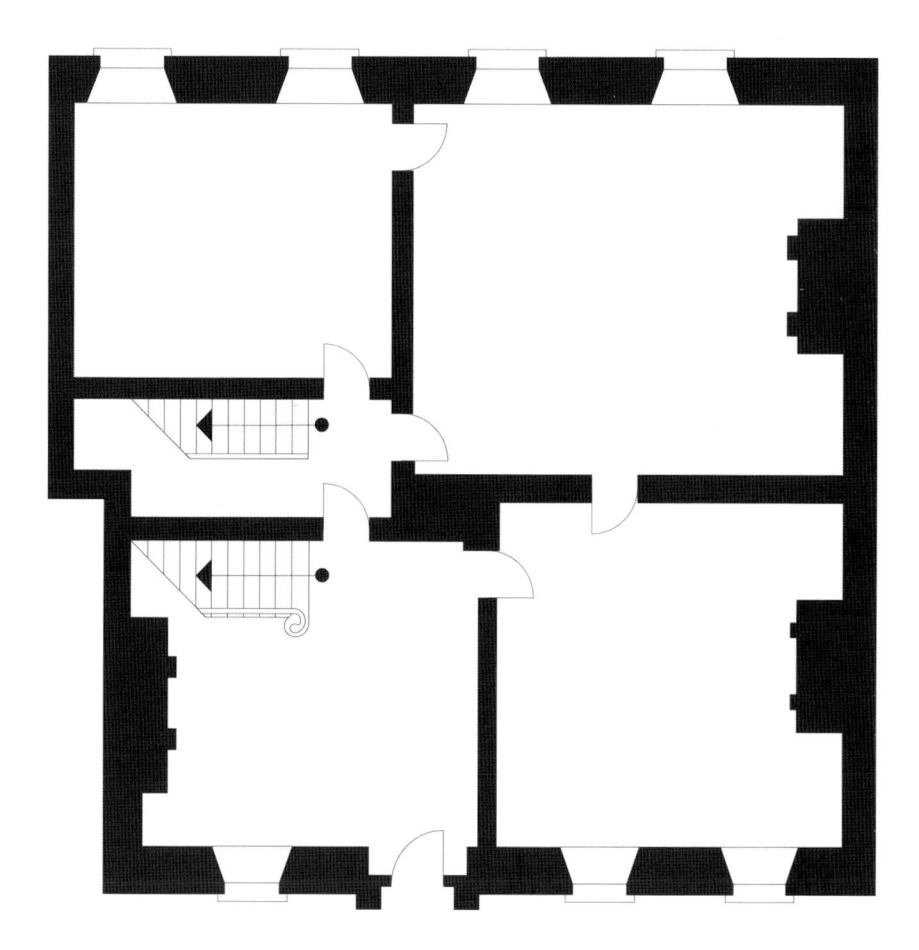

3.8 10 Henrietta Street, Dublin, reconstructed floor plan. © Marcus Lynam.

The front (or 'street') parlour, which was the first room into which waiting visitors were ushered, tended to serve for more everyday entertainment, while the rear or back parlour was often used by the family as an informal dining room.[54] These rooms tended to be of more intimate proportions than the first-floor rooms, though as inventory evidence at Henrietta Street and elsewhere makes clear they were densely packed spaces with a profusion of seating, tables and sideboards, expensive mirrors and art work. Along with a 'mohog.y dining table' and a 'Marble table top', the Street Parlour at 10 Henrietta Street included 'a large pier glass in a white carved frame', a 'chimney glass', a 'Landscape of Powerscourt waterfall', two pictures of King William

21 (2018), 96–107. **54** For similar findings, see McCarthy, 'From parlours to pantries', pp 115–16; K. Lipsedge, *Domestic space in eighteenth-century British novels* (Basingstoke, 2012), pp 53–4; Barnard, *Making the grand figure*, pp 100, 104.

3.9 The breakfast parlour at 10 Henrietta Street, Dublin. Photo William Garner. Courtesy of Irish Architectural Archive.

and Queen Mary, two 'sea pieces over the doors', 'a large history piece', two 'flower pieces', a 'conversation piece in gilt frames', and an unusual piece described as 'Bertual by candle light'. Representative of the duality between formal functions and informal familial use, the rear Breakfast Parlour contained a Dutch massacre, three 'landscapes over the doors', a 'large fruit piece in a gilt frame', and three 'family pieces', likely a reference to a popular type of group family portrait known as a conversation piece. The presence of dining tables and sideboards in the family's Street and Gilt parlours clearly indicates that these spaces were also used for dining. These may have served for informal occasions, perhaps intended for daytime use, as the name of the Breakfast Parlour suggests, with more formal dining taking place on the first floor.[55] In 1744, Mrs Delany referred to both an 'eating parlour' on the ground floor of her suburban house at Delville, which was evidently a substantially-sized room, as well as a 'small parlour' to the rear where 'we breakfast and sup.'[56] Everyday function, however, was generally more flexible, even *ad hoc* in urban dwellings, with pressure on space meaning rooms served a variety of uses, often at once.[57] Barnard

[55] NLI, MS 36,617/1, 'Household Goods Plate Linen and Furniture'. [56] Mrs Delany, Dublin, to Mrs Dewes, Bradley, 12 July 1744 in Llanover (ed.), *Autobiography and correspondence of Mary Granville*, ii, p. 309. [57] See P. Guillery, *The small house in eighteenth-century London: a social and architectural history*

notes that during the 1730s a bed stood in the parlour of Bishop Francis Hutchinson's Dublin lodgings, though here the pressure on space in rented rooms would necessarily have dictated multiple functions (fig. 3.8).[58]

In terms of material finishes the Breakfast Parlour at 10 Henrietta Street exudes an air of controlled Palladian splendour that was cutting edge for its date. Hand-carved joinery, moulded wall panels and geometric plasterwork ceilings were enriched with an ornamental repertoire previously unknown in Irish interiors (fig. 3.9). Pedimented plaster panels and niches enriched the wall surface, Greek-key fret picked out coffered ceiling compartments, and gilded classical orders and oak leaf friezes enlivened carved door-cases. According to Ware, 'the grandest' decorative treatment for the 'inside of rooms' 'is that in stucco'. The choice of plaster for the walls, as opposed to wainscot, which Ware recommend for use in parlours, was also a practical one.[59] Although 'stucco rooms, which are those where the wall is left naked, but ornamented in itself' tended to be colder than wainscot, 'The Stucco room, when heated, becomes the hottest of all'.[60] Lime plaster was also a relatively cheap treatment that was quick to apply and had the added benefit of being fire retardant. Adequately heating these spaces was evidently a concern for the Gardiners. Writing to Clements in London, Luke Gardiner remarked: 'I find there is one Mr Robert Phillips living in great Queen Street that has a patent for making machine Fire Grates, for warming large rooms, and preventing the inconvenience of smoke, enquire whether they answer'.[61] This remarkable invention was characterized as 'a Machine or Wind Grate,' which the *Daily Post* reported:

> infallibly prevents the Smoking of the Chimney in which it is fix'd, and all Smoak coming down from any Neighbours Chimney, and all Smell of Smoke or Soot; when there is no Fire in it, it blows up a Fire in a few Minutes, without any Trouble; it warms Persons all over alike, in any Part of the Room; and if the Room be found too hot at any Time, by a very easy Motion it shifts the Air, and brings in fresh as it shall be requisite; it can air and warm two or three Rooms on the same Floor, or any Rooms just over, to any Degree of Pleasure, which will very much preserve Paintings, and other valuable Furniture, from all Damps; if the Chimney should be at any Time be on Fire; it can instantly be put out by one single Person; it may be removed from one Room and fix'd in another, at any Time. Many Gentlemen who have seen it have much approved of it, as a more curious and useful Machine than any hitherto invented.[62]

Complaints over smoking chimneys were frequent, even in the best houses. At Longleat in Wiltshire, the seat of Viscount Weymouth, Mary Pendarves remarked on

(London, 2004), p. 66.   **58** See Barnard, *Making the grand figure*, p. 84. On beds in public rooms, and *ad hoc* room use, see Vickery, *Behind closed doors*, pp 293–4.   **59** Ware, *A complete body of architecture*, p. 469.   **60** Ibid.   **61** TCD, MS 1741/15, Gardiner to Clements, Dublin, 19 Mar. 1744/5.   **62** *Daily Post*, 14

3.10 'Mountjoy House, Henrietta Street', *Dublin Penny Journal*, vol. 4, 13 February 1836. Public Domain.

how 'since my moving into a new apartment, and that my room does not smoke, I have not taken my morning walks in the gallery, for that broke in a little too much on my morning exercises'.[63] The Gardiners shared chimneystacks with the adjoining house at 9 Henrietta Street, which was built about the same time for Thomas and Mary Carter. As the last house in the terraced range, the threat of fire, as well as the inconvenience of 'Smoke or Soot', was a serious concern.

After the consideration of heat, Ware tells us 'comes that of light': here, he suggests that 'a wainscoted room, painted in the usual way, is the lightest of all, the stucco is the next in this consideration and the hung room the darkest.'[64] The more even the surface, apparently, the most light would be reflected. By Ware's calculations, a wainscoted room took only 'six candles to light it', as opposed to eight for stucco or ten if hung, which was no small consideration given the cost of wax candles.[65] As Hannah Greig notes, distinctions were routinely drawn between tallow and wax candles, the latter were used only in the best rooms, on social occasions.[66] This was

---

Apr. 1729. **63** Mrs Pendarves to Mrs Ann Granville, Longleat, 19 Dec. 1733 in Llanover (ed.), *Autobiography and correspondence of Mary Granville*, iii, p. 425. **64** Ware, *A complete body of architecture*, p. 469. **65** Ibid. **66** Greig, *The beau monde*, p. 42.

even the case at court, where 'firing and lighting' allowances show that white wax candles were only to be used in the state apartments at St James's Palace, yellow wax lights were used in secondary spaces like the 'back stairs', while tallow candles were reserved for private rooms.[67] Although the amount of light given off was similar, the rendered animal fat used in tallow gave off an unpleasant odour when it burned, and filled the room with smoke.[68] Overtime this would have marked the walls and ceilings, and soft furnishings. The choice of lighting fixture was also important. As noted, Luke Gardiner had Clements enquire into 'the ornamental way of Lighting rooms' in London, adding 'I hate lustres or hanging metal branches'.[69] The Breakfast Parlour, however, contained a 'pair double brass branches' valued at £1 6s. Sconces, or wall-mounted candlesticks, were another popular and often showy solution. An inventory of Mrs Balfour's goods 'in her house at Stephens Green', recorded in 1741, lists a 'Scone [sic] & pair of scrolls' in the back parlour, while Nicholas Loftus' house in Henrietta Street (the present number 13) contained a 'pair of silver embossed sconces, on one the figure of Apollo, on the other Diana, with two single silver branches thereto belonging'.[70] In closing his letter to Clements, Gardiner acknowledged his preoccupation with these domestic concerns: 'I believe by this time, you think that I have very little care on my head, when I trouble myself, and you, about these trifles,' and yet clearly such 'trifles' mattered (fig. 3.10).[71]

In August 1755, Luke Gardiner – then a sick and elderly widower, with just one of his children, Mary, still living at home – made a new will. Therein, he 'directed that his said Eldest son Charles should go and reside in his then present Dwelling house in Henrietta Street and it was his will that all his household Goods Plate and Furniture whatever that should be in his said Dwelling House at his decease should be deemed as Heir looms and forever'.[72] While the country house is usually viewed as a symbol of dynastic continuity, urban houses tended to be seen as a commodity, filled with moveable items of personal property that could be easily removed upon death, or at the end of the season.[73] Yet Gardiner clearly viewed his house in Henrietta Street and its contents in a dynastic regard. This not only tells us something about the value Gardiner attached to material acquisition and legacy, but also prompts us to think about these buildings as lived spaces involving a continuous flow of goods, people and ideas: as Stobart notes (in relation to the country house), houses were 'the product of individual and collective taste, but also of domestic negotiation and

---

67 Georgian Establishment Books (EB/EB/31), The Household allowance book for George II, 1727. *Royal Collection Trust, Georgian Papers Online.* Accessed 25 Nov. 2021. https://gpp.rct.uk/Record.aspx src=CalmView.Catalog&id=GEO_EB%2f13.   68 Prosser, 'Experiments with historic light'. See also, J. Cornforth & J. Fowler, *English decoration in the 18th century* (London, 1974), pp 220–3.   69 TCD, MS 1741/15, Gardiner to Clements, Dublin, 19 Mar. 1744/5.   70 NLI, MS 9534, Townley Hall papers, Account book relating to the affairs of the Balfour family of Castle Balfour, Co. Fermanagh, including an inventory of the contents of a house in Stephen's Green, Dublin 1741–3; *Faulkner's Dublin Journal*, 31 Oct. 1755, cited in *GSR*, 4 vols (Dublin, 1909–13), ii, p. 22.   71 TCD, MS 1741/15, Gardiner to Clements, Dublin, 19 Mar. 1744/5.   72 NLI, MS 36,617/1 refers to this clause in Gardiner's will made on 16 Aug. 1755.   73 R. Stewart, *The town house in Georgian London* (London, 2009).

deliberation. We lose sight of these at our peril because, without them, the country house is reduced to a museum; each room is a cabinet displaying treasures, but devoid of life or human context.'[74] Number 10 Henrietta Street stands as a tangible example of Gardiner's taste and vision, and a lasting testament to the wealth and position he had achieved. It was a place of business, an arena for hospitable display and a family home, where the dual tensions of private convenience and public concerns met, and the intangible experiences of life played out.

[74] Stobart, 'Lost aspects of the country estate', p. 40.

The merchant house in eighteenth-century Drogheda

AISLING DURKAN

This chapter focuses on the changing morphology of the town house plan in eighteenth-century Drogheda to meet the needs of an ambitious mercantile class. It explores the arrival in the town of plan types popular in Dublin and London from the early 1700s onwards. House plans are especially informative in terms of design and use. For example, the size and layout of rooms can indicate the wealth of an individual: large-scale houses with wide street frontages suggest a rich patron. Vaulted basements tell of a need for storage, while integral arches may allude to a workshop on site. As room placement changed over time, we can trace changing patterns of behaviour. A good example of this is the dining room, which was often located on the *piano nobile* during the first half of the eighteenth century, after which it was more likely on the ground floor, with a drawing room on the *piano nobile*.[1] The eighteenth-century town house plan developed over the century to conform to changing styles in architecture, business and social practices. Speculative building, the dominant driver of urban domestic construction, encouraged the repetition of economic and practical house plans. Builders' manuals and pattern books introduced formulaic models that could easily be applied in most towns, and eventually replaced the earlier sub-medieval and post-Restoration house plans.[2]

Drogheda's urban domestic architecture offers a microcosm of this complex development, displaying different plan typologies, some of which emerged in the late seventeenth century, and others which display the key characteristics found in typical Dublin and London town house plans of the mid eighteenth century. This study expands on seminal research by Úna O'Tierney on Drogheda's eighteenth-century town house plans by considering them in the broader context of architectural development in the English-speaking world.[3] By analyzing the plan forms of Drogheda's town houses and grouping them by typology, comparisons can be made with house plans found in Dublin and elsewhere of a similar period, and with plans

---

[1] N. Burton & P. Guillery, *Behind the façade: London house plans, 1660–1840* (Reading, 2006), p. 12. [2] Most of the Drogheda house plans used to illustrate this chapter are redrawn from Louth County Council planning permission files or reproduced from Úna O'Tierney. I am very grateful to the late Úna O'Tierney for allowing me to reproduce many of her plans. Other Drogheda house plans were redrawn by the author from LCC Planning Finder: www.louthco.maps.arcgis.com/apps/mapviewer/index.html. House plans are not to scale and are intended as a representation of the original layouts of the houses only. Where possible, later additions and removable partition walls have been edited out; examples of popular building manuals in the early eighteenth century include Joseph Moxon's *Mechanick exercises, or, The doctrine of handy works* (London, 1683, 1703). [3] U. O'Tierney, 'Fair Street and Drogheda – the eighteenth-century town, the street and its houses: surviving to the twenty-first century?' (MUBC, UCD, 1999).

4.1 Gabriele Ricciardelli, *View of Drogheda from Ball's Grove*, c.1755, oil on canvas, 71 x 151 cm. Drogheda Municipal Art Collection, Highlanes Gallery, Drogheda.

found in contemporary building literature, manifesting the various ways in which the Drogheda house was influenced by contemporary building practices found in the rest of Ireland and in Britain. Such comparison also exposes the way in which the Drogheda town house plan maintained and adapted local building traditions alongside more modern developments.

While the transition from timber to brick in domestic architecture is poorly documented in Ireland – Niall McCullough concluded that 'there is simply not enough evidence' – that of the so-called Dutch Billy type and the later Palladian-style town houses that superseded it are somewhat easier to trace.[4] The Dutch Billy seems to have spread in Ireland with the settling of tradesmen from southwest England in Dublin in the course of the seventeenth century, bringing with them their own building techniques.[5] Recognizable by its curvilinear gables that sweep up to a curved or triangular pediment, these tall, red-brick, gable-fronted houses and their distinctive plan became noticeable in the city by the turn of the century, and were common by 1720.[6] In Drogheda, this tradition continued into the mid-eighteenth century, often being built contemporaneously with Palladian houses. While no entire

4 N. McCullough, *Dublin, an urban history: the plan of the city* (2nd ed., Dublin, 2007), p. 186.   **5** R. Loeber, 'Dutch Billies' in R. Loeber et al. (eds), *Art and architecture of Ireland, vol. 4: architecture 1600–2000* (Dublin, 2015), p. 421; P. Walsh, 'Dutch Billys in the Liberties' in E. Gillespie (ed.), *The Liberties of Dublin: its history, people and future* (Dublin, 1973), pp 58–75.   **6** McCullough, *Dublin*, p. 186.

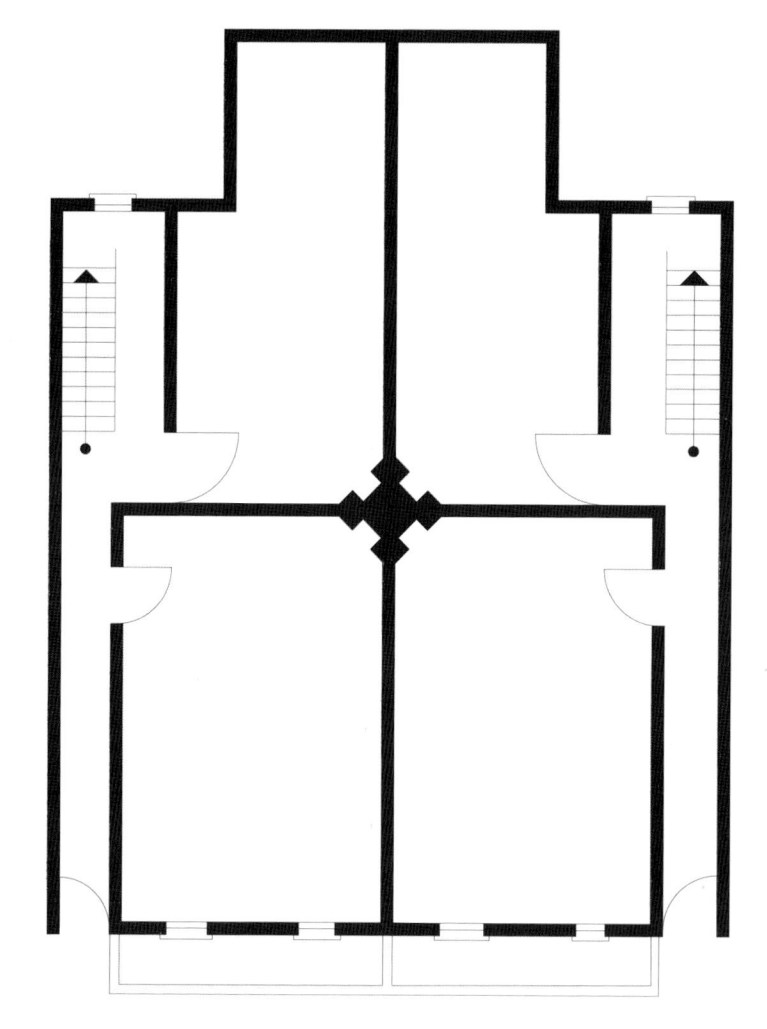

4.2 Ground-floor plans of two Dutch Billy gable houses.
Original drawing by author; redrawn by Marcus Lynam.

Dutch Billies survive in Drogheda, evidence of them is found in paintings, early photographs, and in the remaining built fabric on all the major streets of the town.[7] Even when we look at a mid-century *View of Drogheda from Ball's Grove*, painted *c*.1755 by Gabriele Ricciardelli, we see a mix of old and new, with a large portion of the town built in brick displaying both gabled and more modern Palladian-type town houses (fig. 4.1). This was not unusual in larger towns in eighteenth-century Ireland. Contemporary images of Cork, Limerick, Kilkenny, Waterford, Wexford and Derry

[7] Spelling of *Billies* follows M. Craig, *Dublin, 1660–1860* (Dublin, 1956), and Loeber, 'Dutch Billies', but appears elsewhere as 'Billys.'

4.3 Façade of 21 and 22 Fair Street, Drogheda. Photograph by the author.

also show the endurance of the Dutch Billy alongside more fashionable Palladian town houses, with some surviving into the twentieth century.[8]

The two principal features of the Dutch Billy plan are a corner chimney and a closet return at the rear of the house (fig. 4.2). The corner chimney stack was both economic and practical, as the houses were often built in pairs or terraces and a corner chimney meant that two houses could share a common stack. The closet return allowed for extra room on each floor. Kitchens were in the basement. The position of the staircase varied but was most often to the rear of the entrance hall, or in the centre of the house. While no such houses survive in Drogheda in their entirety, there is evidence that many houses that appear to be 'Georgian' originally had gables which were later altered either to adhere with the fashions of the later eighteenth century, or for structural purposes. Of particular significance here is the fact that features of this plan type, and indeed some related building practices, were reprised in later Palladian-style town houses in Drogheda.

8 John Butts, 'View of Cork from Audley Place', c.1750, oil on canvas, 72.5cm x 120cm, Crawford Art Gallery; NLI, ET C350, Samuel F. Brocas, 'King John's Castle, Limerick', lithograph (Dublin: S. Brocas, 15 Henry St., 1826); Willem Van der Hagen, *View of Waterford city*, c.1736, oil on canvas, Waterford Museum of Treasures; Edmund Garvey, *A view of Kilkenny*, n.d., oil on canvas, 91.4cm x 152.3cm, Ulster Museum; Willem Van der Hagen [attrib.], *A view of Londonderry*, c.1730, oil on canvas, formerly the Guildhall, Derry.

The Dutch Billy was gradually supplanted by a new house type which had emerged in London c.1700. Often referred to as the 'Summerson' type (after architectural historian Sir John Summerson who codified it), the plan consists of a passage or entrance hall on the ground floor, with a staircase (usually a dog-leg staircase in Drogheda) to the rear giving access to all levels. Beside the hall on the ground and first floors were two rooms, one at the front and one at the rear, with separate chimneys in each room. The kitchen was in the basement and a closet wing was often added to the rear. Though established by 1700, as Elizabeth McKellar points out, this 'standard' plan evolved slowly from the seventeenth century.[9]

The standard or 'Summerson' plan was convenient as it provided for one rear window on each storey directly onto the staircase, although this essentially reduced the size of the adjacent rear room. While window light inevitably privileged the stair over rear rooms, unlike a central staircase, it meant that a skylight was not required and thus provided for a simple roof structure.[10] This was important for speculative building, which relied on quick and cheap construction. Niall McCullough identifies this as the most popular plan in eighteenth-century Dublin, which he designates as 'type A'. A good example of this plan type in Drogheda can be seen at 21–22 Fair Street, built c.1770 (fig. 4.3).[11]

PLAN TYPE A

The majority of surviving eighteenth-century town houses in Drogheda were built to this plan.[12] As in London and Dublin, there are often small variations in the type which can be seen equally in the larger town houses on St Laurence Street, and the smaller terraced houses found in Fair Street and Church Lane. Numbers 3–8 Fair Street are simple two-bay, three-storey over basement terrace houses, which exhibit the standard type A plan and appear to date from the 1760s or 1770s.[13] They open into a narrow entrance hall/corridor, with a dog-leg staircase to the rear. There was originally one room to the front and one to the back, adjacent to the hall. Numbers 4 and 5 Fair Street also share a common chimney stack. Numbers 3 and 4 Fair Street are almost mirror images of each other, as are 4 and 5, except that number 4 has a two-storey return to the rear. These are small terraced houses, only two bays wide and three-storeys over a basement, with ground-floor additions to the rear. The three houses have single-pitched roofs set at right angles to the street, disguised by a straight parapet. Number 6 Fair Street is a one-bay wide, three-storey building with

---

9 E. McKellar, *The birth of modern London: the development and design of the city, 1660–1720* (Manchester, 1999), p. 161.　**10** Burton & Guillery, *Behind the façade*, p. 10.　**11** McCullough, *Dublin*, pp 171–2. The plan is found on Parnell Square, Merrion Square, North Frederick Street, South Frederick Street, Baggot Street, St Stephen's Green, Bridgefoot Street, Little Mary Street, Dawson Street, Ormond Quay and Eccles Street.　**12** O'Tierney, 'Fair Street and Drogheda', p. 65.　**13** Numbers 3–8 Fair Street display typical mid-eighteenth-century features for a regional town, such as lugged and shouldered doorcases and windows alongside a round-headed entrance door.

an integral carriage arch at ground level, joined with 7 Fair Street to create a three-bay house. The internal plan of 8 Fair Street is a complete mirror image of number 7, with deep basements and a cellar extending out under the pavement.[14] Neither have return closets. Numbers 7 and 8 Fair Street have corner chimney places in each room. This corner chimney stack saved money in construction and harks back to the earlier building traditions associated with the gable-fronted house.[15] Surviving internal ornamental features again suggest that these houses are of the early to mid-eighteenth century. Externally, it would appear that the windows of the *piano nobile* of 7 and 8 Fair Street, and the ground-floor windows of number 8 were lowered in the later eighteenth century, as they are larger, with the windows on the first floor of number 8 being almost floor-level, with internal splayed surrounds. These houses most probably date from the 1750s through the 70s due to the existence of corner chimney places, lugged and shouldered door and window surrounds, alternative window reveals, and low stair-case rails, all features of the early town house in Dublin and London. This type of detailing appears to have lasted longer into the eighteenth century in regional towns such as Drogheda.

This predominance of the type A plan lasted through the eighteenth century in Drogheda. It can be seen in plan form and in variations on St Laurence Street, Church Lane and Fair Street. Numbers 20–24 St Laurence Street are much wider and taller than the terraced houses at 3–5 Fair Street.[16] Their street frontage is similar in measurement to number 7 (without the extra bay of number 6) and 8 Fair Street.[17] The windows in these houses are much longer, and the buildings are taller than earlier transitional town houses, such as 40 West Street (now Arrow Tours), even though both are of four-storeys over basement. These two-bay, four-storey over-basement houses, dating from *c.*1760, are now separated by the Whitworth Hall (built in 1864 to designs by W.J. Barre). They are each reached by a flight of stone steps and are of the common type A two-room plan with aligned entrance and stair hall. Most have a small original return, and 20 St Laurence Street appears to have been further extended in the twentieth century.[18]

A contemporary of 20–24 St Laurence Street with the same plan can be seen at 1 Church Lane. Standing alone beside St Peter's Parish widows' alms houses, it is not visible on Joseph Ravell's celebrated map of Drogheda published in 1749, but appears on Joseph Taylor and Andrew Skinner's later map of the town published in 1778.[19] It is a three-storey structure, three bays wide with a hipped roof, but the plan

14 The street frontage of 8 Fair Street measures 23 ft 4 in. (7m 13cm); from the ground to the apex of the roof it measures 34 ft 33 in. (10m 47cm), or from ground to top of parapet it is 31 ft 4 in. (9m 55cm). 15 See plans of Bridgefoot Street (A8) and Little Mary Street (A9 and A10) in McCullough, *Dublin*, p. 171.   16 There streetfrontages on average are similar: No. 20 being 22 ft 6 in. (6m 90cm); No. 21 is 23 ft 6 in. (7m 20cm); Nos. 23 and 24 measure the same at 24 ft 6 in. (7m 50cm). In comparison, Nos. 3–5 Fair Street measures only 15 ft 2in. (4m 64cm) in street frontage.   17 8 Fair Street measures 23 ft 4 in. (7m 13cm) to the front.   18 While modern internal partitions have been introduced in most of the plans for office-use and the upper storeys altered for apartments, the footprint of the original ground-floor plan is still clear.   19 M. D'Alton, 'Conservation report, method statement and impact assessment, 1 Church Lane, Drogheda' (2017): http://apps.louthcoco.ie/idocswebDPSS/ViewFiles.aspx?docid=886199&

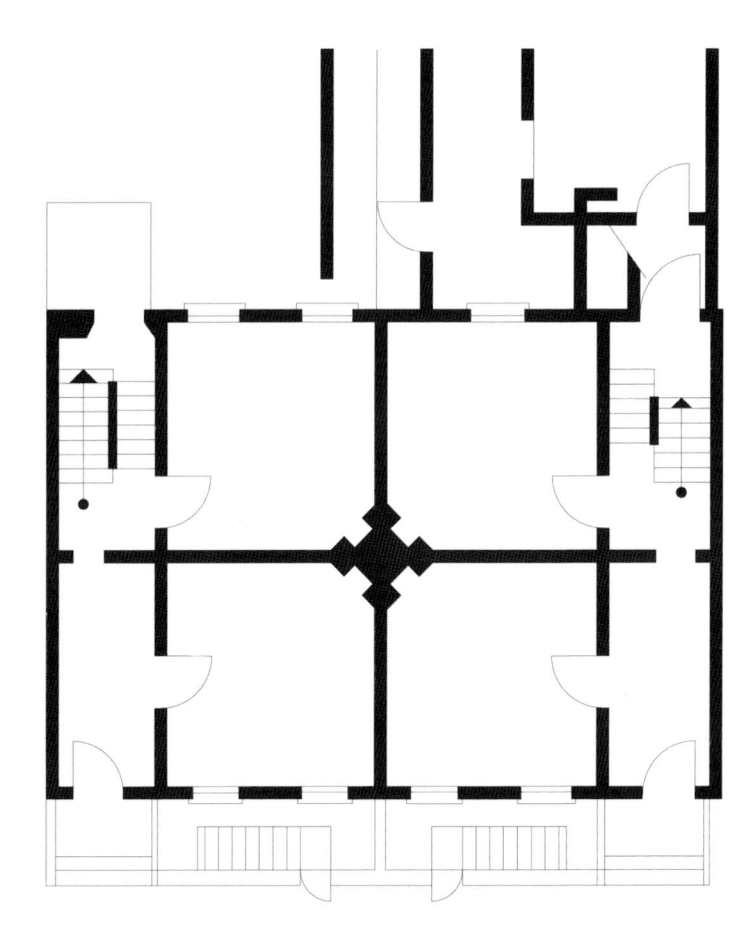

4.4 Ground-floor plans of 21 and 22 Fair Street, Drogheda. Original drawing by Una O'Tierney in author's possession; redrawn by Marcus Lynam.

diverges slightly from the typical type A town house; a central chimney stack is found along the partition wall between front and rear, centrally positioned. While the house has been substantially renovated, with a large extension to the rear, the chimney stack along the partition wall appears to be an original feature and serves to show that house type A was often slightly altered, but retained its overall footprint.[20] Numbers 21–24 Fair Street appear to have been built together. As mentioned, numbers 21–22 display a typical type A plan, and share a central chimney stack, allowing for corner chimney places in both front and rear rooms (fig. 4.4). Clearly the shared diamond chimney stack persists until a late date in Drogheda. Numbers 23–24 Fair Street slightly

format=jpeg accessed 5 Feb. 2018. This suggests that in the late nineteenth and early twentieth centuries it was used as part of the Blue Coat School, as their gardens were attached in the 1879 Ordnance Survey of Ireland map of Drogheda. **20** The house retains its original windows without horns, sash horns being seen only from the 1860s onwards.

4.5 Façade of 33 St Laurence Street, Drogheda. Photograph by the author.

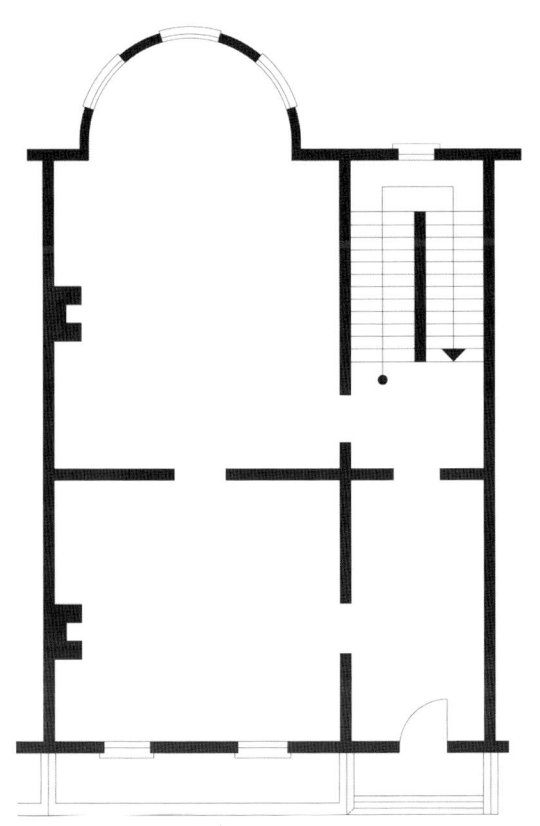

4.6 Ground-floor plan of 33 St Laurence Street, Drogheda. Original drawing by Una O'Tierney; redrawn by Marcus Lynam.

deviate from this, with each house having its own stack at the rear of the house and sharing a chimney stack along the party wall in the front rooms. Numbers 19 and 20 Fair Street have a two-bay entrance hall instead of a narrow entrance hall, which allows for a significantly different threshold experience. Again, this is a two-room plan with front and rear parlours accessed from the front and rear halls.

In the second half of the eighteenth century, bow or bay windows were often added to rear elevations in London and Dublin, increasing internal space as well as giving varied views, with good examples in Parnell Square and Merrion Square.[21] In Drogheda, this plan form can be seen at 33 St Laurence Street, a three-storey over deep basement town house dating from the 1760s (figs 4.5 and 4.6). The 1760s would have been quite early for a bow in a regional town: it is possible that it was a later eighteenth-century addition to the property, although an image of Drogheda from 1774 clearly shows the bow of that house.[22] It has three bays to the ground floor, two bays above and a bow to the rear. The fireplaces in this house are placed along the party walls. Importantly, the houses on the upper south side of St Laurence Street frequently have a deep double basement due to their siting on a steep hill. The lower basement projects onto the garden. It would appear that 30–33 St Laurence Street were developed by Anthony and John Marshall, brothers and building speculators in the eighteenth century, who had leased the land from a local large landowner, John Godley. Both were free merchants of Drogheda and were active in the corporation.[23] When Anthony Marshall died in 1773, his brother John Marshall inherited much of the property, but soon went bankrupt.[24] However, the listed tenants show that the social elite of Drogheda had an interest in these houses, such as Henry Coddington of Oldbridge who leased one of the new houses for his mother to dwell in until her death, when it came into the tenancy of Edward Chesshire, a member of a leading mercantile and political family in the town.[25]

PLAN TYPE B

A further plan type, here referred to as type B, is seen at 15–16 Fair Street, a pair of houses of mid- or late-eighteenth-century date (figs 4.7 and 4.8). They are both attached, two-bay, three-storey over basement town houses.[26] Built as a pair, they have

[21] Burton & Guillery, *Behind the façade*, p. 15; McCullough, *Dublin*, p. 171 (type A1–A3). [22] 33 St Laurence Street is *c.*1762 (RD, 218/550/144703). [23] Louth County Council Office, 'The Freemen Roll of Drogheda Borough, commencing from the Revolution in 1690'. John Marshall was made mayor of Drogheda in 1767, while Anthony Marshall became mayor in 1772. See Council Book of the Drogheda Corporation, vol. 2. [24] Anthony Marshall devised all his real and personal estate to his brother John Marshall, and after the decease of his wife Rebecca Marshall (née Vanhomrigh), he devised a fourth part or an equal value to it of all his leases and lands to John Partington Vanhomrigh. See 'Anthony Marshall's Will' (RD, 302/546/201902). John Marshall's bankruptcy is recorded in the *Dublin Evening Post*, 23 Dec. 1780. [25] Edward Chesshire married Elizabeth Marshall in St Peter's Church of Ireland church on 5 June 1779. See St Peter's Drogheda Registers (1702–1900), marriages. [26] 15 Fair Street has been significantly altered in recent years to provide for a surgery, with a large extension in the rear. The figure shows the plan of the house before these alterations.

4.7 Façade of 15 and 16 Fair Street, Drogheda. Photograph by the author.

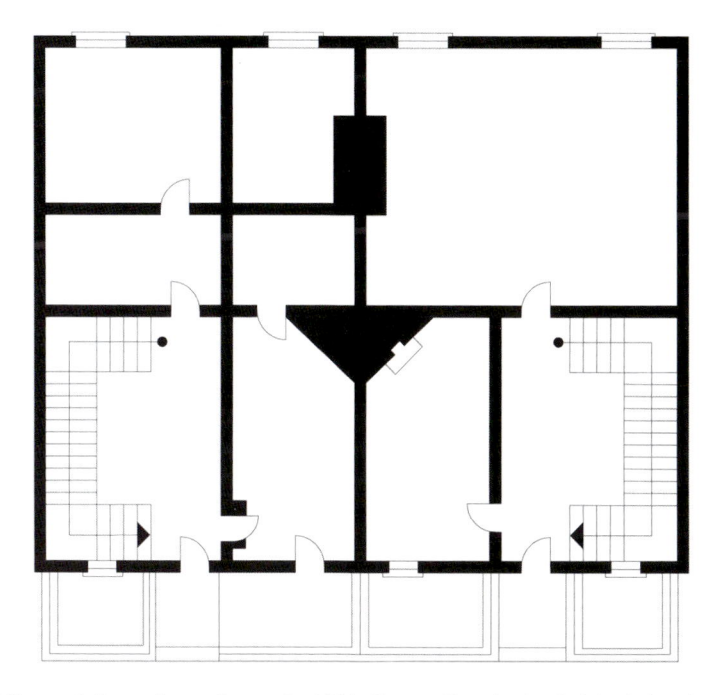

4.8 Ground-floor plans of 15 and 16 Fair Street, Drogheda. Original drawing by Una O'Tierney in author's possession; redrawn by Marcus Lynam.

central entrance doors, an uncommon feature for terraced houses and a choice that had repercussions for the plan. The preference for symmetry over a more practical and regular plan type would suggest a more ambitious master builder, but the overall result is clumsy. The doors are off-centre and the staircase is cramped in the front hall.[27] Although now divided into offices, placing the staircase to the front would have originally left a large room to the rear. At 16 Fair Street, the staircase is open-string, with a goose-neck rail, and appears to be original, though the balusters are a later replacement. There are shared corner fireplaces in the front rooms, while in the rear there is a fireplace along the centre of the party wall dividing the two houses. As O'Tierney pointed out, the plans of numbers 15–16 are very reduced versions of the plan found at number 18 and at number 11 (the former Presentation Convent, c.1776) in this street.[28] Although number 11 is technically a terraced house, it is of substantial size and quality.[29] Interior ornamental features on the ground and first floors, such as lugged and shouldered door surrounds, and straight, non-splayed window cases, would suggest that it dates from the mid-eighteenth century.[30] The type B plan thus appears to date from the mid-eighteenth century. It seems that these houses were some of the houses owned by the Smyth family of Drogheda, who were intermarried with the local political families of Meade, Ogle and Barlow.[31]

PLAN TYPE C

A one-room plan, here referred to as type C, is found at 17–18 Church Lane, a pair of semi-detached, three-bay, three-storey over basement town houses, with entrance hall and stair beside one room. Number 17 has a fireplace in the centre of the side wall, whereas number 18 has a corner fireplace. The two have a similar plan and scale, although recent internal changes have helped to obscure this. Peter Guillery has stated that one-room plans were widespread in London in the late seventeenth and early eighteenth century, and may have provided slightly more affordable accommodation: rooms could be sublet while still providing good accommodation per floor.[32] The one-room plan did not automatically denote poverty. Indeed, both 17 and

---

27 William Garner noted the problematic nature of this design. W. Garner, *Drogheda architectural heritage* (Dublin, 1986), p. 32. Similar plans can be found in Molesworth Street in Dublin: see plan type C1 in McCullough, *Dublin*, p. 171.   **28** O'Tierney, 'Fair Street and Drogheda', pp 66, 78; the former Presentation Convent is now part of 11 Fair Street, Law Chambers, B. Vincent Hoey and Co., Solicitors. RD, 300/148/99111: this lease was granted to James Forde in his own name for 99 years on 10 Jan. 1776 at the General Assembly, but was covenanted to lay out £300 in making further improvements within the first years, making it likely that the house was built c.1776–80. O'Tierney records that James Forde appears to have demised his lease in 1782 to the Revd Brabazon Disney. It later entered into the hands of the Presentation Order. See O'Tierney, 'Fair Street and Drogheda', p. 89.   **29** This plan is discussed by O'Tierney, and referred to as type A/2 in O'Tierney, 'Fair Street and Drogheda', p. 69.   **30** Lugged surrounds are a feature of earlier eighteenth-century Irish architecture but took longer to be phased out in areas outside of the capital.   **31** The Smyth family inherited a large amount of property on Fair Street. See RD, 315/231/210094, 326/41/213280, 326/41/213280, 321/8/211492, 348/440/234642.   **32** P. Guillery, *The small house in eighteenth-century London: a social and architectural history* (London, 2004), p. 50.

18 Church Lane enter directly into a shared stair hall, which would give an element of privacy to tenants by allowing access to each floor without entering another person's quarters. Such refinement would have been quite a luxury when compared to the cabins inhabited by the poorer classes in the town.[33]

PLAN TYPE D

Another plan which deviates from type A is found at Duke House, Duke Street, and this will be referred to as type D.[34] Formerly St Philomena's School, it is now in a very advanced state of deterioration. However, original features survive. It is a two-bay (three-bay on ground floor), four-storey town house, with a single pitched roof hidden behind a stepped pediment. The house is entered through a wide entrance hall to the front. Directly opposite the entrance door is an archway into the stair hall, with a dog-leg stair to the right. There is another entrance way to the rear room from the stair hall, creating an enfilade through the house from the front entrance to the back door. In other words, the house is divided bi-laterally by a central stair hall. There is a fireplace in the front and rear, centrally positioned on the wall opposite the doors, not unlike plans shown in the second edition of Stephen Primatt's *The city and country purchases and builder* (1667).[35] It appears to have been common in London in the late seventeenth century, though it remained a feature of some houses at the lower social scale throughout the eighteenth century. Guillery points out a link between its continuance of use for shopkeepers, though this link may be merely due to the fact that the plan was suited to narrow street frontages, such as houses found on high streets where shopkeepers tended to live.[36] Whether this house on Duke Street was originally used for commercial purposes is unknown, but there are deeds referring to houses being let to merchants on the east side of Mass Lane (now Duke Street) from the eighteenth century so it seems likely.[37] It certainly is similar to house plan types found in Smithfield, Dublin.[38]

---

[33] Evidence for cabins or hovels found in and around Drogheda throughout the eighteenth century can be found in many registered deeds. For example, see RD, 86/7/59023, 393/195/260215, 567/486/382003. Evidence is also found in the Council Book of the Drogheda Corporation, vol. 2., for example, fo. 86 (6 Nov. 1744); fo. 193 (15 July 1760); fo. 239 (13 Jan. 1764). [34] There is no official numbering or Eircode assigned to this property. It is known as Duke House or Alwell House and is listed as 4 Duke Street on Griffith's Valuation, Map of the county and town of Drogheda, 1854: www.askaboutireland.ie/griffith-valuation/index.xml?action=doNameSearch&PlaceID=905449 &county=Meath&barony=Drogheda,%20county%20of%20the%20town%20of&parish=St%20peter&t ownland=%3Cb%3EMoneymore%3C/b%3E, accessed, 30 Nov. 2021. [35] The plans in the second edition of Stephen Primatt's *The city and country purchases and builder* were reissued by William Leybourne in 1680 and are noted in Guillery, *The small eighteenth-century house*, pp 62–4. [36] Ibid., p. 64. [37] RD, 347/14/230674 and 382/554/260310. [38] McCullough, *Dublin*, p. 171 (type B9).

PLAN TYPE E

A singular plan at 17 Fair Street not found elsewhere in the town will be denoted as type E (figs 4.9 and 4.10). The most striking feature is the long and narrow front room adjacent to the entrance hall; it is elongated horizontally over two bays, parallel to the street, with three rooms to the rear. The narrow, horizontality of the front room would have been even more noticeable on the first floor, where the room must have had a corridor or hall-like effect.[39] The house is entered through a large entrance hall with a door to the front room on the right. Directly opposite the front door is an archway leading into a stair hall, with the dog-leg stair on the left and a door into the centre-rear room. This rear room does not allow access to the adjacent rear room, which can only be accessed via the large front room. The front and centre rear room share a chimney stack along the spine wall. Internally, the house has been completely remodelled, with little surviving eighteenth-century fabric remaining. According to *Griffith's Valuation*, the house was occupied by Anne Evans in 1845, who was leasing it from John Smith, most likely a member of the Smith family who had interests on Fair Street.[40] Anne Evans was probably the wife or daughter of George William Evans, mayor of Drogheda in 1795.[41] Evans and his son Charles William Evans were printers based in Drogheda, and appear to have been brother and nephew respectively of Charles Evans, one of the earliest recorded booksellers and printers in Drogheda. While we know that Charles Evans carried on his printing works at a house in St Laurence Street, George William Evans and his son Charles William Evans also went into the printing business and became proprietors of the *Drogheda Journal*.[42] George William Evans appears to have been based at Fair Street from as early as 1825, and in 1832 he placed an advertisement to let a dwelling house in Fair Street.[43] Is it possible that they also carried on their printing business at Fair Street? The long front rooms might have accommodated a printing press, type cases and related equipment and materials.[44]

39 The Street frontage of 17 Fair Street measures 20.97 ft (6.39 m). **40** *Griffith's Valuation*, Map of the county and town of Drogheda, 1854. NAI, 'Residents of a house 17 in Fair Street (Fair Gate, Louth), 1911 Census', House and Building Return (form B1) states that the house was owned by John Smyth. The house is numbered as 18 Fair Street on Griffith's 'Map of the county and town of Drogheda', 1854, and the occupant is listed as Ann Evans, a lessee of John Smith. **41** George William Evans was related to an Anne Evans: see 'St Peter's Church of Ireland, Drogheda, baptism register 1702–1899', p. 90: https://www.ireland.anglican.org/cmsfiles/pdf/AboutUs/library/registers/StPeterDrogheda/Baptisms.pdf, accessed 30 Oct. 2021. On his death, Charles Evans is recorded as the proprietor of the *Drogheda Journal, or Meath and Louth Advertiser*, in the *Berkshire Chronicle* (26 May 1832), and in the same year George W. Evans advertised a dwelling house to let in Fair Street (*Drogheda Journal*, 3 Mar. 1832). Both men are listed as printers in House of Lords, *The sessional papers, 1801–1833*, 118 (1820), pp 136, 140. **42** RD, 590/520/403927; *Drogheda Journal*, 17 Jan. 1837, 25 Apr. 1837. By 1838, the journal had been taken over by St John Collins. See *Drogheda Journal*, 29 Dec. 1838. **43** J. Finegan, 'The role of the printed word in Drogheda up to 1815: a case study of print production and consumption in provincial Ireland', *Journal of the County Louth Archaeological and Historical Society*, 23:2 (1994), 189. **44** George William Evans died in 1849, only a few years before the Griffith's Valuation map was made, while Charles Evans Jnr died in 1832, and an Anne Evans died aged 81 in 1874 in the Church Alleys. See 'St Peter's Church of Ireland, Drogheda, burial records 1702–1899', p. 87: https://www.ireland.anglican.org/cmsfiles/pdf/AboutUs/library/registers/StPeterDrogheda/Burials.pdf, accessed 30 Oct. 2021.

4.9 Façade of 17 Fair Street, Drogheda. Photograph by the author.

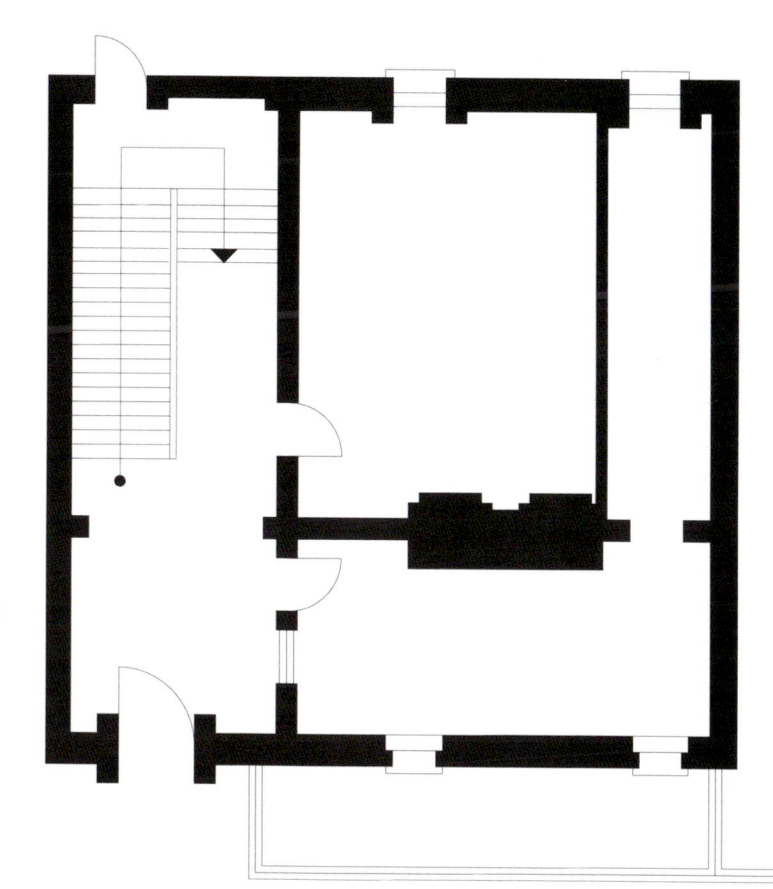

4.10 Ground-floor plan of 17 Fair Street, Drogheda. Original drawing by Una O'Tierney in author's possession; redrawn by Marcus Lynam.

While it is now difficult to say for certain, the unusual horizontality of the long front rooms would suggest a specific, purpose-built function.[45]

PLAN TYPES: OUTLIERS

At St Peter's Place or Church Lane, widows' alms houses, known locally as 'the Alleys', were developed by Archbishop Marsh and Archbishop Boulter respectively.[46] Primate Marsh built and endowed the alms houses at Drogheda for the reception of twelve widows of 'decayed' clergymen, to whom he allotted a lodging and £20 a year for maintenance (these are the three southernly ranges, currently numbered 5–16).[47] Boulter's four later houses on the north were finished by July 1738, and are recorded in an indenture dated 21 November 1739 between him and Ambrose Philips, Richard Morgan and Henry Tomes, esqs of the city of Dublin.[48] In the deed he states that:

> he hath lately at his own expense built four alms house in the town of Drogheda for the reception and habitation of the widows of four poor clergy men which said four alms houses are contiguous to each other and are situate on the east side of the church yard of St Peter's Church in the town of Drogheda and are bounded on the south side with other alms houses formerly built by the order and appointment of the late Lord Primate Marsh for the Widows of the poor.[49]

Marsh died in 1713, and had stipulated in his will (dated 1707) for alms houses or a hospital to be built: these were in fact already built by October 1713, when he was granted a fee farm forever for land 'on the north side of the ground he built the alms houses on, at a pepper corn a year, if demanded, the same being to enlarge the said houses'.[50] The houses are now covered with cement render which is broken off in areas to reveal red brick. They retain notable eighteenth-century features, such as

45 This spatial arrangement was retained and employed successfully as a doctor's surgery for a long period of the twentieth century. **46** Council Book of the Drogheda Corporation (CBDC), vol. 1, fo. 304 (9 Oct. 1713). **47** Marsh's Library, Dublin, Z2.3.12, 'Last will and testament of Narcissus Marsh, Archbishop of Armagh and Primate and Metropolitan of All Ireland', made 22 Feb. 1707. A copy of the will with codicils and proof dated 22 Feb. 1711 and 20 Apr. 1713 is in PRONI, T. 209–10. **48** On 20 July 1738, Richard Morgan paid Alderman Rencher (most likely John Rencher, a Drogheda alderman and builder of the Free School-Master's House) the 'late £100' on account of Archbishop Boulter for 'building the widows' houses at Drogheda'. See TCD, MS 6399, 'Account Book of Richard Morgan for Archbishop Hugh Boulter, 1724–41', fo. 115; S. Sullivan, 'St Monumentum Requiris, Circumspice', *Journal of the Old Drogheda Society*, 1 (1976), 14. **49** Ibid. **50** According to the OED, a fee farm is 'a kind of tenure by which land is held in fee-simple subject to a perpetual fixed rent, without any other services; the estate of the tenant in land so held; rarely, the land itself'. The Lord Primate was granted a fee farm forever of land from the corporation north of where he built the alms houses, 'the same being to enlarge the said houses'. See CBDC, vol. 1, fo. 304 (9 Oct. 1713): 'Grant of probate, George Horner, Cliftonville, Belfast, Oct., 1897'. In his last will and testament written in 1707, Narcissus Marsh stated that he wanted to leave land in Drogheda to his executors, Marmaduke Coghill and John Sterne, to give to his successor, the archbishop of Armagh, the mayor of Drogheda, and the vicar of St Peter's (CoI), Drogheda, and their successors, to 'build and erect or cause to be built and erected one good and sufficient

large 6 over 6 sash windows on the ground floor with small 3 over 3 attic sashes. The houses are two-storey over-basement structures with small arched windows visible above ground, fronted by iron gutters. They have simple, single-pitched roofs with long, slender chimneys, some of exposed red brick and others rendered in cement. The four terraces are joined at the end by a terminating house with a bow end in the central bay. The secluded nature of the area has changed little, fronting St Peter's church-yard to the west. This would have been an ideal location for the wives of deceased clergymen, as it would have offered a place of seclusion and safety not always afforded to single women without money. The houses are depicted on Ravell's map (1749) as four ranges of infill above Henry Singleton's House and to the right of St Peter's church-yard.

The alms houses built in Drogheda in the early eighteenth century are excellent examples of charitable urban housing and remain intact. Neatly organized into four terraces of four-bay, two-storey houses, they are also notable in being more proportionally homogenous than any other eighteenth-century terraced houses in Drogheda. The two ranges to the south are arranged in the same manner; the entrance leads into an entrance hall, with staircase to the rear, not unlike the standard plan. However, there is one large living room adjacent to the entrance hallway, from which two separate smaller rooms can be reached. In the houses of the southernmost range the chimney is in the centre of the wall which divides the living room and the two closets or smaller rooms. This is also a feature seen in the veteran's rooms in the Royal Hospital in Kilmainham, designed by Sir William Robinson in 1680–4, and later in the master builder Michael Wills' design for the Erasmus Smith School-Master's House on St Laurence Street in Drogheda.[51] In the second southernmost range the chimney stack is recessed into the smaller rooms, which allows the living area more space but makes the smaller rooms somewhat cramped. The fireplace could efficiently heat the small rooms and internal chimney stacks ensured that heat was retained, whereas an external stack had no such lateral value. This plan is altered in the northernmost ranges, which Edward McParland correctly identified as being later in date than the southern ranges.[52] In the later houses the chimney stack is built up on the external wall and placed in the centre of the rear wall of the living room, thus giving more space to the area but sacrificing heat retention. These plans are not found in any of the eighteenth-century houses throughout the town.

Alms houses were not unusual. In 1695, the Trinity alms houses of Mile End Road, London, were built according to designs by William Ogborne. However, internally their layout is not similar to that of Drogheda.[53] Relief for the clergy's

alms house for the habitation of minister's widows'. However, if the alms houses were already built in his lifetime, he wanted the archbishop, mayor and vicar to 'expend and lay out yearly and every year out of the rents, issues and profits of my said estate in the County of Lowth [sic] in repairing the said alms houses any sum not exceeding the sum of ten pounds per annum'. Marsh died in 1713, so it is possible the houses were begun between 1707 and 1713.   **51** For the plan see E. McParland, *Public architecture in Ireland: 1680–1760* (New Haven and London, 2001), p. 59.   **52** Ibid., p. 72.   **53** Alderman Rencher was paid between 1732 and 1737 for building the widows alms houses, but it is believed that some of the houses pre-date this. See TCD, MS 6399, 'Charge upon Richard Morgan for the Half Years rents and

widows was an important philanthropic undertaking by the Church of Ireland in this century, with funds set up in 1749 by the Society for the Relief of the Widows and Children of Clergymen of the Diocese of Dublin.[54] While there were many alms houses in Ireland, such as in Dublin, Kilkenny, Limerick and Cork, none resemble the neat, well planned terraces of those in Drogheda.[55] The builder of the north range was John Rencher, a local alderman who was simultaneously building the Erasmus Smith Free School-Master's House (to designs by Wills, as noted above). Rencher largely followed the design of the earlier widows' alms houses erected under Primate Marsh before 1713. Their spare and efficient nature suggests the hand of a master builder trained in engineering and barrack architecture: Wills worked as a clerk to the distinguished Dublin architect Thomas Burgh,[56] who visited Drogheda at least once to view the ground and make a plan for the Erasmus Smith School-Master's House. (The surviving plan, elevation, and section of that building were drawn by Wills, acting as Burgh's clerk and draughtsman.) Nonetheless, Burgh's influence is felt at the alms houses, albeit to a more simplified degree befitting regional architecture, having been mediated through Wills and then Rencher.[57] Such neat and uniform houses clearly made a statement about the power that the Church of Ireland had in shaping the urban landscape of Drogheda. Their institutional aspect meant that they had to be seen as being of good quality design and workmanship, befitting the status of clergymen's widows. They were not ostentatious, but as an ensemble they are noticeably more refined than many of the speculatively-built houses in the town.[58]

PLAN TYPES: CONCLUSIONS

The surviving evidence suggests that the standard town house plan of type A was the most common type utilized in eighteenth-century Drogheda, though within this standard there were some minor variations. This follows the basic pattern of Palladian design found so often in Dublin from 1720 to 1770. There is evidence of more idiosyncratic layouts too, as seen in the uncommon placement of a central door in a pair of town houses with cramped front-hall staircases at 15–16 Fair Street. However, surviving evidence would suggest that such idiosyncratic plans were infrequent. Furthermore, the persistence of the diamond chimney stack suggests a general contentment with this plan. For builders, it may have simply been the layout that they were well-practised in. It also represented a convenient way of heating the house

duties due to his Grace Hugh, Lord Arch Bishop of Armagh, Primate and Metropolitan of All Ireland, out of his Arch Bishopric of Armagh'. **54** *The fundamental rules unanimously agreed to for the better support of widows and children of clergymen of the diocese of Dublin* (Dublin, 1749). **55** Examples of alms houses active in Ireland at the time include Egan House (former widows' alms house), St Michan's church-yard, Dublin (built *c.*1720); Skiddy's alms house, Cork city (built *c.*1718–19); Shee alms house, Kilkenny (built *c.*1582); and Dr Hall's widows' alms houses, Limerick city (*c.*1691, made a linen-board school in 1740). **56** McParland records that Burgh was mentioned in at least one of Robinson's wills. McParland, *Public architecture*, p. 146. **57** Erasmus Smith Archives, Dublin, BG/512, 'Treasurer accounts, 1706–45' [bound volume], 24 Dec. 1730. **58** McParland, *Public architecture in Ireland*, p. 59.

while saving on materials. As for patrons, those not preoccupied by the stylistic developments of the capital may have simply found the corner fireplaces to be less intrusive than one in the centre of the party wall. In any case, their persistence in the town would suggest that it satisfied both patron and builder.

HOW WERE THESE ROOMS USED?

What is less obvious is how these rooms were originally intended to be used. If they followed the same pattern of usage as Dublin, as they did with plan patterns, it would seem that most of these houses were used as businesses as well as dwellings. Research on room usage in eighteenth-century Ireland has largely been confined to the country house and, to a lesser extent, the elite Dublin town house, although the fluidity of function has been acknowledged.[59] Unfortunately, there is not nearly as much record of room usage in Drogheda, but there are a few examples that hint towards how town houses were used in general. These are documented in registered deeds and newspaper advertisements from the period. For example, in 1734 a local Drogheda cordwainer let half his house on Peter's Street to a stay-maker.[60] The deed specified that there was to be one common entrance and stair and that there was equal access to the garden and backside. The fact that such access had to be specified not only suggests multiple occupancy, but also addresses the types of disputes that may arise when one had to share spaces. Another lease from 1760 records a house in West Street, which had a 'work house' in the back, while the shopfront was used to display a milliner's hats for sale.[61] In this instance the rest of the house was occupied by other tenants, showing a clear mix of public and private function within one property. Other houses were perhaps built to attract a different social calibre. In 1765, a house on St Laurence Street was advertised for letting: boasting a front parlour, dining room and four bedchambers, with a 'beautiful prospect of the Town and River', the description suggests the lessor's astute commercial awareness of marketing a house with a view.[62] In 1776, a house on the North Quay was advertised as being three storeys tall with three rooms on each floor, offices behind the house, and a stable and coach house that included an apartment for servants.[63]

Such descriptions are not exhaustive by any means, but they are good indicators of the variety of ways rooms and houses were employed and experienced by different people occupying the same domestic space. Indeed, while we see an abundance of 'standard' typology of town house plans in Drogheda in the dominant type A, such arrangement was by no means the rule, and even where this plan was utilized there does not appear to have been set functions for rooms. Rather, the eighteenth-century inhabitants of Drogheda adapted and negotiated spaces to meet their needs, with multiple occupancy being not uncommon.

59 P. McCarthy, *Life in the country house in Georgian Ireland* (New Haven and London, 2016); C. Casey (ed.), *The eighteenth-century Dublin town house* (Dublin, 2010). **60** RD, 77/122/58034. **61** RD, 205/462/136927. **62** *Dublin Journal*, 27 Apr. 1765. **63** *Saunders's News-Letter*, 3 Apr. 1776.

'Baubles for boudoirs' or 'an article of such universal consumption': ceramics in the Irish home, 1730–1840

TOBY BARNARD

In the 1780s, an arrogant lawyer, John FitzGibbon, soon to be lord chancellor and earl of Clare, contacted an acquaintance, conveniently British ambassador in Paris. FitzGibbon desired a porcelain dessert service from Sèvres, by the 1780s regarded as the acme of ceramic luxury.[1] He was prepared to spend upwards of £200 on the purchase, but left the selection to the emissary. In the event, it was the latter's wife who chose. FitzGibbon fretted about how best to have the precious cargo transported. Apart from its value, it offended against the current patriotic repudiation of expensive imports. The difficulties were overcome, and evidently FitzGibbon was well pleased: more pieces were ordered from Sèvres, and the dessert service was valued enough to be mentioned in his will.[2] It was unusual for either ceramics or glass, unlike silver and jewellery, to be thus specified.[3] FitzGibbon had happily added tea-ware to his French commissions, but declined to order soup plates. He was content with the silver dishes that he had already commissioned, taking malevolent glee when the footmen burnt their fingers on the hot rims.[4]

The FitzGibbon episode unusually brings ceramics for the Irish table into the foreground of domestic hospitality. In general, other features in a home have attracted closer attention: the rooms themselves and their decoration, together with fixtures and fittings of high value such as paintings, seat furniture and textile hangings. Even when the table is approached, the kinds of food and drink on offer, how they are arranged and served, are what is noted, together with comments on profusion and extravagance or seemliness and moderation. Only occasionally are the dishes on which the offerings were placed and from which they were eaten or drunk mentioned. The earthenware and 'china' were often outshone by the dazzle of the silver implements and ornaments and the sharply facetted glass.[5] What follows will attempt to bring the apparently overlooked but ubiquitous component of daily living from the shadows. In doing so it will focus on drabber regimes than FitzGibbon's.

[1] P. Ennès & B. Ducrot, *Un défi au goût: 50 ans de creation a la manufacture royale le de Sèvres (1740–1793)* (Paris, 1997); S. Erikson & G. De Bellaigue, *Sèvres porcelain: Vincennes and Sèvres, 1740–1800* (London, 1987). [2] D.A. Fleming & A.P.W. Malcomson (eds), *'A volley of execrations': the letters and papers of John FitzGibbon, earl of Clare, 1772–1802* (Dublin, 2005), pp 44, 51–2, 58, 59, 62, 104, 411, 412. [3] An exception was John Brown, squire and land agent of Mount Brown (County Limerick), who bequeathed glass lustres, a carpet and a dessert service to a daughter. Palatine Heritage Centre, Rathkeale, Brown MSS, box 2, bundle 5(a), will of John Brown, 17 Sept. 1803. [4] Fleming & Malcomson (eds), *'A volley of execrations'*, p. 58. [5] A. Moran, '"The eye as well as the appetite must be car'd for": glass and dining in Ireland, about 1680–about 1830' in C.L. Maxwell (ed.), *In sparkling company: reflections on glass*

The study of ceramics in eighteenth- and early nineteenth-century Ireland has concentrated, understandably, on local manufacture.[6] Irish potteries were few and mostly short-lived. If some of their wares were distinctive and in demand, nevertheless they constituted a very small proportion of the earthenware and china on sale and in use. In contrast, imports were ubiquitous, of ever-increasing variety, and variously priced. Innovations proliferated throughout the eighteenth century. Coarse pottery for utilitarian uses had long been known, and had even been made in Ireland. These earthenwares and stonewares were progressively refined in composition and decoration, mostly by continental European potters. Frequently, the robust pottery, majolica and faience were lumped together under the generic name of 'Delft', from the Dutch town which specialized in their making. It was this commodity which was manufactured and sold briefly in mid-eighteenth-century Dublin by Henry Delamain.[7] A few copied his initiative but with no lasting success. However, a taste for such wares existed and grew, and to satisfy it, cargoes were shipped regularly from London, Bristol, Liverpool and European ports.

The volume and value of earthenware entering Ireland from England was increasing sharply throughout the eighteenth century. In 1747, annual imports were valued at £3,367; by 1783, at £17,401. Despite unfriendly tariff regimes and disruption through warfare, the volume and value of the trade continued to grow. It was reckoned to be worth £90,000 by 1808.[8] Specialist retailers opened establishments in Dublin and general traders sold glass and china. The number recorded in the printed directories, having hovered between four and six during the 1770s, rose to around seventeen by the 1790s and to thirty-nine in 1824.[9] Meanwhile, as early as the 1760s, specialist shops were appearing in the larger provincial towns. In 1769, Limerick, for example, had no fewer than five.[10] By 1789, numerous small towns had suppliers. In Old Leighlin (County Carlow), the Misses Davies presided over a 'china and glass warehouse'.[11] At Carlow, John Coffey combined trade in ceramics with cabinet-making, auctioneering and selling timber. Premises were sometimes described, like the Davies', as a 'warehouse'.[12] This may have denoted a wholesale trade, aiming at pedlars and casual sellers at fairs and patterns, alongside satisfying the townspeople. Also, it may imply that scant attention was devoted to showing the stock alluringly. It is doubtful whether the sophistication enlivening city shops across western Europe, and touching Dublin by the end of the century, spread into provincial Ireland.[13]

in the eighteenth-century British world (New York, 2020), pp 194–229. 6 P. Francis, *Irish delftware: an illustrated history* (London, 2000); idem, *A pottery by the Lagan* (Belfast, 2000); R. Meenan, 'Post-medieval pottery in Ireland' in A. Horning, et al. (eds), *The post-medieval archaeology of Ireland, 1550–1850* (Dublin, 2007), pp 393–404; M. Reynolds, 'Irish fine ceramic potteries, 1769–96', *Post-Medieval Archaeology*, 18 (1984), 251–61. 7 Francis, *Irish delftware*. 8 Francis, *Irish delftware*, p. 178; M.S.D. Westropp, *General guide to the art collections, pottery and porcelain, Irish pottery and porcelain* (Dublin, 1935), p. 33. 9 *Pigot and Co's city of Dublin and Hibernian provincial directory* (London, 1824), p. 66. 10 J. Ferrar, *The Limerick directory* (Limerick, 1769), pp 12, 14, 16, 18; R. Lucas, *A general directory of the kingdom of Ireland*, 2 vols (Dublin, 1788), ii, pp 168, 176. 11 Lucas, *The Cork Directory*, ii, p. 145. 12 Ibid., pp 104, 111, 128, 129, 139, 140, 153, 159, 163, 168, 189, 191. 13 T. Barnard, '"China-men" in

II

Two parallel developments converged to create a more abundant variety and supply of pots. Technical, stylistic and marketing innovations had first brought the much-admired porcelains from China and Japan to Europe, shipped by the several national East India Companies. Increasingly, the ware was decorated to please Europeans. Spurred by the demand and likely profits, several European factories, led by Meissen in Saxony, experimented and eventually perfected the firing of porcelain that replicated the oriental wares. By the 1740s, the potting techniques had been learnt by a few English manufacturers to produce soft-paste porcelain. The formula for hard-paste of the Chinese type, with its prized translucency, eluded them until the 1790s.[14] Thereafter, as will be seen, British factories competed fiercely to introduce further refinements in composition and style, always fearful that adventurous continental establishments would outpace them. The robust and gaudily painted 'ironstone' was one popular variant of the early nineteenth century.[15] Other than the short-lived operations of the Downshire pottery between 1787 and 1806, no prestigious ceramics were made in Ireland until the opening of the Belleek venture in 1857.[16]

The ships from the Orient, ballasted with china, transported another profitable commodity: tea. Its consumption, initially restricted by cost to grandees, slowly percolated downwards as prices dropped. The preparation and service of tea were elaborated into sociable rituals. In 1769, an employee of the Dublin Society published a notional estimate of the annual spending by the household of a substantial 'strong' farmer. Total outgoings of £132 included £1 2s. 5 on 'earthenware'. The more rarefied china or porcelain is not mentioned. The sum compares with a mere 6s. 6d. for glass and 11s. 3d. on wooden ware. The consumption of tea, assumed to be entrenched in such a family, took an annual £2 13s. 3d.[17] For tea accessories and utensils were fabricated, thereby adding to the refinement and – at first – expense of the habit. Some – tea tables and caddies – were of wood; others, the kettle, pot, milk jug, sugar basin, spoons and tongs, and the caddy too, might be fashioned in silver or

---

Dublin between 1790 and 1843: Samuel and George Alker', *Journal of Royal Society of Antiquaries of Ireland*, 150 (2020), 246–56; idem, 'Hedgehogs in Cavan; Wolfes in Dublin: selling English ceramics in Ireland, c.1770–1850', *Proceedings of the Royal Irish Academy*, 121C (2021), 284, 301; C. Fairchilds, 'The production and marketing of populuxe goods in eighteenth-century Paris' in J. Brewer & R. Porter (eds), *Consumption and the world of goods* (London, 1993), p. 238; S. Foster, '"Ornament and splendour": shops and shopping in Georgian Dublin', *IADS*, 15 (2012), 12–33; J.H. Furnée & C. Lesger (eds), *The landscape of consumption: shopping streets and cultures in western Europe, 1600–1900* (Houndmills, 2014); A. Moran, 'Selling Waterford glass in early nineteenth-century Ireland', *IADS*, 6 (2004), 56–90; J. Stobart, A. Hann & V. Morgan (eds), *Spaces of consumption: leisure and shopping in the English town, c.1680–1830* (Abingdon, 2007); C. Walsh, 'Shop design and the display of goods in eighteenth-century London', *Journal of Design History*, 8 (1995), 157–76.   **14** S.L. Marchand, *Porcelain: a history from the heart of Europe* (Princeton, 2020), pp 23–59; S. Richards, *Eighteenth-century ceramics: products for a civilised society* (Manchester, 1999).   **15** K. Curry, 'Empire of China', *Irish Arts Review*, 21:1 (2004), 116–23; R. Haggar & E. Adams, *Mason porcelain and ironstone 1766–1853* (London, 1977), p. 61. Cf. *Belfast News-Letter*, 31 Oct. 1815; *Belfast Commercial Chronicle*, 20 Apr. 1816.   **16** Francis, *A pottery by the Lagan*.   **17** J.W. Baker, *To his excellency the Right Honourable, Lord Visc. Townshend … the following remonstrance* (Dublin, [1768]), p. 89.

base metals.[18] By the 1780s, if not earlier, ceramics were preferred to silver on practical grounds (ease of handling and cost) for pots as well as cups.[19]

From the 1730s, ceramics, both ornamental and useful, are frequently mentioned in Ireland. Jonathan Swift's 'china', cheap earthenware, and six blue-and-white coffee cups hardly surprise.[20] More suggestive of a wider spread of the commodity comes from a land agent and farmer in County Limerick. From 1748, Nicholas Peacock was buying tea occasionally in the nearby city. Two years later he noted buying some cups.[21] In 1769, the Cork Franciscans bought their first recorded stock of tea, probably the cheapest variety of bohea, and sugar. Two years later, a teapot and 'cup and saucer' followed, costing 1s. 6d.[22] By 1822, the same institution owned half a dozen cups and saucers, valued at 7s. 6d. Changing conventions are also hinted at by an entry of 1825 when 'tea for a stranger' was costed in the accounts at three and a half-pence.[23]

Until 1784, tea was heavily taxed. Smuggling was rife and seized consignments were regularly auctioned by the customs officers. After the dramatic reduction of the import duty, consumption grew, as did the ingenuity of manufacturers in supplying and multiplying the accompanying paraphernalia.[24] Bohea was most commonly drunk because the cheapest: in 1776, a pound could be bought for 2s. 3d. at a central Dublin supplier.[25] But this very democratization of tea-drinking encouraged the smart to differentiate themselves by serving one of the more expensive blends. Vance, the Dublin retailer, listed eight separate varieties. If 'good plain green' cost four shillings for one pound, 'fine London green' was priced from ten to fourteen shillings.[26] These gradations in cost further challenged those wishing to keep pace with or outstrip their neighbours.[27] At the same time, the greater availability of cheaper but eye-catching

---

18 A. FitzGerald, *Silver in Georgian Dublin: making, selling, consuming* (Abingdon, 2017), pp 100, 103, 172; B. Cunningham, *Gentlemen's daughters in Dublin cloisters: the social world of nuns in early eighteenth-century Dublin* (Dublin, 2018), p. 31; D. FitzGerald, Knight of Glin, & J. Peill, *Irish furniture* (London, 2007), pp 238–41; M.L. Legg (ed.), *The diary of Nicholas Peacock, 1740–51* (Dublin, 2005), p. 160. Cf. R. Roth, *Tea-drinking in 18th-century America: its etiquette and equipage* (Vancouver, WA, 1961). **19** FitzGerald, *Silver in Georgian Dublin*, pp 100–1. **20** P.V. Thompson & D.J. Thompson (eds), *The account books of Jonathan Swift* (London, 1984), pp 164, 244, 266. **21** T. Barnard, *Making the grand figure: lives and possessions in Ireland, 1641–1770* (London, 2004), p. 130; Legg (ed.), *The diary of Nicholas Peacock*, pp 184, 203, 211, 219, 224. **22** L. Kennedy & C. Murphy (eds), *Account books of the Franciscan House, Broad Lane, Cork, 1764–1921* (Dublin, 2012), pp 15, 19. Cf. Cunningham, *Gentlemen's daughters in Dublin cloisters*, p. 22. **23** Kennedy & Murphy (eds), *Account books of the Franciscan House*, pp 66, 86, 96. **24** R. Emmerson, *British teapots and tea-drinking* (London, 1992), pp 4–27. **25** NLI, Talbot-Crosbie MSS, folder 57, Lady A. Crosbie to M. Collis, 15 Sept. 1757; Emmerson, *British teapots and tea-drinking*, p. 11; *The letter-book of Richard Hare, Cork merchant, 1771–1772*, ed. J. O'Shea (Dublin, 2013), p. 219, and passim; *Hibernian Journal*, 22 Mar. 1776; T. Hunt, *The radical potter: Josiah Wedgwood and the transformation of Britain* (London, 2021), p. 29; J. Pettigrew, *A social history of tea* (London, 2001), pp 40–7. **26** L.A. Clarkson & E.M. Crawford, *Feast and famine: a history of food and nutrition in Ireland 1500–1920* (Oxford, 2001), p. 50; L.M. Cullen, *Anglo-Irish trade 1660–1800* (Manchester, 1968), pp 151–2; C. Nierstraz, *Rivalry for trade in tea and textiles: the English and Dutch East India companies (1700–1800)* (Houndmills, 2015), pp 91–123; C. Nierstraz, 'The popularization of tea: East India companies, private traders, smugglers and the consumption of tea in western Europe, 1700–1760' in M. Berg (ed.), *Goods from the east, 1600–1800: trading Eurasia* (Houndmills, 2015), pp 263–76. **27** *Hibernian Journal*, 17 May 1773, 10 Dec. 1773, 22 Mar. 1776; *Saunders's News-Letter*, 8 and 21 May 1783.

tea-wares accompanied the spreading habit. Reduced prices for tea and of ceramics popularized both. Earlier, both commodities along with exotic textiles, frequently smuggled into the island to evade duties, exuded the allure of the illicit.

The beverage (along with coffee) came to be served in the evening after lavish dinners and entertainments, as well as earlier in the day. Bishop Thomas Barnard of Limerick, staying at Ardfert Abbey in County Kerry during 1798, praised his hosts. Lord and Lady Glandore presided over 'one of the most regular and best conducted houses that I have been in in Ireland'. They dined at 4.30 p.m., after which there was 'no soaking'. In the evening there would be a game of cards, with tea and coffee offered, supper at ten and retire to bed at 11.30 p.m.[28] Despite the bishop's praises, just how widely this cultivation extended may be exaggerated. Although the requisites were readily acquired even in the provinces, when Maria Edgeworth was stranded in a ramshackle Connemara mansion during the 1840s, the place boasted only a single teapot. Those wanting its use, notably the servants, had to wait.[29]

The spread into lower levels of society of tea-drinking and the acquisition of the necessary accessories are well-attested. And yet there are ambiguities. Observations in the 1820s from rural areas across the country revealed variously the popularity or the rarity of tea. The notion that it harmed health and undermined industry was not altogether discarded.[30] Numerous hopeful suppliers of china and earthenware moved into the Irish trade; many, most famously Wedgwood, were disappointed.[31] Demand, buoyant when tea and its consumption were novelties, may have stagnated. Figures of imports reached its zenith during the Napoleonic Wars. At the same time, per capita consumption by the Irish has been calculated to have been only a third of that in England. With coffee, the difference – one fifth in Ireland – is yet more startling. A great upsurge in the Irish consumption of tea happened only in the late 1830s and the following three decades.[32] How far, especially in the poor and rural population, these beverages had been adopted and become staples of diet must remain hazy, and with it the optimistic, perhaps over-optimistic, estimates of the possession of useful ceramics.[33]

III

During the seventeenth century, ceramics noted in Ireland were usually ornamental (large vases, figures and chargers) not useful. By the early eighteenth century, smaller and more humdrum pieces are mentioned more regularly. Terminology is usually too

---

28 A. Powell (ed.), *Barnard letters, 1778–1824* (London, 1928), pp 110–11.   29 M. Edgeworth, *Tour in Connemara and the Martins of Ballinahinch*, ed. H.E. Butler (London, 1950), p. 45.   30 Clarkson & Crawford, *Feast and famine*, pp 64, 68, 83, 195.   31 Barnard, 'Hedgehogs in Cavan', 273–5, 283–5; G. Blake-Roberts, 'Wedgwood's Dublin showroom', *Journal of the Royal Society of Arts*, 138 (1990), 840–3.   32 Clarkson & Crawford, *Feast and famine*, pp 51–2, 103; T. Cusack, '"This pernicious tea-drinking habit": women, tea and respectability in nineteenth-century Ireland', *Canadian Journal of Irish Studies*, 41 (2018), 178–209; H. O'Connell, '"A raking pot of tea": consumption and excess in early nineteenth-century Ireland', *Literature and History*, 21 (2012), 37–47.   33 By 2015, Irish *per capita* consumption surpassed

vague to allow precise identification of the objects. A fundamental difference in origin and monetary value stretched between the authentic hard-paste porcelains shipped from China and slowly becoming available from German manufacturers, then from the French and ultimately the English, and the humbler earthenwares and delft. Descriptions such as the bald 'china', 'burnt china' and 'flint ware' usually sufficed. One observer distinguished between 'fine and coarse china ware' supplied by the East India Company.[34] These high quality and costly products remained a small proportion of what circulated in Ireland. There were further distinctions – in look, price and desirability – between crocks for the nursery, dairy, kitchen and drainage, which might have been made in the locality, and the vividly embellished pottery arriving from the Netherlands, Rhineland, Iberia, France and England.

It was the ornamental and seemingly useless against which critics inveighed. In 1748, a disgruntled County Cork squire asserted 'a house is not thought to be furnished that has not a parcel of jars and images of china in it'.[35] Such strictures against ostentation notwithstanding, by the middle of the eighteenth century, showy ceramic need-nots formed a very small proportion of what entered Ireland. Nor did these pieces always amount to rash extravagances, as the austere contended. The ports of Munster on the trade routes from the Orient were favourite stops for unloading saleable articles, whether authorized or not and at bargain prices.[36] Yet, even with easy access to coveted East India wares, it was the more utilitarian ceramics, increasingly originating in Britain or continental Europe, which flooded into Ireland.

Evidence of ownership through the haphazard survival of invoices, receipts, and inventories starts to be supplemented: first by printed auction catalogues and then – from the mid-century – by regular retailers' advertisements. The very existence of these types of records suggests changes: the presence of more artefacts within Irish homes and an eagerness to buy, both the new and the second-hand. But ascertaining what exactly was on offer, when it had first arrived in Ireland and from where, and how then it was used and regarded: all remain frustratingly opaque. In 1729, many of Edward Wingfield's goods were auctioned, including the contents of the 'china closet' in his William Street Dublin house (the later Powerscourt House). Most goods were for the service of meals. Included with 'sundry other china too tedious to mention' was the highly prized and priced 'burnt china', either from the east or Europe.[37] Two years later, the china – together with the linen – accumulated in the Ingoldsbys' central Dublin residence generated a separate printed catalogue.[38] Almost all was intended for presenting food and drink. These owners belonged to the highest echelons of Irish Protestant landed society. How far travel within and beyond Ireland or the women of their households determined choice is entirely unknown. The

English: E. Rappaport, *A thirst for empire: how tea shaped the modern world* (Princeton, 2019), p. 376. **34** FHL, J. Wight, journal, 20 July 1756. **35** NLW, Aberystwyth, Puleston papers, MS 3580E, E. Spencer to F. Price, 25 Apr. 1748, now printed in D. Fraser & A. Hadfield (eds), *Gentry life in Georgian Ireland: the letters of Edmund Spencer (1711–1790)* (Cambridge, 2017), p. 143. **36** FHL, J. Wight, journal, 20 July 1756; Barnard, *Making the grand figure*, pp 132–3. **37** *A catalogue of the goods and stock of the late Edward Wingfield, Esq.* (Dublin, 1729), p. 3. **38** *A catalogue of the China Ware and Linnen of*

records of spending and ownership relate typically – and distortedly – to men. In 1736 it was a prospering Dublin physician who asked an acquaintance in Liverpool to send over 'two nests of pots for baking puddings, etc.' To this request was soon added another for two dozen Liverpool earthenware plates.[39] Rigid conventions about gender roles in running a household were liable to break down in practice. It is also impossible to gauge the influence over acquisitions of housekeepers, stewards and butlers. Astute retailers might well cultivate these lesser and shadowy figures on whom so much day-to-day marketing fell.

Lord and Lady Kenmare arrived in Dublin from County Kerry during December 1753. Their lodgings were only partly furnished. In common with other temporary sojourners, they had to find for themselves such accessories as linen, glass, metal-ware and crockery.[40] Dublin retailers were on hand. The Kenmares were immediately accommodated with an extensive service of 'delf ware' for £3 1s. 10d.[41] A few days later they bought a second, large service of 'china'. Separately, a china bowl and a teapot were acquired for eighteen shillings.[42] The origins of the 'china' – in the Orient, continental Europe or England – can only be guessed. The supplier of their earthenware is known to have dealt with the Delamain's Dublin factory.[43] The need to have, as it were, 'a best' and an everyday service showed the enlarged demands of polite urban life, at least in the Kenmares' circles (figs 5.1 and 5.2).

The demand for such ceramic accoutrements among the propertied elite of Irish society by the mid-eighteenth century and the attention devoted to meeting it can be illustrated by two further examples. They challenge the views that acquisitions were of superfluous luxuries and instigated mainly by women. George Cockburn was a well-connected merchant and military agent who lived permanently in central Dublin.[44] The contents of the amply furnished residence in a fashionable north-side street were meticulously listed in 1763.[45] They included copious useful crockery, some of it described as 'Roan [Rouen] Ware'. Much of it was kept in or near the kitchen in a painted press lined with paper, seen only by the family and visitors at meals. Some vessels were described as 'old'. Indeed one 'old bowle', despite being cracked, was still valued at two shillings. Either it had sentimental or possible resale value. Damage could be repaired. The frequent payments for riveting, 'hooping' or sticking china suggests frugal rather than profligate housekeeping.[46] In a society not yet habituated to the microwave, convenience food and the dishwasher, there was an inclination to hoard and re-use rather than to throw away.

The Cockburns' reception rooms were originally bare of ceramic ornament. Only in 1773 was a garniture of five vases by Wedgwood and Bentley bought and placed in

the late Henry Ingoldsby, Esq ([Dublin, 1731]).   **39** NLW, Puleston papers, MS 3584E, T. Kingsbury to F. Price, 8 June 1736, 12 Sept. 1738.   **40** NLI, PC 446, M. Ledwidge to W. Smythe, 22 Jan. 1754. **41** Westropp, *Irish pottery and porcelain*, p. 33.   **42** PRONI, D 4151/R/2, Kenmare account book, from 18 Dec. 1753, s.d. 14, 15 and 18 Dec. 1753.   **43** Francis, *Irish delftware*, p. 62.   **44** J. Meredith, 'A "good figure": the story of George Cockburn (1764–1847) as revealed through contemporary letters and papers', *IADS*, 9 (2008), 104, 107.   **45** BL, Cockburn papers, Add MS 48,314, inventory, 1 Jan. 1763.   **46** NLI, Personal accounts of Richard Edgeworth of Edgeworthstown, MSS 1522, 1533, 1534, accounts, s.d. 22

5.1 Irish delft small platter, chinoiserie, mid-eighteenth century. Private collection.

5.2 Irish delft small platter, chrysanthemum, mid-eighteenth century. Private collection.

the street parlour, the room into which a visitor would first be shown. Since Cockburn was now a widower, it may be assumed that the vases were his choice.[47] Otherwise, the owner's dressing room was embellished with porcelain, notably with figures of Flora, 'Hunting', the five senses, 'a man and a woman hunting' and six 'real china' figures. 'Real china' may have distinguished what was made in China or Japan from the imitations being manufactured in continental Europe, led by Meissen, and lately copied by English factories. Hunting subjects were especially favoured by German manufacturers such as Meissen and Frankenthal.[48] These were costly bibelots: the pair of Flora and 'Hunting' were valued at £3. However, the value pales into insignificance against individual articles of silver, jewellery and watches, or even the carved chimneypieces from the Darley stonemason's shop in the principal rooms.

Men's interest in these seemingly trivial details of domestic management is again demonstrated by another widower, Edward Synge, bishop of Elphin. Furthermore, Synge sheds a little welcome light on attitudes: as to what was thought appropriate for city or countryside and the reasons for particular choices. Synge, born into the episcopal purple, was a wealthy and forceful man, conscientious in discharging the duties attendant on his position. Spending each summer in his diocese, Synge at Elphin found himself short of suitable plates. In 1749, he requested supplies from Dublin, leaving others to choose so long as 'they be pretty and strong'.[49] By 1750, Synge was expecting a service of Rouen-ware to arrive, and intended to use it at a visitation dinner as an alternative to pewter.[50] Although he had hoped for more plates edged in blue to match those that he had already, he confessed, 'I make a motley figure with blue dishes and other colour'd plates'. He disliked colours that he considered 'glaring', but went on, 'if they be more strong and lively, I may possibly like them, for the faintness of those disgusted me most'.[51]

Synge and the Cockburns benefited from the new availability of the vividly decorated faience from Rouen. That it became popular in Ireland from the 1740s is attested by records of its purchase and ownership. It is even found among the accoutrements of *The Phoenix*, an inn in Werburgh Street.[52] Bolder and brighter than most conventional delft, including the English and Dublin versions, the reasons for its success in Ireland await convincing explanation. Rouen was only one maker – and not the most prominent or prolific – of brightly decorated earthenware in France. By the 1750s, its style of ornament was looking *retardataire* in comparison with the

May 1756, 16 Oct. 1767, 4 Nov. 1768; Barnard, *Making the grand figure*, p. 130.   **47** BL, Cockburn papers, Add MS 48,312, Cockburn's wife died at Spa in 1769. For examples of such vases: R. Reilly, *Wedgwood*, 2 vols (London, 1989), i, pp 68–71; H. Young (ed.), *The genius of Wedgwood* (London, 1995), pp 102–17.   **48** M. Miller (ed.), *Höfische Jagd in Hessen: Ereignis; Privileg; Vergnügen* (Petersberg, 2017), pp 91, 127–31; U. Pietsch, *Triumph der blauen Schwerter: Meißner Porzellan für Adel und Bürgertum* (2010).   **49** M.L. Legg (ed.), *The Synge letters: Bishop Edward Synge to his daughter, Alicia, Roscommon to London, 1746–1752* (Dublin, 1996), pp 99, 108, 179, 190.   **50** Legg (ed.), *The Synge letters*, pp 194, 197, 255. See also T. Kellaghan, '"I have no mind to buy more pewter": an examination of elite consumption trends in ceramic tableware in Georgian Ireland' in M. McWilliams (ed.), *Food and material culture: proceedings of the Oxford symposium on food and cookery 2013* (Totnes, 2014), pp 200–3.   **51** Legg (ed.), *The Synge letters*, pp 294, 300, 303.   **52** *Saunders's News-Letter*, Mar. 1773, 6 Aug. 1773, 6 Apr. 1774.

'Baubles for boudoirs' or 'an article of such universal consumption'   113

5.3 Rouen faience wall-fountain, mid-eighteenth century. Private collection.

factories at Strasbourg, Niederviller, Marseilles and Moustiers, but they were sources less readily accessible to Ireland.[53] A petition in 1753 alluded to the costly imports into Ireland of Rouen, 'Burgundy' and Marseilles earthenware.[54] It could be that

---

53 H.P. Fourest & J. Giacometti, *L'oeuvre des faïenciers Français du xvie à la fin du xviiie siècle* (Lausanne, 1966), pp 150–65; A. Lane, *French faience* (2nd ed., London, 1970), pp 20–4; M.-J. Linou (ed.), *À Table: les arts de la table dans les collections du Musée Mandet de Riom, xviie–xixe siècles* (Clermont Ferrand, 1997), pp 70, 99.   54 Westropp, *Irish pottery and porcelain*, p. 14.

'Rouen ware' became a generic term, akin to 'burnt china', 'delft' or (later) 'Staffordshire' to describe the similar products of several potteries.

The mystery is who had first thought to profit from importing the faience into Ireland. The same question can be repeated in relation to the first introduction into Ireland of other ceramic (and consumer) novelties. Entrepreneurial traders with extensive overseas links are the most obvious explanation. It then raises the conundrum of who shifted taste and consumption so dramatically: the manufacturer, an intermediate agent, or the trend-setting customer? Shipments from Rouen were easy, long established and regular, but were distinct from those of wine and brandy handled by other French ports. Rouen at this time had a substantial colony of Irish *emigrés*, involved chiefly in the textile manufacture.[55] When Bishop Synge ordered his Rouen dishes, the commission was entrusted to his Dublin wine-merchant, Daniel Sullivan. Presumably Sullivan and others who dealt regularly with France had correspondents there who could satisfy special orders. In 1765, for example, a wine-merchant undertook to procure a curious double-barrelled gun made in Paris.[56] During warfare with France between 1756 and 1763, the regular trade stopped.[57] Some years later, a consignment including baskets containing six Rouen services was auctioned in Dublin. Alongside the faience were red and white wine and champagne. The cargo was completed by 308 chamber pots, also of French manufacture. They were being shipped from Le Havre, down-river from Rouen at the mouth of the Seine, in a vessel registered at Whitehaven.[58] Rouen-ware was still being advertised by a central Dublin shop early in the 1770s, alongside a galaxy of other imported earthenware, mineral waters, beer, cider, and hams (fig. 5.3).[59]

IV

In the 1740s, one of the Taylors of Bective spent £107 on a service 'of the finest Saxon painted ware in imitation of china'. Arresting as the purchase is, Meissen porcelain was a rarity in any Irish house – as was hard-paste porcelain from any source.[60] Notwithstanding the stir caused by this, FitzGibbon's Sèvres or the Cobbes from Newbridge (County Dublin) with their assemblage of gay Worcester, such show was untypical.[61] Spending on this scale explains why the acquisition of ceramics has been categorized as an element in the quest for luxury. But these purchases remained exceptional (and therefore noteworthy). They do not account for the widening spread in the possession of useful china and pottery through Hanoverian Ireland.

'Chinamen' and potters, facing intensifying competition, sought new formulae for glazes, bodies, and decoration. In addition, they adapted their products to fresh

---

55 R. Hayes, 'Irish footprints in Rouen', *Studies*, 26 (1937), 427–8. 56 NLI, MS 35,561/1, F. Hodder to Lord Castlecomer, 12 Apr. 1765. 57 Francis, *Irish delftware*, p. 60. 58 *Freeman's Journal*, 5 Dec. 1767. 59 *Saunders's News-Letter*, 23 Mar. 1774, 21 July 1775. 60 Barnard, *Making the grand figure*, p. 133. 61 NLI, A.P.W. Malcomson, 'Report on the Headfort Mss', F/3/19, Jane Edwards, bill to Dean Robert Taylor, 1740s; Barnard, *Making the grand figure*, p. 133; A. Cobbe, *Birds, bugs and butterflies: Lady*

5.4 Higginbotham invoice for utilitarian wares, 13 May 1843. Cobbe papers: Alec Cobbe division.

uses: as well as the service of meals, there was their preparation in the kitchens and preliminaries in the dairy. Gardening, indoors and out, made work for potters. The display and nurture of bulbs, exotic blooms and plants brightened rooms. Pot-plants such as geraniums required pots.[62] Nicety about cleanliness promoted tiling, sanitary and medical wares. Ewers and basins for hot water, chamber pots, foot baths, slop-pails, dishes for soap and razors, and then the novel water closet brought orders for those who pioneered their fabrication.[63] Seals, fobs, buttons and false teeth were all fashioned in ceramics (fig. 5.4).

The glut of goods bewildered. Steering a course between the extremes of parsimony and extravagance was taxing. If guidance abounded, individual fancy frequently prevailed. The unsure were instructed with formulae as how properly to set the table for special events.[64] Laying out the several confections enticingly

Betty Cobbe's 'Peacock' china (Woodbridge, 2019).   62 Barnard, 'Hedgehogs in Cavan', 295; Richards, *Eighteenth-century ceramics*, pp 113–20.   63 C. Lucey, 'Marketing the necessary comforts in Georgian Dublin' in J. Stobart (ed.), *The comforts of home in western Europe, 1700–1900* (London, 2020), pp 67–72.   64 N. Cullen, 'Women and the preparation of food in eighteenth-century Ireland' in M. MacCurtain & M. O'Dowd (eds), *Women in early modern Ireland* (Edinburgh, 1991), pp 269–75; A. FitzGerald, 'Taste

necessitated an assortment of dishes of graduated sizes. Despite the ability of a few households to maintain unstinted hospitality, formality and largesse were hard to sustain day after day. Neither space nor income allowed them. The illustrations of the meticulous arrangement of the table, like the contemporary manuals of polite conduct, represented an ideal for which to strive not the muddled reality.

At the mercy of slovenly servants and boorish visitors, more relaxed habits, even a degree of confusion, probably attended meals and hospitality. On some occasions, already prepared dishes were laid out in advance, according to a plan; they could then fall prey to gluttonous gourmands wanting a sample and to four-legged visitors.[65] The frequency of food poisoning in eighteenth-century Ireland has not hitherto been investigated. How many families could reserve some utensils, whether of glass, metal or ceramics, for red-letter days, and meanwhile content themselves with lower-value equivalents for daily use? In 1789, Dorothea Herbert, a member of a well-to-do and well-connected family living mainly in Carrick-on-Suir, bemoaned the fuss in preparing 'a state dinner, therefore troublesome to us'.[66] In the flurry, some details had to be fudged. Two tables, needed for the guests, were decorated. As well as foliage and fruit, kitchen utensils and even an earthenware chamber pot were enlisted.[67]

Confronted with such challenges, equipment and caterers could be hired. Even Trinity College Dublin was obliged to hire china from a local merchant when, in 1768, the installation of a new chancellor was celebrated.[68] For a lavish dessert arranged in 1747 by the O'Haras, up from the west, not only were glasses and dishes supplied by the confectioner who made the sweetmeats, but also two pineapples. Lord Gormanston availed of a comparable service from another Dublin confectioner in 1772. This time the pineapple was an ice, and the hired china, 'Dresden'.[69] Indeed, pineapples came to symbolize unstinting hospitality, given the expense of growing them successfully. Mary Delany, a vigilant observer of social niceties, was gratified to have fresh pineapple at a grand Dublin dinner, adding that it was served in 'fine old china'.[70] Sir James Caldwell, touring his neighbours' mansions in Ulster a few years later, reported coolly on a dessert composed of 'a pineapple, not good, a small plate of peaches, grapes and figs but a few, and the rest pears and apples'. It was served on the newly fashionable 'queen's ware' pottery.[71] By 1828, Dublin specialists advertised

in high life: dining in the Dublin town house' in C. Casey (ed.), *The eighteenth-century Dublin town house* (Dublin, 2010), pp 120–8; Moran, '"The eye as well as the appetite must be car'd for"', pp 199–200; Richards, *Eighteenth-century ceramics*, pp 152–63. **65** *Retrospections of Dorothea Herbert, 1770–1806* (2nd ed., Dublin, 1988), p. 40. **66** Ibid., p. 194. **67** F. Finnegan (ed.), *Introspections: the poetry and private world of Dorothea Herbert* (Piltown, 2011), pp 32–3. **68** TCD, MUN/P/4/56/1, Bursar's receipts, 15 Nov. 1768. **69** NLI, MS 36,483/3, N. Hickey, account with C. O'Hara, 19 Oct. 1747; NLI, Gormanston MSS, folder, trade receipts, 1760s and 1770s, H. Hoffman, account with Lord Gormanston, 26 Mar. 1772; D. Cashman, 'Sugar bakers and confectioners in Georgian Ireland', *Canadian Journal of Irish Studies*, 41 (2018), 74–99. The home cultivation of pineapples, in hot-houses, was the ultimate in horticultural snobbery. NLI, Talbot-Crosbie MSS, folder 54, W. Crosbie to Sir M. Crosbie, 8 Feb. 1757; JRL, B 3/10, Lord Farnham to Sir James Caldwell, 5 Sept. 1768, pp 855–6; R. Levitt, '"A noble pursuit of truth: the transatlantic history of pineapple cultivation', *Garden History*, 42 (2014), 106–19. **70** Lady Llanover (ed.), *The autobiography and correspondence of Mary Granville, Mrs Delany*, 6 vols (London, 1861–2), iii, p. 582. **71** JRL, B 3/29/32, Sir James Caldwell to Lady Caldwell, 18 Oct. 1772.

5.5 Irish delft shaped sweetmeat or pickle dishes, mid-eighteenth century. Private collection.

that they hired out attractive dishes for dinner and supper parties. Pineapples were not mentioned.[72]

The ingenuity and opportunism of manufacturers, and the fierce competition for sales, led to the proliferation of dishes for particular purposes. A meal might necessitate asparagus servers, butter- and sauce-boats, argyles (for keeping gravy hot and pouring it), perforated plates (mazarines) for draining the liquor from meats and fish, bowls reserved for salad and punch, oyster plates, ice-pails, wine-coolers and monteiths for rinsing drinking glasses, water-fountains and filters. Already in the 1760s, distinctive cups – of a larger size – appeared at breakfast.[73] Similarly in affluent homes, coffee was drunk from cups different from those for tea (fig. 5.5).

Opportunities to eat outside the home, whether in intimidating state or in unbuttoned ease, expanded. Taverns had long served food, as did many of the coffee houses that multiplied during the eighteenth century. It has been noticed already that

---

[72] *Saunders's News-Letter*, 10 May 1828. [73] NLI, MS 40,083/22, G. Newton, accounts with Lord Louth [1760s].

5.6 Mason's ironstone shaped dish for Monaghan grand jury, *c*.1835. Private collection.

one inn in central Dublin was equipped with Rouen-ware. Clubs, hunts, county grand jurors, masonic lodges, knots of friendly brothers, regiments and looser convivial groupings dined together regularly (fig. 5.6). Some commissioned ceramics emblazoned with their own insignia; all required dishes from which to be helped and to eat. By the early nineteenth, as travel became easier with better roads and ultimately railways, hotels opened. In all these public gatherings, expectations of certain standards of accommodation and refreshment obliged the proprietors to invest in the appropriate furnishings, including the china and earthenware. One Belfast trader made a deliberate pitch for such custom.[74]

Invitations to grand establishments introduced the uninitiated to unfamiliar modes and implanted a yearning for novelties. When Bishop Synge fussed over the look of his visitation dinners in County Roscommon, one motive was to familiarize the parish clergy with more refined ways (just as his predecessor had hoped to foster an interest in reading among them). Until advertisements were well illustrated – with more than crude woodcuts – it was impossible for most to envisage what was meant by the arcane terminology ('burnt china') of origins, shape and purpose. Seeing examples alone made them real and aroused longing. If the urge to possess was undoubtedly emulative, underpinned by aspiration and ostentation, more personal fancies sometimes explained the acquisitiveness. Ceramics could give visual and tactile delight.

[74] Barnard, '"China-men" in Dublin between 1790 and 1843', 252; Barnard, 'Hedgehogs in Cavan', 289; Curry, 'Empire of China', 116–23.

Austere men disparaged 'people of fashion' who risked beggaring themselves by rushing after 'great bargains of china and other fine need-nots'. In 1748, two returning East India ships docked at Kinsale for unscheduled repairs. 'Most of the women' from the Cork hinterlands were said to have descended on the alluring cargoes.[75] Such reports belonged to a tradition of misogyny in which female desire for ceramics, dangerous in itself, was a surrogate for more destructive lusts. In eighteenth-century Ireland, owing to the nature of the evidence, men appear much more active in selecting, ordering and paying for china. Few women – the first duchess of Ormond and Lady Grandison in County Waterford during the 1750s – are identified as owners of significant collections.[76] Yet, with household management treated largely as a woman's work, care and pride as to how comestibles were stored and served would seem a natural part of these responsibilities. Yet, who decided what novel items were to be bought and for what reasons have left almost no traces.

If the craze was censured by men, it is also through them – more surprisingly – that engagement with and responses to china in eighteenth-century Ireland have largely to be reconstructed. Ostentation can certainly be attributed to FitzGibbon with his costly shopping. With other purchasers different motives are discernible. Unexpectedly, the simpler pleasures excited by the bright, brittle objects are communicated by the attribute of 'prettiness'. Bishop Synge, as has been mentioned, used the term of his Rouen-ware, as did a contemporary squire in County Westmeath who judged one pattern, 'much the prettiest of all'.[77] Richard Lovell Edgeworth, a wearisomely inventive squire, did not hesitate from advising Wedgwood, whom he knew from social and intellectual circles in England. In addition to practical suggestions as to how the design of sauce-boats and inkstands might be improved, Edgeworth when ordering creamware on his family's behalf in 1787, specified that it should be 'your newest and prettiest ware'.[78] By 1840, Anson Floyd, trading on a grand scale at Wellington Quay, Dublin, advertised tea and breakfast services as 'the newest and prettiest' ever offered.[79] Prettiness is far removed from grandeur.

V

Given the outlay on china and earthenware, together with its bulk and fragility, care was needed in its storage. Ornamental pieces were designed to be seen. They, however, constituted a fraction of the ceramic holdings in most households. The useful wares posed a greater problem. Those who owned only a rudimentary collection of crocks, probably unmatched and imperfect, differed from those able to

---

75 NLW, Puleston MSS 3580E, E. Spencer to F. Price, 25 Apr. 1748; Barnard, *Making the grand figure*, p. 132.   76 PRONI, T. 3131/F/2/17, Inventory of Dromana, 12 Aug. 1755; J. Fenlon, '"Her Grace's closet": paintings in the duchess of Ormond's closet at Kilkenny castle', *Bulletin of the Irish Georgian Society*, 36 (1994), 30–47.   77 NLI, PC 436/41, W. Smythe to R. Smythe, undated [*c*.1750]; Barnard, *Making the grand figure*, p. 131.   78 F. Doherty, 'An eighteenth-century intellectual friendship: letters of Richard Lovell Edgeworth and the Wedgwoods', *PRIA*, 86C (1986), 256.   79 *Dublin Evening Post*, 8 May 1840.

acquire the extensive dinner services – from 144 to 206 pieces – supplemented by smaller sets reserved for breakfast, tea, coffee, dessert and supper. Too bulky to be left about in rooms, some nevertheless were used daily and had to be readily accessible. Others by their nature were required only for specific and intermittent functions; also, the prized was brought out for 'best'. In the intervals, space had to be found for the wares. Only in the largest houses could dedicated china closets be made for storage, as in the Wingfields' Dublin house or at Fota in County Cork.[80] An alternative, although again it assumed room to spare, was to arrange a buffet or 'beaufette' [buffet] in which choice ceramics, glass and *objets d'art* could be seen by visitors. This ornamental device was contrived for a dancing master in Cork city, as part of the *mise-en-scène* to persuade pupils of the refinement of their tutor and what they were about to learn.[81]

Dotting china on available surfaces was all very well with garnitures of vases or figures intended to embellish chimneypieces and shelves (as *chez* Cockburn), but not practicable or desirable with heftier articles in regular use. Cupboards and closets were an obvious answer but an alternative growing in popularity was the dresser. It coupled safe storage with showing off visually pleasing possessions. In houses of pretension, dressers were found in the servants' quarters: they were convenient to the kitchen and the preparation of meals and also shelved the utilitarian vessels used by underlings. What has yet to be demonstrated is how far upwards dressers edged: not only in the kitchens in which most of the waking life of a family was passed but into the eating rooms and parlours where those of greater aspirations and means gathered to eat and socialize. Through the surviving artefacts and rare paintings of domestic interiors, the dresser as an adaptable and vital item of furniture has been documented, notably by Claudia Kinmonth.[82]

A degree of improvisation frequently attended these matters. Notwithstanding the orderly arrangements prescribed by manuals and trendsetters, situations were hardly standardized. Whatever was at hand had to be deployed in organizing a household. Accidents happened. A woman, visiting a modest country dwelling, on retiring to bed, knocked a nail (for hanging her clothes) too vigorously into what she took to be the partition wall. She had hit the back of a dresser that divided her sleeping apartment from another room. A cascade and breakages followed. There was further dismay that the losses could not be made good until someone went to Carrick-on-Suir for replacements.[83]

---

80 *A catalogue of the goods and stock of the late Edward Wingfield*, p. 3; R. Sexton, 'Food and culinary cultures in pre-Famine Ireland', *PRIA*, 115C (2015), p. 291.   81 Barnard, *Making the grand figure*, pp 112–13; *The poems of Olivia Elder*, ed. A. Carpenter (Dublin, 2017), p. 8. For the evolution of the buffet: P. McCarthy, *Life in the country house in Georgian Ireland* (New Haven and London, 2016), p. 100; P. Thornton, *Seventeenth-century interior decoration in England, France and Holland* (New Haven and London, 1978), pp 238–9, 282–4.   82 Barnard, *Making the grand figure*, pp 48, 64, 107, 126; C. Kinmonth, *Irish country furniture and furnishings, 1700–2000* (Cork, 2020), pp 179–239; C. Kinmonth, *Irish rural interiors in art* (London, 2006), pp 50, 51, 52, 53, 61, 64, 65.   83 *Retrospections of Dorothea Herbert*, p. 300.

VI

An Irish official enquiry in 1823 concluded that ceramics are 'an article of such universal consumption, and of such simple manufacture'.[84] There was dismay that no manufacturer in Ireland currently met the demand. Instead, utilitarian and other wares were imported (fig. 5.7). The scale of the trade and of consumption was suggested by what is known to have been despatched from Staffordshire via Liverpool into Ireland between 1821 and 1823. The bulk was shipped to Dublin and larger towns such as Belfast, Cork, Drogheda, Limerick and Waterford, but smaller and remoter ports (more than thirty) received consignments (fig. 5.8).[85]

5.7 Minton, Staffordshire dish, 'bird and bough', marked for 'Donovan', Dublin, *c*.1800. Private collection.

[84] Commissioners for enquiring into the collection and public management of the public revenue in Great Britain in *Dublin Mercantile Advertiser*, 24 Feb. 1823.   [85] Barnard, 'Hedgehogs in Cavan', 288.

5.8 Blue and white platter (made by Tams, Staffordshire, c.1830) with view of General Post Office, Dublin. Private collection.

Further systematic investigation is needed to connect what can be retrieved about the availability of goods, especially through advertisements and directories, to wider economic and social developments. Embourgeoisement and modest urbanization occurred from the later eighteenth century, if not on the same scale as in western Europe and Britain. Population increased rapidly until the 1840s, together with the spending power of some. The practices of shopkeeping and the conventions for living respectably and creditably evolved, to which suppliers of ceramics responded. Indeed, sometimes they can be suspected of engineering the adoption of new habits.[86] Innovations in design, production and marketing multiplied. As in central and western Europe, so in Britain, makers and sellers of ceramics had realized that

---

[86] D. Dickson, 'Death of a capital? Dublin and the consequences of Union' in P. Clark & R. Gillespie (eds), *Two capitals: London and Dublin, 1500–1840*, Proceedings of the British Academy, 107 (2001), 111–31; D. Dickson, 'Society and economy in the long eighteenth century' in J. Kelly (ed.), *The Cambridge history of Ireland, vol. 3, 1730–1880* (Cambridge, 2018), pp 173–4; FitzGerald, *Silver in Georgian Dublin*, pp 191–3; F. Lane, 'William Thompson, class and his Irish context' in F. Lane (ed.), *Politics, society and*

5.9 Trade card for Higginbotham, Mary's Abbey and Pill Lane, Dublin, *c.*1810. Cobbe papers: Alec Cobbe division.

commercial success relied on a broad, middling spectrum of society, not just on a courtly coterie.[87] The 'mock court' in Dublin had done little to promote an indigenous earthenware industry. By the 1820s, provincial retailers were offering a range of moderately priced ceramics for meals. They – and their suppliers – invented novelties such as game-pie dishes 'representing the most beautiful and accurate devices in poultry, game, etc.'.[88] By 1839, the bait of 'a Christmas supply' was announced by a Tralee shop.[89] Gift-giving for other occasions was also encouraged. In 1840, one prominent trader on the Dublin quays addressed customers seeking wedding presents. If a china clock at £30 was singled out as 'the finest piece' currently on sale in Dublin, the advertisement stressed the 'boundless stock of blue and common goods' in the shop.[90]

the middle class in modern Ireland (Houndmills, 2010), p. 24; C. O'Neill, *Catholics of consequence: transnational education, social mobility, and the Irish Catholic elite 1850–1900* (Oxford, 2014). **87** Marchand, *Porcelain*, pp 176–7, 195, 234. **88** *Cork Examiner*, 13 Dec. 1847; *Southern Reporter and Cork Commercial Chronicler*, 16 Dec. 1848. For examples: D. Edwards & R. Hampson, *English dry-bodied stoneware: Wedgwood and contemporary manufacturers 1774–1830* (Woodbridge, 1998), p. 71; Reilly, *Wedgwood*, i, pp 502–3. **89** *Kerry Evening Post*, 11 Dec. 1839. **90** *Dublin Evening Post*, 8 May 1840.

Adroit dealers stocked both the ornamental and the utilitarian. A salesman from Cheltenham, who staged an auction in Dublin during 1825, promised 'ornamental china, adapted to the mantelpiece, boudoir or pier table'. He would sell massive vases for vestibules and halls, pot-pourri jars and 'baubles for boudoirs'. There is a suspicion that out-of-fashion and unsaleable English wares were being unloaded onto gullible Dubliners through this stratagem.[91] Elsewhere in the city, a large emporium catered for all tastes and purses. Among its assorted stock were 'cheap Staffordshire goods', aimed at 'those who may not be particular in their choices' (fig. 5.9).[92]

With no Irish manufacture of finer wares between about 1806 and 1857, even scrupulous patriots were spared heart-searching about buying imports. Despite the size and value of this apparently captive Irish market, manufacturers in Britain seldom fabricated pieces aimed blatantly at Hibernian sensibilities. Irish customers were apparently happy with the products popular in Britain and continental Europe. The china in use or on show rarely asserted a distinctive Irish identity.[93] What it did betoken was the willing Irish embrace of a commodity of 'universal consumption'.

91 *Dublin Morning Register*, 8 Mar. 1825; *Saunders's News-Letter*, 3 Mar. 1830.   **92** Curry, 'Empire of China', 116–23; *Saunders's News-Letter*, 18 July 1830.   **93** Barnard, 'Hedgehogs in Cavan', 285–7; S. Beltrametti & W. Laffan, 'William McCleary and the trade in printed caricatures in early nineteenth-century Dublin: part I – "Unlawfully participating in the profits of their labour"', *IADS*, 23 (2021), 112–33.

Communality and privacy in one- or two-roomed homes before 1830

CLAUDIA KINMONTH

This essay explores aspects of communality and privacy for people such as labourers and workers living inside Ireland's smallest rural dwellings in the long eighteenth century (c.1700–1830).[1] Initially it looks at sleeping habits, then at how people ate, and includes a description of a marriage in a small home. Building on the author's previous publications on material culture and art history (especially relating to beds, mattresses and tables, or paradoxically the lack of them), it presents some previously unpublished material.[2] It includes elements of architectural history, poetry and some contemporary texts primarily by Quaker author Mary Leadbeater (1758–1826), and Maria Edgeworth (1768–1849), juxtaposed with the Edgeworth family's sketches.[3]

HISTORIOGRAPHY

After the 1830s, there is a marked increase in evidence from travelling writers, reporters, government officials, diarists and artists describing arrangements inside the smallest homes. Sources during the long eighteenth century are fewer and less accessible (although digitization is redressing that imbalance). The Dublin Society's Statistical Surveys (c.1800 to c.1830) provide helpful insights. However, most of these proudly describe 'improved' housing for the authors' tenants, from the stylistic (Gothic windows) to the convenient (upstairs bedrooms, boarded floors, sashed windows), rather than the uncomfortable reality of the unimproved, overcrowded, dark and damp conditions that most workers endured.[4] Earlier, grander sources provide valuable precedents. In 1620, Luke Gernon, a condescending English official, observed how people slept when he visited Irish castles (rather than 'cabins'). His

---

1 The author is grateful to the following people who kindly helped in various ways with this work. Sean Barden (Armagh County Museum), Jayne Clarke (Mid & East Antrim Museum & Heritage Service/Braid Museum, Ballymena, Co. Antrim), Louis M. Cullen, Konstantin Ermolin (RIA Library), Conor Lucey, Finola O'Kane, Thomas and Valerie Pakenham, The Bodleian Library, Sinead Reilly (Fermanagh & Omagh District Council, Fermanagh Co. Museum), Jean Walker and Gerard Whelan (RDS Library). 2 C. Kinmonth, *Irish rural interiors in art* (New Haven, 2006), pp 126–51; C. Kinmonth, *Irish country furniture and furnishings 1700-2000* (Cork, 2020), pp 292–389; C. Kinmonth, 'Rural life through artists' eyes: an interdisciplinary approach' in P. Murray (ed.), *Whipping the herring: survival and celebration in Irish art* (Cork, 2006), pp 34–45, 152–3, 164–7. 3 See also V. Pakenham (ed.), *Maria Edgeworth's letters from Ireland* (Dublin, 2018). 4 R.A. Thompson, *Statistical survey of the county of Meath: with observations on the means of improvement: drawn up for the consideration, and under the*

account resonates, considering later evidence for people sleeping communally: 'you shall have company ... When you come to your chamber, do not expect canopy and curtaynes. It is very well if your bedd content you, and if the company be greate, you may happen to be bodkin in the middle'.[5] A travelling Frenchman, Monsieur Le Gouz de la Boullaye, adds material detail about sleeping arrangements in 1644: 'They have little furniture, and cover their rooms with rushes, of which they make their beds in summer, and of straw in winter.' Like subsequent writers he noticed that people deliberately blocked chimneys to conserve heat and fuel with the result that smoke issued through the front door.[6]

Written evidence is scarce about the domestic arrangements of people lowest down the economic scale who, unlike the aristocracy, rarely published their own accounts or had their homes or their portraits painted.[7] Terminology can be confusing and misleading about such people and their dwellings.[8] Those we are concerned with here were variously described as farmers, fishermen, labourers, cottiers, cottars, paupers or indeed a range of artisans. These people lived in the smallest one- or two-roomed homes, labelled 'scalps' or bothies, cabins, 'cabbins' (formerly 'creats'), 'hutts', hovels and farmhouses.[9] Many cohabited under the same roof as their farm animals in 'byre dwellings'. Others practised transhumance, moving along with their dairy cattle in summer, to 'upland booley huts', away from their main settlement.[10]

Alan Gailey discusses a complexity of terminology for small dwellings, especially when English visitors described the Irish cabin as a 'cottage' (a label which didn't come into intermittent use in Ireland until after the period considered here).[11] So abject was the cabin dwellers' or labourers' situation that, according to Leadbeater, they habitually described themselves as 'slaves', with phrases such as 'I am a poor slave from Connaught, that is looking for work'.[12] Detailed descriptions of farmhouses (farmers usually employed labourers or cottiers) are as elusive as for those 'beneath' them economically. The system of 'conacre', where land was rented for a single season, mitigated against improvement of labourers' cabins. Rents were highest

---

direction of the Dublin Society (Dublin, 1802), pp 69, 72.   **5** L. Gernon, *Discourse of Ireland anno 1620* (2014), p. 361.   **6** T. Crofton Croker (ed.), *The tour of the French traveller de la Boullaye Le Gouz in Ireland, A.D. 1644* (London, 1837), pp 40–1.   **7** With some exceptions, see sketches in L.M. Cullen, *Life in Ireland* (London, 1968), pp 120, 122–3.   **8** J. Bell, 'Miserable hovels and substantial habitations: the housing of rural labourers in Ireland since the eighteenth century', *Folklife*, 34 (1995–6), 43–56.   **9** A. Gailey, *Rural houses of the north of Ireland* (Edinburgh, 1984), pp 197–9. Regarding house terminology see https://www.bl.uk/picturing-places/articles/an-irish-cabin-on-the-commons-of-bray See also F. O'Kane, 'Arthur Young's published and unpublished illustrations for "A Tour in Ireland 1776–1779"', *IADS*, 19 (2016), 120–1, 123–6, 133.   **10** E. Costello, *Transhumance and the making of Ireland's uplands (1550–1900)* (Woodbridge, 2020), pp ix–x, 1, 11–12, 35, 41, fig. 2.4.   **11** Gailey, *Rural houses*, pp 197–200; M. Leadbeater, *The Leadbeater papers. The annals of Ballitore, since the year 1766*, 2 vols (London, 1862), ii, p. 198: 'I was ardent in my wish to alter "Cottage" to "Cabin" in the title ... but was told that in England it would be understood to mean the cabin of a ship' – quoted from Leadbeater's correspondence in 1810 concerning the title of her forthcoming book *Cottage dialogues among the Irish peasantry, with notes and a preface by Maria Edgeworth* (London, 1811).   **12** Leadbeater, *Cottage dialogues*, pp 285–6.

6.1 'Bed & Floor Matts', sketch, 180 x 116 mm, inscribed 'Floor and Bed mats' from *The cries of Dublin, drawn from the life by Hugh Douglas Hamilton*, 1760. Examples of plaited straw or woven rush mats survive in museums.

closest to towns and varied according to the quality of the land.[13] Some sources provide useful insights into internal arrangements and into people's rituals, aspirations, and priorities, even if the material is scarce.

13 Cullen, *Life in Ireland*, pp 118–22.

SLEEPING ARRANGEMENTS AND BED TYPES

The rare descriptions of one- or two-roomed dwellings, usually by surprised, shocked, or blatantly disgusted travellers, show how for poor people a bed of straw, either loose or made into a plaited mattress, was commonly used for sleeping on. 'A Poor Man's Petition' is a long poem by Andrew M'Kenzie from 1807, explaining the hard life of a County Down labourer with a wife and 'six naked children'. It clearly refers to their lack of a raised bedstead:

> And in a corner by the wall,
> We have a bed that *cannot* fall,
> But let this not create surprise –
> Securely on the ground it lies;
> To furnish it no flocks of geese,
> Were plundered of their downy fleece,
> Plain straw it is ... and o'er this bed,
> The ruins of a quilt are spread.[14]

People sleeping on straw either laid it down loose or had it skilfully plaited into mattresses or palliasses. Especially desirable was an additional mattress on top, of feathers and/or down, and one surviving palliasse (now in the Ulster Folk Museum) still has fragments of what appears to be goose down clinging to its upper surface.[15] Although straw objects from Irish museums rarely pre-date the early twentieth century, there is evidence suggesting that plaiting, or 'coiling and binding' techniques, have a far longer continuity.[16] Cabins usually had earthen or flagged floors that had the disadvantage of becoming muddy in winter and dusty in summer. Surviving straw floor mats, with suspension holes suggesting they could be hung up after washing, must have helped people to keep their feet and bedding clean. A rare sketch of a salesman weighed down with 'Bed and Floor Matts', created in 1760 by Hugh Douglas Hamilton, reveals how similar they look to examples that survive in museums (fig. 6.1).[17]

A two-roomed dwelling could be created from a single room, subdivided by some sort of partition to form a smaller space for a 'room' (distinct from the kitchen, often referred to as 'the room') usually at the end furthest from the hearth. By the nineteenth century, furniture was certainly incorporated into such partitions, and this may have been usual (in some households) during the eighteenth century too. In 1812, the writer Edward Wakefield published a historical description (originally recorded on 27 January 1747) that vividly records the interior spatial arrangement of such a dwelling:

14 A. M'Kenzie, *Poems and songs on different subjects* (Belfast, 1810), pp 119–20.   15 Kinmonth, *Irish country furniture and furnishings*, figs 320–1.   16 Pakenham (ed.), *Maria Edgeworth's letters*, pp 173–4.   17 W. Laffan (ed.), *The cries of Dublin drawn from the life by Hugh Douglas Hamilton, 1760* (Dublin, 2003), pp 120–1; Kinmonth, *Irish country furniture and furnishings*, pp 116–17, figs 103–4, 111.

> Robert Barry, a labouring man, being in bed with his wife and two children in a close room, the door of which, opposite to a chimney in an outer room, was shut, a flash of lightening broke down some part of the top of the chimney, and split the chamber door, forcing one half of it into the room where the people lay … The lightening forced its way through the wall behind the fireplace, making a hole, which was larger on the outside of the house, than within. A pig was found dead near the chimney.[18]

This suggests that the plan of Barry's two-roomed home had a kitchen (the 'outer room') with its hearth situated within an external gable wall, and a second 'close room' (suggesting it lacked windows) separated by a partition, within which was a door. Plans for that type of house have yet to emerge from 1700 to 1830, but occasionally commentators describe such two-roomed, or one-roomed arrangements. Partitions were of wattle, straw or wicker and probably other locally available materials such as stone, mud or turf. Writing in 1813, Reverend James Hall described how the Irish poor kept out the cold:

> in places where fuel is scarce, they have a partition of platted straw, higher than their heads, with slender wood in it, at the head and foot, moveable like a screen; it being suspended by straw ropes from the roof. They lift the cap of this when they go out or in, and remove it wholly, or not, in summer.[19]

Repeatedly, writers were disgusted to find animals in dwelling houses (in so-called 'byre dwellings'), and people sleeping communally, or, as in this case, together in one room. It is not therefore a coincidence that in Wakefield's account the pig was found dead 'near the chimney', because this valuable, intelligent animal, beneficial to the labourer's income, was habitually housed indoors. Wakefield commented that 'the pig is an inmate in every Irish cabin, and remains there for a considerable time: the hog, indeed is as much a domestic animal in Ireland as the dog, and becomes so habituated to the warmth of the cottage, that he seldom strays far from home.'[20] Hall goes further, telling how

> animals live not only about, but literally in the house with the family, the hog seems most at home, and at his ease. At breakfast, dinner, and every meal, he draws near the board, squats on his hams like a cur, and grunts his request … [they] give him the peelings and the worst potatoes. In fact, he breakfasts, dines, and sups with his master.[21]

Pigs fattened well on cooked potatoes, peelings and scraps. Kept safely indoors by night, they could be 'house trained' like dogs and added warmth to the cabin and its

---

18 E. Wakefield, *An account of Ireland, statistical and political* (London, 1812), p. 208.   19 J. Hall, *Tour through Ireland; particularly the interior & least known parts*, 2 vols (London, 1813), ii, p. 86.   20 Wakefield, *An account of Ireland*, p. 354.   21 Hall, *Tour through Ireland*, ii, p. 87.

6.2 A family of eight 'Sleeping in stradogue'. By landlord James Connery, *The reformer*, c.1830.

occupants (fig. 6.2). The same advantage applied to fowl kept partially indoors, where they were safer and produced more eggs (especially during naturally barren, wet winter months). Arthur Young wrote in the late 1770s that every cottage 'swarms with poultry, and most of them have pigs' (fig. 6.3).[22] Wakefield's compassion for animal welfare led him to describe as barbarous the practise of plucking living geese, resulting in them running around conspicuously devoid of feathers.[23] This presumably was driven by people's desire to augment their own bedding, or profit from the sale of feathers.

In 1813, James Hall aligns with other accounts about the times working people went to sleep: 'to save fuel, they always go early to bed, particularly when it is cold; and that, except in the middle of summer, they always get up by day light'.[24] The material sleeping conditions for one poor family in Connemara were recorded in 1823–4. A woman who had just given birth to her seventh child, lay in a cabin

> without a window, the holes in the floor were filled with rainwater, and of the two opposite doors one was open to give light to the room, the other, off its hinges, rested against the framework, and but partially protected the woman from the effects of a thorough draught of air [...] Her scanty bed of straw was spread upon the damp floor: a single blanket her only covering, while her head was literally supported by a block of wood.[25]

22 A. Young, *A tour in Ireland, 1776–1779* (London, 1780), p. 21, cited in O'Kane, 'Arthur Young's published and unpublished illustrations for "A Tour in Ireland"', 132.   **23** Wakefield, *An account of Ireland*, p. 359.   **24** Hall, *Tour through Ireland*, ii, p. 82.

Communality and privacy in one- or two-roomed homes before 1830

6.3 Pen and wash drawing entitled 'An Irish Cabbin'. One of three naked children reaches into a huge bowl of potatoes (contemporarily described as the 'communal platter'). From Arthur Young's own extra illustrated edition of *A tour in Ireland … 1776–1779*, vol. 1/1 (London, 1780). Courtesy the National Library of Ireland.

In households lacking bedsteads the 'shake down' of straw on the floor was widespread, and had practical advantages. The common complaint in inns throughout the British Isles was of fleas and lice that hid in the cracks of wooden bedframes and emerged to torment sleepers who, horribly 'pestered with buggs', were driven from their night-time slumbers.[26] But a 'shake down' could be renewed or disposed of easily if it became 'lousy'. In 1811, Mary Leadbeater, writing from County Kildare, advised cottagers sleeping on straw 'to spread lime on the floor, under your straw, it will help keep the damp from you; and change your straw often'; for those better equipped she recommended they 'spread lime … under the bedstead, to prevent the damp from rising up to you. I wish your windows opened' she continued.[27] Lime may also have deterred vermin. Leadbeater's *Cottage dialogues* was a manual of helpful

---

[25] K. Whelan (ed.), *Letters from the Irish highlands of Connemara, by the Blake family of Renvyle House (1823–1824)* (Clifden, 1995), p. 43. [26] L. Wright, *Warm and snug, the history of the bed* (London, 1962), pp 165–7. In 1786, a guest stayed at London's Bell Savage, but by 4 am upped and went for a walk until breakfast time. The following night he deserted the same bed to sit 'up in the great Chair all night'. [27] Leadbeater, *Cottage dialogues*, p. 177.

advice to the poor that provides useful historical insights. She self-consciously observed her own text, stating 'it may serve for the information, perhaps for the amusement of future antiquaries ... to mark what is now esteemed luxury, and economy, in a certain rank [the 'peasantry']'.[28]

We hear that 'often a poor woman can't leave the cabin with any safety or convenience' because the cabin, often simultaneously a byre dwelling, was a dangerous environment for children.[29] Although ownership of a pig (or pigs), preferably a sow to produce a valuable litter, was desirable, the perils of cohabiting with such large, greedy omnivores are presented at the outset when Leadbeater recounts the discovery of a small child 'all in a gore of blood, and its face so eaten by the nasty sow, that the life was out of it'.[30] Such drama presumably caught the most ambivalent reader's attention and was reinforced by the tale of an infant unwisely left 'in the cradle by himself, and while he was asleep, an ugly brute of a pig came in, and ate off his poor little hand, as it hung over'. These cautionary tales were primarily aimed at discouraging women from working outside their homes, but they add evidence of the threat that cohabitation with pigs represented, especially to infants and children. The floor-level, ever-burning turf fire was another danger, its heat and light acting like a magnet (fig. 6.2). In such a cabin, 'another child that was left by itself ... got out of the cradle and crawled to the hearth, and its little petticoat took fire, and it was burned to death.'[31] In this regard, the 'half door' was another functional barrier between small children and animals, for those who could afford one. It also saved the cost of glass windows as it allowed in light. Its similarity to a stable door, usually made in two halves, is striking. Many different designs were resorted to: sometimes a full height front door had an additional half height door hinged on the outside, both usually opening inwards (unlike stable doors).

The *settle bed* is traceable as far back as the 1640s in inventories and must have appealed as it served as an extra bed in homes that lacked separate bedrooms.[32] It was most often placed adjacent to the hearth, as were the best beds. A long wooden bench by day that also doubled as a worktop, a series of hinges allowed it to fold out forwards, creating a high-sided, floor level double bed at night. It features in numerous eighteenth-century inventories, as do press beds. The settle bed's configuration as a floor level bed also served perfectly as a playpen, to separate infants from the open hearth, or from animals roaming or tethered indoors. The *press bed* was another type of folding bed that occupied less floor space than the settle bed. Concealed behind what looked like a pair of wardrobe doors, the bedframe was stored vertically, folding downwards once the doors were opened, to create a double bed that kept the bedding off the floor. Recently discovered inventories reveal that they were common in big houses throughout the long eighteenth century.[33] Like the settle bed,

28 Ibid., p. 280.   29 Ibid., p. 73.   30 Ibid., p. 3.   31 Ibid.   32 Kinmonth, *Irish country furniture and furnishings*, pp 150, 143–66. J.C. Walton, 'The household effects of a Waterford merchant family in 1640', *Journal of the Cork Historical and Archaeological Society*, 83:238 (1978), 102 ('One Settle bedd or bench bedd contayneinge a flox bed a boulster and one coverlet valued 1£').   33 T. Murdoch (ed.), *Great Irish households: inventories from the long eighteenth century* (forthcoming). The author is grateful to John

the press bed was also used in the 'big house' to accommodate servants. Those working people subsequently built their own versions which were appropriate in their far smaller, overcrowded homes.

The widespread practise of the family sleeping together in front of the fire was commonly referred to as 'in stradogue', although other terms were used for this communal way of sleeping on the floor. Fascinated travellers typically encountered this in remote rural cabins, when caught out beyond the reach of inns. In the late 1770s, Arthur Young wrote that 'A "shake-down" when I was in Ireland meant some clean straw spread upon the floor, with blankets and sheets'.[34] Touring County Mayo in 1800, Caesar Otway described how the communal bed was made up afresh each night, and specifically arranged 'with the parents in the centre, the daughters on the mother's side, the boys on the father's, then the travelling pedlar, or tailor or beggar [with] great propriety of conduct'.[35] The sole illustration of this practice dates from *c*.1830 and is a landlord's sketch, showing what he found upon visiting his tenants in the middle of the night (fig. 6.2). It supports what numerous travellers described, with one covering over eight people lying top to tail, and a man's coat placed on top. The proximity of the fire and of the sow (with as many of her own offspring) clearly demonstrates the benefit of mutual body heat. Writing in 1832, landowner James Connery mentions how the man of the family was on the floor as 'the fleas ejected him some time before from the bed in which he usually lay, in a dungeon of a room he had.'[36] His naïve drawing reveals an open thatched roof, with the sleepers' heads extremely close to the hearth.

Leadbeater's 'Dialogues between Nancy and Rose' suggest evidence for how cabins might be kept badly or well in early nineteenth-century Ireland. So we hear from (comparatively slovenly) Nancy: 'We lie very snug in the chimney corner in winter: in summer that's too warm, and we lie in *the room* [as the second room was called]; but the straw grows damp and fusty; and Tim threatens [promises] to get a bedstead for ourselves, and another for the children.'[37] The 'chimney corner' was, for reasons of warmth, the favoured place to sleep. Some considered it a 'nicety to wish for a bedstead to raise one up from the floor, a straw bed [mattress] in coarse sacking, and a warm pair of blankets'. Less ambitious, according to Leadbeater, was Tim's description that 'a man and his wife may be very comfortable on the floor, by the side

---

Adamson for advancing proofs of this prior to publication and pers. comm. Settle beds and press beds appear frequently in grand inventories, in servants' quarters. Listings newly published here indicate that settle beds (one listed as deal, another oak) were mainly relegated to stable quarters and outhouses associated with grooms, the blacksmith, shepherd or gardener (pp 49, 50, 91, 158, 172, 294, 296, 299, 301, 303). Press beds/press bedsteads predominated instead indoors, associated with a nurse, a maid, a housekeeper, a butler etc., with some listed as deal but also oak or mahogany (pp 141, 145, 151, 157, 171) and in the form of a desk (pp 189, 191, 205, 212, 223, 224, 225, 232, 329). M. Hayes, *The best address in town, Henrietta Street, Dublin and its first residents, 1720–80* (Dublin, 2020), pp iv, 168–9. **34** M. Betham-Edwards (ed.), *The autobiography of Arthur Young with sections from his correspondence* (London, 1898), p. 72. **35** C. Otway, *Sketches in Erris and Tyrawly* (Dublin, 1841), pp 32, 13. **36** J. Connery, *The reformer* (Dublin, 1832), quoted in C. Kinmonth, *Irish country furniture 1700–1950* (New Haven, 1993), p. 151. **37** Leadbeater, *Cottage dialogues*, pp 176, 320. 'Threatened' is explained in her endnote as 'promises'.

of the fire; a few stones will keep in the straw, as well as the sacking; and as to blankets, sure one will do, along with the big coat about ones' feet'.[38] The same 'big coat', which was such an important part of the labourer's outdoor clothing, certainly appears as part of the bedclothes in Connery's sketch. Leadbeater describes how the 'Irish *trusty* is a frieze great coat of uncommon thickness.'[39] Dress historian Mairead Dunlevy wrote that for men the popular *trusty* 'fitted loosely and was described as similar to a surtout or greatcoat'. In one instance, recorded in County Armagh in 1804, this outside coat cost £1, nearly a quarter of the cost of their entire wardrobe; in general, labourers 'were so poor that they could expect to replace their greatcoat only once every three years'.[40]

A *bedstead*, or any sort of frame that enabled people to raise their bedding up away from the floor, was desirable but beyond the means of the poorest families of labourers. Surviving early vernacular examples are rare, but illustrations reveal their structure and how they were draped with peoples' clothing, specifically in an example in a gate lodge recorded in a sketch by British artist Maria Spilsbury Taylor (1777–c.1823).[41] Cross referenced with texts and surviving objects, we can reconstruct how some of them may have looked.[42] Such beds, both 'high' and 'low posted', can be seen in the Irish Agricultural Museum, County Wexford.[43] Similar in construction are a pair of high posted eighteenth-century bedsteads made of bog oak bearing pitsaw marks, now in the Ulster American Folkpark, Omagh.[44]

With the above sleeping arrangements in mind, it is telling that around 1810 the term 'in the straw' referred to a woman who was about to give birth.[45] Connery's image, considered along with Leadbeater's dialogues, reveals how people sleeping in a byre dwelling alongside their animals might lack a bedstead yet own a table, a chair and stool, a dresser and basic utensils such as a water jug, plates and a piggin for milking their cow. Leadbeater's discussions relate that 'the parents and children all pig together, on the same wisp', yet the mother might desire 'a dresser to put her crockery ware on … and a chest for our clothes, a cupboard, and some chairs, and a table: in short everything necessary for a family that don't wish to live like savages'.[46]

Some houses in the coldest northwesterly counties incorporated a sleeping alcove set into the wall, called an *outshot bed*. Its low ceiling, raised bedframe and close proximity to the fire helped keep people warm and dry in otherwise unheated cabins. Its distribution has already been closely mapped (predominately in Ulster and Western Scotland, and coinciding with byre dwellings) and described in considerable detail.[47] Many bed outshots had curtains: along the north coast and County Donegal it was screened behind timber doors and hidden from visitors. It created an equivalent space to a bedroom, providing relative privacy within an otherwise shared space. In 1802, this was observed in houses in County Mayo and described as 'a little recess

38 Ibid., p. 74. 39 Ibid., p. 303. 40 M. Dunlevy, *Dress in Ireland* (London, 1989), pp 121, 139. 41 Kinmonth, *Irish rural interiors*, fig. 134, p. 133. 42 Kinmonth, *Irish country furniture and furnishings*, p. 308, fig. 319, p. 314, fig. 322. 43 IAM, Reg.6/8/95. 44 NMNI, Reg. No: OMAFP 1984.98/9, from Crosh townland, Newtownstewart, Co. Tyrone. 45 Leadbeater, *Cottage dialogues*, p. 121. 46 Ibid., pp 75–6. 47 Gailey, *Rural houses*, pp 153–7, figs 165, pp 161–4.

called *hag*, which is made into the side wall ... for one bed [with] straw mats, which hang parallel with the wall from the roof, by way of a curtain.'[48] In old age, bedridden grandparents were not isolated and could warn children away from the dangers of the fire. The outshot may also have been used as a private space to get dressed behind the curtains.

EATING COMMUNALLY

The Ordnance Survey Memoirs of Ireland, authorized by the Duke of Wellington (the Prime Minister) in 1824, comprises notes intended to accompany the series of published maps. An excerpt from County Tyrone provides detail about wages and employment of 'the lower orders of inhabitants', specifically those gaining their incomes from weaving, spinning or labouring (as opposed to begging). Disparaging in tone, especially regarding 'order, cleanliness or neatness', one fairly typical account sheds light on communal dining as a choice rather than a necessity, as the people described clearly had some financial savings at their disposal:

> you may see pigs and fowl eating in the kitchen and everything dirty and confused, the furniture a few pots and noggins, a stool or a broken chair. The potatoes at meals are thrown out in a basket and so laid on the table or on a stool, and the whole family gather round, master, mistress, children and servants in a mass, and eat out of the basket without knife, fork or any other appendage at meals. A man who can give his daughter in marriage 50 pounds or 100 pounds will live [in] this manner. But ... sometimes everything is seen comfortable, neat and clean ... the furniture good and decent, the kitchen neatly tiled.[49]

Accounts by military personnel lacked interest or understanding. Detailed, sympathetic accounts typically come from artists or travelling writers who were welcomed into cabins in remote places, and often invited to stay overnight without expectation of reimbursement. From such sources we learn that people traditionally ate potatoes from a shallow basket or skib. But one drawing by artist Daniel Maclise prior to 1829 shows a woven hoop being used to encircle a steaming heap of potatoes on a table top, from which a County Kerry family eat. Irish antiquary Thomas Crofton Croker wrote enthusiastically about their offerings of 'potatoes, and butter, and eggs, and milk ... I shared the potatoes of these poor people with an appetite and a relish' and gave them a shilling in return for the meal. Such generosity was received with 'a hundred thousand blessings'.[50] Others took advantage of openhanded

---

48 J. McParlan, *Statistical survey of County Mayo* (Dublin, 1802), p. 63. **49** A. Day & P. Williams (eds), *Ordnance Survey memoirs of Ireland, vol. 5, Parishes of County Tyrone 1, 1821, 1823, 1831–36 North, West & South Tyrone* (Belfast, 1990), p. 59. Gailey, *Rural houses*, p. 210, indicates a date of 1825 for this quote from Clogher barony in east Tyrone. **50** T. Crofton Croker & R. Adolphus Lynch, *Legends of the lakes,*

6.4 The earliest sketch known to the author of a communal potato dinner, shared from a flat basket resting on a cooking pot close to the hearth. Pencil sketch attributed to Charlotte Edgeworth, *c.*1806. Courtesy Bodleian Library.

hospitality. In her journal, Leadbeater relates how the elderly, corpulent, 'respectable' but greedy Joseph Wills 'frequently walked into his neighbours' houses, which opened with latches, and enquired what they had for dinner, at the same time poking his staff into the pot, for they mostly sat in their kitchens in the forenoons. This familiarity was of course not always acceptable.'[51]

Valerie Pakenham's meticulous juxtaposition of Maria Edgeworth's correspondence with selections from the Edgeworth family's sketchbooks reproduced a sketch of a communal meal recorded in County Longford in *c.*1806 (fig. 6.4). By way of establishing a context, Edgeworth describes in April 1829 the single storey 'dry lodgings' with 'little gardens' that she had built for 'future lodgers' at Edgeworthstown, her family seat in Longford. Visiting her tenants there on a daily

or sayings and doings at Killarney, 2 vols (London, 1829), ii, p. 154. The original of this 'Sketch of Interior of a Cabin at Feeding Time' survives in Trinity College Library, and is published in C. Kinmonth, 'Noggins, "The nicest work of all": traditional Irish wooden vessels for eating and drinking', *IADS*, 18 (2015), 134, fig. 4. **51** Leadbeater, *The Leadbeater papers*, i, p. 34.

6.5 Pen sketch inscribed 'C E Invent' and on mount 'Peggy Tuite and Her Family', by Charlotte Edgeworth, c.1806. Courtesy Bodleian Library.

basis, her correspondence reveals her involvement with working people. In 1821, another of her projects was to improve the main street of Edgeworthstown by building a 'gutter & pathway [which] will employ twenty men for a fortnight or 3 weeks and feed them well with meal'.[52]

Four sketches by Maria's half-sister Charlotte Edgeworth (1783–1807) also show how well she knew local families, whose homes both women were welcomed into (figs 6.4–7). The drawings, all apparently sketched by Charlotte Edgeworth (annoted 'C.E.'), are uniquely informative of the artist's careful observation of arrangements, especially when seen together. One is mounted (presumably regarded as a complete rendering), and depicts five well-dressed people, four sitting on low seats around the customary basket of potatoes which rests on the cooking pot (fig. 6.5). Inscribed with the names of individuals discussed in the family correspondence, they are identified as 'Peggy Tuite and Her Family'. Edgeworth depicts details of faces and a hand, but also of furniture, including a splay-legged stool of a type with staked or wedged legs that survives in sufficient numbers in museum collections for it to be readily familiar

---

[52] Pakenham (ed.), *Maria Edgeworth's letters*, pp 236, 295.

6.6 Pencil study inscribed 'Old Mrs Tuite', 'Old W. Tuite', 'CE', by Charlotte Edgeworth, *c*.1806. Courtesy Bodleian Library.

as an object.[53] The legs of at least three of these little stools protrude from beneath the clothing of the eaters, who sit with their hips lower than their knees. To the right, part of a *súgán* chair is visible, with a pronounced curve to its back (figs 6.4–7). A young woman stands to serve the customary buttermilk as 'kitchen' (or seasoning), from a tin mug. Both women wear bonnets, indicating that they are married. Some sit with plates resting on their knees, and one of the young men, on the left, uses a knife and fork, although most people ate potatoes without cutlery. Deep in conversation, old Mrs Tuite seems to hold a potato in one hand. The third sketch in pencil is the only one providing architectural detail, showing a stone-built hearth nearby on the right of the composition (fig. 6.4).

Tenants at Edgeworthstown were possibly better equipped than others, or, as indicated in the poetry below (p. 143), adopted greater formality for guests. In 1812, an insight into the gentry's influence on working people emerges from Mary Leadbeater who describes bringing a Dublin friend to Ballybarney village (where neatness had been encouraged with 'premiums') to 'Biddy's cabin [which] is always clean, though unprovided with what they call "tea-tackle." This her neighbours supply, and we always bring our tea, &c.'[54]

[53] Kinmonth, *Irish country furniture and furnishings*, p. 58, fig. 39 (right).   [54] Leadbeater, *The Leadbeater*

6.7 Ink sketch inscribed 'CE'. Four figures sitting on low stools and a *súgán* chair (right) eating potatoes from a basket balanced on the cooking pot. The young man has cutlery and he and old Mrs Tuite use plates, while she uses her fingers to eat. By Charlotte Edgeworth, *c*.1806. Courtesy Bodleian Library.

A letter from Maria Edgeworth (13 April 1829) to Fanny Wilson describes something similar on the occasion of her visiting 'the widows' houses:

> The widow Campbell, your old friend ... had been confined to her bed .... I went to see her – found her sitting up by her fire with her white hands nicely pinned across & her poor thin yellow face & dark eyes looking as cheerful as it was possible for sickness & misery to look – a little girl sweeping up the hearth & her son appointed to her sitting with hands on knees skinning an excellent manly looking potato, a flat basket of hot dittoes before him on a stool, a tin can of milk, his mother happily full – and when I asked is this your youngest son? – His mother's eyes doating on him as she murmured, Yes and the best of boys he is to me, these poor people have a happiness in their sympathy and affection for each other.[55]

Other drawings reveal the family's affection for their tenants. The earliest sketch to come to light depicting a coiled straw armchair, by Frances Edgeworth, shows 'Old Robin Woods' who was terminally ill. Once again, Maria provides the context:

papers, i, pp 51, 235.   55 Pakenham (ed.), *Maria Edgeworth's letters*, p. 295.

> His good old Margery is in great grief – they will never sit opposite to one another again with their dish of potatoes between them and their mug of milk – One day that I went in when they were at dinner I said 'How happy you two look!' 'Yes miss, we were that every day since we married'.[56]

Maria's description of being invited to the Catholic wedding of tenants, a ceremony normally held at home rather than in a church, offers a glimpse of how a marriage and customary 'breakfast' (or reception) might be conducted in the reduced accommodation provided by a typical early nineteenth-century cabin. In one instance she recalls being ushered in

> through [the] kitchen with blazing hearth & preparations of roast & baking & pots of flesh ... and through another door the boiling pot[atoes] seen in the yard ... Go on to the main rooms – a bedchamber of good size – remarkably clean & nice with nice patchwork quilt & pillows white as snow – two windows, plenty of light. In this room was the bride ... [and bridesmaids] all very neatly & plainly dressed seated on a range of chairs at one side – and opposite a range for us – a great French chest at the end of the room under the window – this serving for a table.[57]

Edgeworth describes a space so small that it wasn't easy for the bride and groom to lower themselves to their knees before the priest for the ceremony, which involved a ring but also money, passed to the bride. Such a detailed account is rare, describing how it was 'all rightly done – no running away', alluding to the so-called 'runaway match' which was common but clearly disapproved of by Maria.[58] A lithograph of artist J.P. Haverty's painting *Matrimony* (c.1840), of slightly later date to the period under review here, illustrates how this ceremony probably looked. It shows a priest conducting a couple's marriage service, with guests seated around the edges of a room; a parlour windowsill is used to lay out the priest's accoutrements.[59]

There was a customary lack of tables. People were creative and economical in the absence of four-legged versions. This included people eating from a basket or skib (that was easily washed then hung up on a wall to dry), and that latter arrangement has physical and cultural parallels. Stump-legged tray-tables, or platters, served the same function as the wicker skib. One example retrieved from a bog in County Armagh has cut marks across its upper surface and a rectangular suspension hole (for hanging to dry), indicating its use in the preparation and eating of food. It awaits carbon dating but appears to be eighteenth century or earlier.[60] A closely comparable Bronze Age 'tray' recently came to the author's attention and it is hoped that further examples may emerge (fig. 6.8).

56 Ibid., pp 173, 174.   **57** Ibid., pp 297–8.   **58** Kinmonth, *Irish rural interiors*, pp 152–65, fig. 167. After publishing Haverty's lithograph, the author found Haverty's substantial oil painting in a private collection, but its poor condition reveals less discernible detail than the lithograph.   **59** Kinmonth, *Irish rural interiors*, pp 152–65, fig. 167, NMI Reg. W. 31 is yet another example.   **60** Kinmonth, *Irish country furniture and furnishings*, p. 367, figs 372–3. E. Estyn Evans, *Irish folk ways* (London, 1979), pp 88–9, fig. 26. Both illustrations cited here feature the same 'table'.

6.8 Bronze Age platter or table/tray, view of top and underside. Hewn from one block of wood, with integral stump legs, 50 x 170 x 38 mm. Cut marks indicate use for communal eating. Dated to 3546+/-37BP, calibrated to 2010 to 1740BC. Courtesy of Mid and East Antrim Museum & Heritage Service.

There are parallels too with the 'falling table':[61] known in inventories and from surviving examples, it usually takes the form of a single rectangular board attached to a side/back wall of the house providing a temporary eating surface. Like the 'trays', it saves timber and space by being attached to a wall, and was easily hinged up into a vertical position after use. Skibs, stump-legged boards and falling tables share common characteristics; each is economical with materials, allows for communal eating, but can be stored on the wall when not in use, freeing the space for other

61 Kinmonth, *Irish country furniture and furnishings*, pp 375–85, figs 380–8.

activities (sleeping, dancing, wielding a flail). Falling tables featured in farmhouses throughout Ireland and like settle beds and press beds were also used in grand houses. The most recent to come to light appears in a newly published inventory of Carton House, Co. Kildare, recorded in 1818; here listed as '2 Oak falling leaves, (fast)' in the 'Groom of the Chambers Room'.[62]

Practices related to communal dining dictated innovate craft solutions. Salt was prioritised along with soap and candles as desirable to labourers' families. It was crucial for preserving fish, meat and butter but also to flavour or 'kitchen' the predominant diet of potatoes.[63] Another verse from the poem by Andrew M'Kenzie includes a reminder:

> But words I will not multiply,
> Potatoes all our meals supply;
> A little milk to them we add –
> And salt, when that can not be had.[64]

Different craftspeople competed for similar markets using different materials. So the wood turner competed by turning a bowl or a shallow, circular communal tray-like platter to hold potatoes, eggs and in the centre salt, each separated by a raised circular ridge (fig. 6.9). This form echoes the basketmaker's skib (which sometimes incorporated a raised circular ridge to secure a noggin of milk firmly in the centre of the potatoes).[65] Similar to an example of a platter from Armagh County Museum (accessioned as being for 'salt, eggs and potatoes'), this more elaborate version recently came to light but was accessioned simply as an 'egg holder'. But its design is perfect for keeping salt dry and separate inside the raised central part (with its tapered lip for facilitating the taking of small pinches of salt), eggs (presumably boiled) in the surrounding ring, and potatoes within the largest, outermost ring. Innumerable small, slightly curved indentations suggest wear from fingernails: we know people ate with their fingers. This intensely communal vessel so perfectly tailored to the potato diet, flavoured with eggs and salt, but carefully decorated with incised lines, raised up on a hollow base, may be eighteenth century (but awaits carbon dating). Like the example at the Armagh museum, its characteristically warped form tells us it was made using a pole lathe: its soft, green wood was dried after being turned. Using one object at mealtimes, without cutlery, minimized the

---

62 Murdoch (ed.), *Great Irish households*, p. 274. **63** Leadbeater, *Cottage dialogues*, pp 308–9. Her glossary explains that: *Kitchen* means 'butter, or any kind of sauce that is eaten with meat or vegetables, to make them more palatable; *Two kitchens to one bread* means butter and milk eaten with one piece of bread.' This is a comparatively early definition of this term, more widely used after 1830. On salt, see D. Downey, L. Downey & D. O'Donovan, *Historical Irish dairy products* (Dublin, 2021), pp 61–74. See also: C. Kinmonth, 'Rags, riches and recycling: material and visual culture of the Dublin Society 1731–1781', *IADS*, 21 (2018), 79. **64** M'Kenzie, *Poems and songs*, p. 121. **65** Kinmonth, *Irish country furniture and furnishings*, p. 367, figs 372–3; pp 431–2, figs 427, 443; Kinmonth, 'Noggins', p. 135, fig. 5.

6.9 Communal eating platter, side-view and top-view. Made on a pole lathe, hence uneven shape, 70 x 240 cm, undated. Sections for salt (centrally), eggs (inner ring) and boiled potatoes (outermost ring) with fingernail indentations.
© Museum Services, Fermanagh & Omagh District Council.

amount of water needed for washing. Given that it was customarily the women who collected and carried water from afar, this was seen as advantageous.

Again, we turn to M'Kenzie's rhymes to understand the common frugality of the typical family home. Something to eat off seemed interchangeable with a basket, which in turn also served other purposes. He suggests how temporary a table needed to be, perhaps only needed to impress or to accommodate extra visitors:

> Three stools, one larger than the rest
> Our table when we have a guest:
> A basket variously employ'd,
> Tho' nearly by old age destroy'd,
> It holds potatoes raw, or boil'd,
> And serves to rock our youngest child.[66]

In the smallest homes before 1830, wall-mounted or temporary arrangements served in lieu of more conventional tables: archaeological evidence suggests such arrangements arise from ancient traditions (fig. 6.8).[67]

---

[66] M'Kenzie, *Poems and songs*, p. 118.   [67] J. Derricke, *The image of Irelande with a discoverie of woodkarne* (London, 1581), plate 3, 'An Irish chieftain's feast', or see Kinmonth, *Irish country furniture and furnishings*, pp 366–7, figs 371–3, 375; p. 431, fig. 427.

CONCLUSION

Frugality, adaptabilty and communality were the shared experiences of people inhabiting the smallest dwellings in the long eighteenth century in Ireland. A sense of communality, with people gathered closely, their hands and elbows touching, around a central platter, basket, stool or falling table to share food (one of life's primal pleasures), is sensed from these elusive objects and from the vivid descriptions of artists, antiquaries and landowners who encountered these lives. Wooden versions of common utensils probably enabled people to cut meat on special occasions, yet served more frequently in lieu of a kitchen or dining table. At the lowest economic levels the concept of one object fulfilling multiple functions, rather than multiple objects each serving individual functions (in more affluent households), endured well into the twentieth century.

The communality of sleeping was partially influenced by Ireland's cool, damp climate and by poor people's lack of fuel. But it had been observed during the seventeenth century in castles where even aristocratic guests were not necessarily accommodated in separate beds, and accounts tell of beds lacking hangings and of straw or rushes being used instead of mattresses or carpets. Communal sleeping not only helped people keep warm in small homes, but had parallels with its physical closeness with communal eating traditions. The tradition of 'sleeping in stradogue' probably evolved as a survival strategy in poor housing and was carefully regulated as to exactly where each person lay. In Ireland's coldest north easterly counties, some privacy was afforded within a raised, roofed and curtained bed outshot for the luckiest, or oldest. The ubiquitous space-saving, draft-excluding settle bed was used in Ireland since the seventeenth century. Each accommodated several people, raised slightly up from a damp, cold floor, or allowed children to sleep packed in 'top to tail', who may also have been accommodated in a press bed (also known from eighteenth-century inventories).

The habit of sharing meals extended spontaneously to any wandering beggar or stranger. It was noticed and even criticized by Richard Pococke who thought that such open-handedness impoverished the hosts. He observed that it was considered unusual when he shared the food he brought along with him, or gave money when he was fed.[68] A lack of formality, and a sense of close proximity, is also striking, with Maria Edgeworth's rare description of a home wedding, with people squeezed into a tiny room, contrasting with the colder formality of a church. The objects and spaces described here share that communality and sense of closeness, like the shared, encircling, inclusive, welcoming meals. This sense of inclusion, that in terms of hospitality welcomed in the travelling huckster, pedlar, working craftsperson, writer and artist as equally as the curious stranger writing a travel journal, seems innately Irish.

---

68 J. McVeagh (ed.), *Richard Pococke's Irish tours* (Dublin, 1995), pp 81–2.

Entertaining royalty after the Union: space, decoration and performance in Charleville Castle, Co. Offaly, 1809

JUDITH HILL

To choose the Gothic style in the early nineteenth century when classicism reigned was to make a deliberate statement. But how is this to be interpreted? Lord and Lady Charleville, both patrons involved in the designing of their new castle, entertained the viceroy and his entourage on their southern tour of Ireland in 1809 shortly after Charleville Castle was completed. In this case, not only do we have evidence relating to the design process, and some indication of how the rooms were furnished, but we can also reconstruct elements of this important visit; we have both stage set and performance. The encounter, occurring nine years after the passing of the Act of Union, was one in which both the viceroy and his hosts had invested heavily, and all knew what they wanted. Culture – planning, furnishings, military, domestic and social rituals – was the vehicle for political aspirations at a time when both viceroy and the Irish Protestant landed class needed to assert themselves. Untangling this, it is the aspiration of this essay to define a particular species of aristocratic house: the post-Union Irish castle.

AMBITION

Designed by architect Francis Johnston and built between 1800 and 1809 on an estate near Tullamore in King's County (now County Offaly), Charleville Castle is a formidable limestone-built complex (fig. 7.1). It is composed of a square, three-storey keep with corner towers and turrets of various designs, and a rambling two-storey wing. This comprises a chapel, kitchen and stables centred on two courtyards extending at a forty-five degree angle from the octagonal northwest tower of the keep. The castle stands within a low curtain wall rising over a fifteen-foot ditch, at the edge of an ancient deciduous woodland in the centre of a large demesne. Although it was not the first castle-style house to be built in Ireland, it was a pioneering design, alert to contemporary British trends in its feeling for the Picturesque, with its references to mid- and late-eighteenth-century buildings such as Strawberry Hill, Twickenham and Inveraray Castle, Argyllshire, and its awareness of the work of contemporary English architects, James Wyatt and John Nash.

The Charleville Estate, part of a large inheritance, came to Charles William Bury in 1785 from his father's maternal uncle, Charles Moore, who had been created earl of Charleville in 1758. The title extinct on Moore's death, Charles William Bury was

7.1 Charleville Castle, Co. Offaly, from the northwest. Photograph by the author.

keen to regain the earldom, which he did in stages: baron Tullamore, October 1797; Viscount Charleville in 1800 as a reward for voting for the Union; earl of Charleville after hard petitioning in February 1806. Bury began his work at Charleville in 1786 by commissioning Thomas Leggett, the Dublin-based landscape gardener, to aggrandise the demesne.[1] Leggett proposed a lake to the south of a newly sunken section of the Birr to Tullamore road, wooded islands and cascades for the River Clodagh on the west boundary of the estate, and a grandly curving avenue for a new mansion to replace the existing seventeenth-century house.[2] Of several surviving proposals for demesne structures, none seem to have been realized, but a four-storey triangular tower with rubble stone walls and stepped battlements bearing a superficial resemblance to a late medieval Irish tower house was constructed. This folly, known

[1] 'Plan of intended improvements at Charleville, the estate of Charles William Bury Esq. by Thomas Leggett, 1786' (private collection). [2] This was largely realized. See C. Coote, *Statistical survey of the King's County* (Dublin, 1801), pp 179–80; first edition Ordnance Survey map (survey dated 1838).

as Camden Tower, was decorated with a mid-seventeenth-century plaque bearing the Moore coat of arms. It can be read as a symbol of the family connection, valued by Bury as the source for his own elevation to the peerage, while the name paid homage to his patron, the earl of Camden, the viceroy who had presided over his promotion to the peerage in 1797.[3]

In 1798, Bury married Catherine Maria Tisdall, a wealthy, well-educated widow with two children, who provided the inspiration, drive and many of the design ideas for Charleville.[4] Together, the Burys commissioned five paintings of the recently dramatized River Clodagh in 1801 from the much sought-after landscape artist, William Ashford.[5] Ashford, subtly amplifying the scale of the riverine landscape, and presenting it at maturity, underscored the romantic nature of the landscape improvements and established a picturesque context for the new castle now under construction.

The Charlevilles' ambition did not stop at the Irish peerage. In 1801, the year of the Union, Bury successfully petitioned to be the first replacement representative peer in the House of Lords, succeeding Lord Rossmore in November.[6] His son was not eligible for the position, so that if the family was to obtain hereditary privileges in Westminster it needed to acquire a British title. Catherine Maria spelled this out in a letter written to her eldest son in November 1812:

> I believe I told you I din'd in compy at the Park with Mr Peele [Robert Peel, Chief Secretary] who has a very sharp countenance & unaffected manner, but nothing very polish'd or genteel in his address or person. [...] There are promotions, & we might have got up a step – but our object is the English Peerage; & the Marquisate [the next step in the Irish peerage] we do not chuse because it wd. impede the other, & because we are not rich enough to desire further elevation. The Eng. Peerage will not *now* be granted, but ... I hope soon it may be accomplish'd. For it I am extremely anxious, because thereby my son wd. be secure of that hereditary seat in the grand council of the Nation which he lost by the Union, & which is now only to be obtained for the life of a peer by court favour & yielding up probably the freedom of opinion to a party.[7]

---

3 It is marked 'Camden Tower' on the first edition Ordnance Survey map. For plan and elevation of Camden Tower, see J. Howley, *The follies and garden buildings of Ireland* (London, 1993), p. 59.   4 J. Hill, 'Catherine Maria Bury of Charleville Castle, Co. Offaly, and the design of the country house, 1800–1812' in T. Dooley, M. O'Riordan & C. Ridgway (eds), *Women and the country house in Ireland and Britain* (Dublin, 2018), pp 116–38.   5 *Fine art auction ... to be held at Charleville Castle, Tullamore*, 1–5 Nov. 1948, Allen & Townsend, Dublin, lot 509, 5 oil paintings, Charleville Forest. For illustrations and catalogue see A. Crookshank, 'A life devoted to landscape painting, William Ashford (*c*.1746-1824)', *Irish Arts Review Yearbook*, 11 (Dublin, 1995), pp 126, 128.   6 Offaly County Library, Howard Bury papers, uncatalogued box, original letters to Viscount Charleville responding to his request for votes in the election to be held for a representative peer for Ireland, 21–3 Sept. 1801, passim. Twenty-eight representative peers had been elected on 2 Aug. 1800 from the peerage of Ireland to sit in the House of Lords. Viscount Charleville, the first replacement, was sworn in at the spring session of 1803.   7 Letter

This demonstrates that after the Union political and social status for elite Irish families was closely connected to the British social hierarchy, more so than previously. The Burys' hopes were disappointed; on 15 October 1812, Peel wrote to Charleville: 'Lord Liverpool does not feel himself authorised to hold out any expectations in regard to the English Peerage'.[8]

DESIGN

I have argued elsewhere that the Gothic revival style used for Charleville Castle was deliberately chosen to support the Charleville's social and political ambitions.[9] There is evidence that its expressive potential to evoke dynastic roots and a quasi-feudal grandeur was fully appreciated by its builders. Gothic at Charleville was, unusually in this period in Ireland, extended to the interior decorations. However, in this arena contemporary standards of comfort were equally important. This was outlined in the brief as related by Johnston in 1820, who described it as 'a very extensive building imitating as near as modern convenience and comfort would admit an old British castle'.[10]

Convenience and comfort at this period meant generous, usually square, well-lit rooms, preferably with sash windows. This was articulated by the landscape designer Humphry Repton who extended his remit to country house architecture in his 1803 publication, *Observations on the theory and practice of landscape*.[11] Communication between the rooms was important too. When James Wyatt was contemplating the replanning of Wilton House in 1800, the earl of Carnarvon outlined the contemporary ideal to Wyatt's patron, the earl of Pembroke:

> A House according to the present state of Society cannot be perfect unless it consists of one or more Drawing rooms, a Library, a dining room and a Billiard room, and apartments for the Male and Female proprietors of the House on the same floor. The perfection of the House also requires ... that the Gentleman's private apartment should connect immediately with the Library and the Ladies apartment to the Drawing Room ... the Library should likewise open to the Drawing Room; and the Billiard room and Dining room to one or other of those rooms.[12]

---

dated 8 Nov. 1812, quoted in R. Warwick Bond, *The Marlay letters, 1778–1820* (London, 1937), pp 233–4. 8 University of Nottingham Manuscripts and Special Collections, Papers of Catherine Maria Bury, 1st Countess of Charleville and her husband Charles William Bury, 1st Earl of Charleville (hereafter Marlay papers), MS My 169, letter from Sir Robert Peel to C.W. Bury, 15 Oct. 1812.   9 J. Hill, 'Perceptions and uses of Gothic in Irish domestic and ecclesiastical architecture, 1800–1815' (PhD, TCD, 2016), chapter 3.   10 F. Johnston, 'A letter from Francis Johnston', *Quarterly Bulletin of the Irish Georgian Society*, 6:1 (1963), 4.   11 H. Repton, *Observations on the theory and practice of landscape gardening including some remarks on Grecian and gothic architecture* (London, 1803).   12 Quoted in J.M. Robinson, *James Wyatt 1746–1813, architect to George III* (London, 2012), p. 73.

This evokes the 'social house' described by Mark Girouard in his ground-breaking book on English country houses published in 1978.[13] Girouard postulated that from the mid-eighteenth century, relaxation of the rules governing the social demonstration of hierarchy led to new types of socializing such as balls and supper entertainments where guests were invited into the main reception rooms of the house and various activities could take place simultaneously in different rooms.[14] This had a decisive effect on interior planning. In older houses, enfilades of state rooms were converted into sequences of reception rooms, where the 'saloon' was no longer the ceremonial centre of the house. Castletown, Co. Kildare, first built in the 1720s and remodelled by Louisa and Tom Conolly in the 1760s and 70s, is an example of a house where state apartments were converted into a 'social house' with a suite of reception rooms.[15] Newer houses were designed with first-floor reception rooms which were interlinked and usually connected to a stair. Both plans facilitated the circulating of guests. Girouard suggested that the essential minimum for a ball and supper was three rooms; one for dancing, one for cards, one for meals. In the mid-eighteenth century, a house such as Hagley Hall, designed in c.1752 by Sanderson Miller, could juxtapose older orderings – here, the grand, centrally positioned hall-and-saloon, and apartments for the family – with more modern planning; the staircase to the east served a drawing room, dining room and gallery, which were linked for entertaining.[16] By the end of the century a house such as Castle Coole, Co. Fermanagh, designed by Wyatt in 1790, could focus on a comprehensive circuit encompassing entrance hall, library, drawing room, saloon, dining room and breakfast room.[17]

These public reception rooms, listed by Humphrey Repton in 1803, were formulated to facilitate the evolving social life of the late eighteenth century.[18] Most notable was a dedicated splendidly decorated dining room.[19] Louisa Conolly created such a room out of two smaller ones at Castletown. Larger houses also had a common eating parlour for everyday family use. The largest room on the circuit could be referred to as a saloon or gallery, dependent on its shape.[20] Where the drawing rooms in the more formal houses of the early eighteenth century had been attached to individuals and associated with their bedrooms, by the later eighteenth-century the drawing room was accessible to all the family and their guests. The creation of a large library, where guests and family could read, write, consult prints and converse, represented another trend. Repton's list also included music room, billiard room and conservatory, suggesting further pursuits.[21]

The prioritizing of sensibility and spontaneity in the later eighteenth century was translated into a taste for asymmetry in house design and informality in furnishing

---

13 M. Girouard, *Life in the English country house: a social and architectural history* (London, 1978). 14 Ibid., pp 181–212. 15 C. Moore, 'Lady Louisa Connolly mistress of Castletown 1759–1821' in J. Fenlon, N. Figgis & C. Marshall (eds), *New perspectives: studies in art history in honour of Anne Crookshank* (Dublin, 1987), pp 123–42; David J. Griffin, 'Castletown, Co. Kildare: the contribution of James, first duke of Leinster', *IADS*, 1 (1998), 120–45. 16 Girouard, *Life in the English country house*, pp 201–2. 17 Robinson, *James Wyatt*, p. 119. 18 Repton, *Observations*, p. 178. 19 Girouard, *Life in the English country house*, p. 203. 20 Ibid., p. 201. 21 Bedrooms were smaller by the end of the eighteenth century,

and social interactions.²² The connection between furnishings and sociability is nicely illustrated by an entry in the diary of Fanny Burney describing a visit to a house off Berkeley Square in London, where the hostess was keen to replace a formal old-fashioned circle with a scattering of furniture: 'Some new people coming in, and placing themselves in a regular way, Miss Monckton exclaimed: "My whole care is to prevent a circle", and hastily rising, she pulled about the chairs, and planted the people in groups with as dexterous disorder as you would desire to see.'²³

With her decoration and furnishing of the long gallery at Castletown in the mid-1770s, Louisa Conolly demonstrated her appreciation of this trend. Previously used to display pictures, when Louisa's craftsmen, artists and suppliers had finished, the gallery was able to accommodate a good many guests happily engaged in a number of different activities in an easy-going and comfortable manner. This was described by Louisa to her sister Emily in January 1776 when the guest of honour was the Lord Lieutenant, 1st earl of Harcourt:

> Our gallery was in great vogue, and really is a charming room, for there are such variety of occupations in it, that people cannot be formal in it. Lord Harcourt was writing, some of us played at whist, others at billiards, Mrs Gardiner at the harpsichord, others at work, others at chess, others reading, and supper at one end; all this without interruption to the different occupations. I have seldom seen twenty people in a room so easily disposed of.²⁴

Written during a three-week Christmas visit, it illustrates another social trend of the late eighteenth and early nineteenth century: the house party. This increasingly popular event, in which visitors had to be accommodated during the day – eating breakfast, playing billiards, reading, writing, playing music – as well as for more formal dinners followed by cards and supper, had, Girouard has argued, a decisive influence in the making of the public reception rooms and their interconnectivity.²⁵

When Johnston wrote that Charleville was a building 'imitating as near as modern convenience and comfort would admit an old British castle', he alluded to tension between the older and newer design models. His phrase suggests that convenience and comfort were primary, but an analysis of the plan suggests that castellar grandeur was allowed to compromise contemporary standards of interior design.

The *piano nobile*, accessed by a grand processional flight of stairs from the mezzanine-level entrance, contains a group of rooms that conformed to Girouard's sociable three: gallery, dining room and breakfast room (fig. 7.2).²⁶ However, unlike the examples mentioned above, movement between the rooms was across the landing at the top of the stair. The rooms themselves conformed to contemporary standards

usually on an upper floor, and often retained the apartment concept with attendant dressing rooms and sometimes a closet.   **22** Girouard, *Life in the English country house*, pp 213–44.   **23** Quoted in ibid., p. 238.   **24** B. Fitzgerald (ed.), *Correspondence of Emily, duchess of Leinster*, 3 vols (1957), iii, p. 181.   **25** Girouard, *Life in the English country house*, pp 231–9.   **26** The breakfast room would later be named the drawing room.

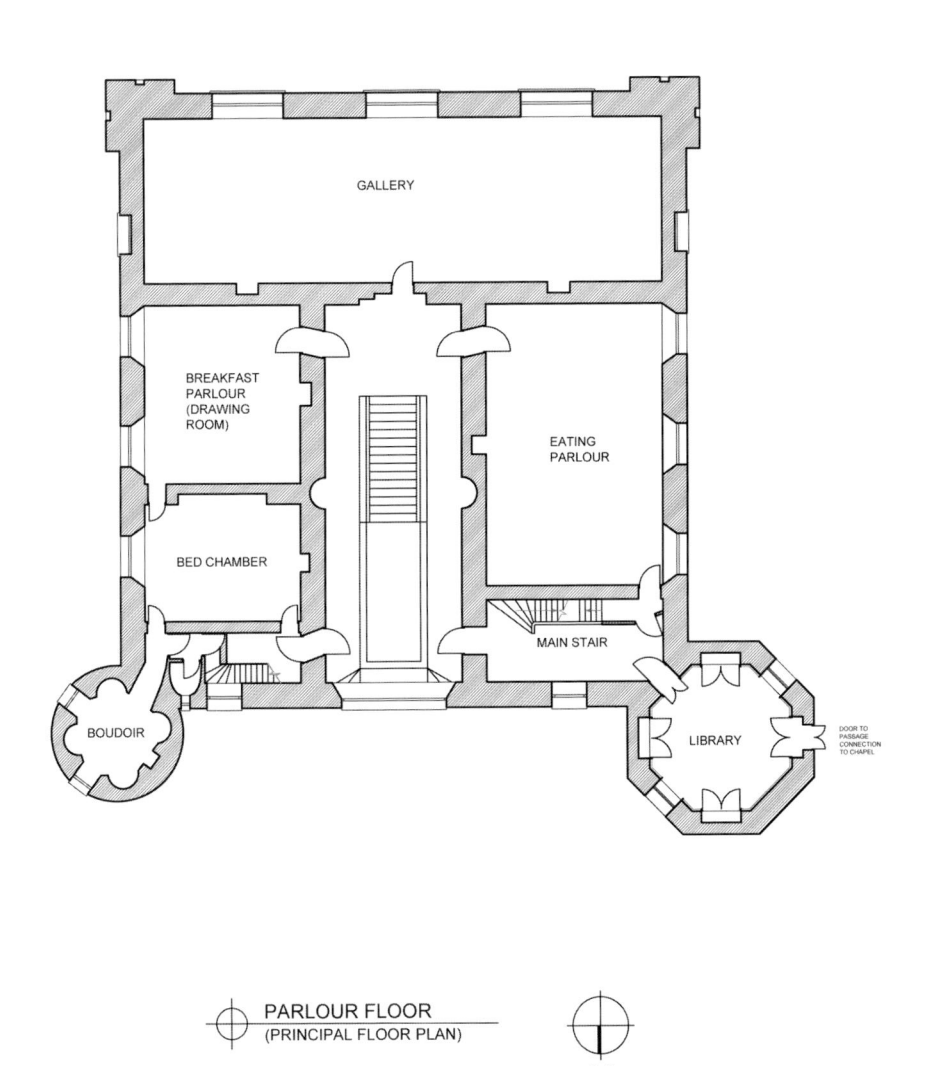

7.2 Charleville Castle, Co. Offaly, plan of principal floor. Drawing by Wojciech Kumik, 2016.

of comfort and convenience. The dining room (called an eating parlour at this period) and breakfast room, both large, rectangular and well proportioned, are Georgian rooms decorated with Gothic-style plasterwork and joinery, which is based on family heraldry prioritizing the connection between Bury and Moore (fig. 7.3).[27] All three rooms have large rectangular mullioned and transomed windows: a compromise between classical proportions and Gothic aesthetic. Two surviving sketches of a

27 Hill, 'Perceptions and uses', p. 157.

7.3 Dining room at Charleville Castle, Co Offaly, lithograph from a drawing by Lady Beaujolois Bury, *c*.1843. Courtesy of the Irish Architectural Archive.

section through the centre of the house attributed to Catherine Maria Bury, which show alternative decorative schemes based on established themes, indicate the likely furnishing style of the hall and gallery (fig. 7.4).[28] Both rooms are decorated with Gothic revival plasterwork, but whereas the hall is conceived as a formal space for the display of armour and family shields, the gallery is presented as a drawing room with sofas, pictures and curtains. That this represented current English fashion is appreciated by comparing the sofas supported by curved legs and the symmetrical display of portraits and landscapes around the window, seen in the lower sketch, with

28 IAA, Charleville Forest Drawings Collection, 89/88, alternative decorative schemes for entrance hall and gallery [1801–1804], attributed to C.M. Bury, illustrated in D.J. Griffin & S. Lincoln, *Drawings from the Irish Architectural Archive* (Dublin, 1993), p. 47.

7.4 Two proposed sections through the entrance hall and gallery of Charleville Castle, Co. Offaly, showing alternative decorative schemes, attributed to C.M. Bury, 1801–4. Courtesy of the Irish Architectural Archive.

J.W.M. Turner's depiction of the drawing room at Farnley Hall, Yorkshire, painted in 1818, where similar sofas are arranged on either side of a chimneypiece, itself the focus for a display of landscapes and portraits.[29] Turner's image evokes a morning or afternoon in which three women are harmoniously engaged in separate pursuits, writing at a table, sewing on a sofa and playing the piano. If, as Catherine Maria's drawings suggest, the Charleville gallery was furnished as a drawing room, it may have been modelled on the gallery at Castletown, for Catherine Maria was a close friend of Louisa Conolly's as their surviving correspondence reveals.[30] At 76 feet, the Charleville gallery was about half the size of that at Castletown, but it is a generously proportioned room and could easily have absorbed multiple simultaneous activities.

29 Illustrated in Girouard, *Life in the English country house*, pl 24.   **30** Several letters are published in Bond, *The Marlay letters, 1778–1820*.

7.5 Grand staircase, Windsor Castle, by James Wyatt, 1800–4. Engraving from a drawing by C. Wild, published in W.H. Pyne, *The history of the royal residences*, vol. 1 (London, 1819). © Victoria and Albert Museum, London.

The Charleville plan incorporates elements associated with the formal house and rooms that have more association with castles. A bedchamber to the east connected via a passage to the boudoir in the round tower were specifically for Catherine Maria's use and inserted private, apartment planning into the principal, public floor. The library, shoe-horned into the octagonal tower, had the air of a private study for Charles William, and, with its door concealed within the bookcase joinery to a hidden passage leading to the chapel, it injected castellar mystery into the planning of the castle. The rib vaults and deeply set windows of both tower rooms gave them the claustrophobic atmosphere of castle chambers. Husband's and wife's domains might have had an unfashionable private character on the *piano nobile*, but they conformed

7.6 Newspaper photograph of Charleville Castle, Co. Offaly, published 5 June 1873, showing front elevation with heraldic glass. The Biddulph Collection.
© Offaly History Centre, Tullamore, Co. Offaly.

to some extent to Lord Carnarvon's prescriptions: Catherine Maria's apartments opened onto the informal drawing room (breakfast room), and one could move easily from Charles William's library to the dining room. Further, the arrangement of the doors reveals that these rooms could be incorporated into an extended circuit focused on the processional stair.

The centrality of this stair, designed for formal access from the entrance to the main reception rooms, is striking. It was more than likely modelled on the stair designed in *c*.1800 by James Wyatt at Windsor Castle for George III to connect his remodelled entrance to the state apartments (fig. 7.5).[31] The role of the Charleville stair – grand, axial, royally resonant – as the beating heart of the house was augmented by the great perpendicular window above the entrance, decorated with heraldic glass, which would have stood out against the dark woodwork of the vestibule and stair (fig. 7.6).[32]

The expectation that guests would receive the full measure of Charleville magnificence as they descended the stair was described in a poem commissioned from John Doran:

[31] W.H. Pyne, *The history of the royal residences*, 1 (London, 1819). The use of Windsor as a model by the Burys is discussed in Hill, 'Uses and perceptions', p. 117. [32] The original decoration is discussed in M. Girouard, 'Charleville Forest, Co. Offaly, Eire', *Country Life* (7 Sept. 1962), 711.

7.7 Pencil drawing of the main stair taken from outside the gallery, Charleville Castle, Co. Offaly (post 1809). Courtesy of the Irish Architectural Archive.

> Ten thousand rays dart from the blushing stains
> And scarlet suns are dancing through the panes
> His dignified arms from their centre glares
> With royal splendour view it from the stairs
> Right pointing from the great hall unite thee
> Famed Charleville's long line of majesty.[33]

[33] WCL, Howard Bury Collection, P1/33, John Doran, *A poem on Charleville and castle, addressed to the Rt Hon the Earl of Charleville* [1809].

The idea that that particular view was a central experience of Charleville is also conveyed by two nineteenth-century pencil drawings of the window seen from the landing outside the gallery at the top of the stair (fig. 7.7).[34]

Bisecting the plan and prioritizing the central processional route over informal circulation between the individual rooms, this processional stair with its assertion of grandeur – formal procession, hereditary glory, royal resonance – compromised the contemporary model of the social house. This did not occur in contemporary British castles such as Robert Smirke's design for Lowther Castle, Westmoreland (1802–c.1813), where the concentric plan, although centred on the galleried stair, had layers of circulation: one around the stair, another through the surrounding public rooms.[35] At Culzean Castle, Ayrshire, designed and built by Robert Adam (finished in 1787), the interconnecting reception rooms were wrapped around three sides of an impressive oval stair.[36] In both of these examples grandeur was integrated into planning for contemporary entertainments.

TOUR

The seven-week tour of southern Ireland undertaken by the duke and duchess of Richmond from 28 August to 16 October 1809 was the first viceregal tour after the passing of the Act of Union. It took the viceroy, vicereine and their entourage from the Phoenix Park in Dublin to Kilkenny, Waterford, Cork, Kerry, Limerick and Offaly, ending at Charleville Castle. From here the party boarded a canal passage boat for Edenderry where carriages waited to take them back to Dublin. Their progress was characterized by the splendour of formality, flags, fire, guns and congregations of people, and they were shadowed by obsequious journalists whose reports, celebrating their advance through the country, were printed in local papers as well as the *Freeman's Journal*.[37] In the towns, where they were welcomed by people lining the streets, and by cannon fire, illuminations and bonfires, the viceregal party received delegations of civic dignitaries and clergy, inspected new public buildings and detachments of yeomanry, dined in commercial buildings and attended balls in assembly rooms. They stayed in the houses of Protestant landowners, military generals and bishops, including the marquis of Waterford at Curraghmore, the bishop of Waterford, General Floyd, commander of the Southern District, in Cork, the earl and countess of Glandore at Ardfert Abbey, the countess of Clare at Mount Shannon, and the earl and countess of Rosse at Parsonstown (now Birr); in all instances there were dinners, balls and suppers attended by the local gentry. The viceroy held a levee in Killarney where military promotions were announced, inspected the canal works at Edenderry, and spent a night aboard the frigate *Virginie* in Cobh harbour.

[34] IAA, Collection of Knight of Glin, 13/53P2, J[ohn] Blore, 'Sketch of hall & staircase at Charleville Castle. Unfinished' [1841]; 13/53P3, 'View of hall and staircase at Charleville Castle', n.d. [35] Plan of the principal floor of Lowther castle illustrated in J. Macaulay, *The Gothic revival, 1745–1845* (Glasgow, 1975), p. 301. [36] Floor plan illustrated in ibid., p. 100. [37] It was customary at this time for some

The tour was a public relations exercise, strengthening the connection between the viceroy and his subjects. It is clear from reports in the *Freeman's Journal* that the subjects he was mainly– though not exclusively – focused on were landed and Protestant. The language employed to describe the relationship between viceroy and subjects embraced the concepts of loyalty – the *Freeman's Journal* reiterated that people were given the opportunity to show allegiance to the representative of George III in Ireland – and popularity: according to one newspaper, the duke of Richmond had, at the conclusion of the tour, 'become one of the most popular Viceroy's [*sic*] that ever represented our beloved sovereign in this kingdom'.[38]

Although the viceregal tour was an established pre-Union phenomenon, it was particularly apposite in 1809.[39] The post-Union viceroy differed from his predecessors; whereas Ireland's separate status was a given before 1800, the passing of the Act of Union had raised the expectation that Ireland would be incorporated into Britain. The continuing presence of the viceroy in Ireland was a demonstration that this was not the case.[40] And, as Theodore Hoppen has argued, British policy in Ireland in the first thirty years of the union was based on the assumption that not only Irish Catholics – antagonized by the failure of Westminster to honour the Union promise of emancipation – but also the Protestant elite – who had lost power and status at the Union – were untrustworthy.[41] Ireland was also a weak link in the defences against the French.[42] Ireland was thus distinguished from the rest of Britain, a situation which, it was initially felt, called for separate, usually repressive, measures, tailored to Irish circumstances. Not only was the viceregal role open to scrutiny, but British policy in Ireland did not perforce promote harmony.

The duke of Richmond was appointed as Lord Lieutenant (April 1807) at a time when Catholics were renewing their pressure on the government to stand by its Union promises with regard to Catholic rights. The government of Richmond's predecessor (the duke of Bedford) had resigned due to the failure of its attempt to make concessions to Catholics.[43] Catholic activists decided to postpone their petition, but they were confronted with a new viceroy who was a strong opponent of Catholic emancipation and willing to govern in his party's interest, elevating leading parliamentary opponents of emancipation. S.J. Connolly has noted that this apparent support for militant Protestants was reflected in what seemed to be an increase in growing sectarian violence, with Orange outrages against Catholics more frequent

---

articles to be reproduced in different papers, sometimes with variations.   **38** *Freeman's Journal*, 12 Sept. 1809, p. 3; Marlay papers, My 1130/2, newspaper cutting, 17 Oct. 1809. It is substantially similar to *Freeman's Journal*, 18 Oct. 1809, but has added sentences.   **39** Very little scholarly attention has been paid to viceregal tours. One exception is R. Wilson, '"An admirable vice-queen": the duchess of Rutland in Ireland 1784–7' in M. Campbell (ed.), *Vicereines of Ireland: portraits of forgotten women* (Dublin, 2021), pp 92–121.   **40** K.T. Hoppen, 'An incorporating Union? British politicians and Ireland 1800–1830', *English Historical Review*, 123:501 (April 2008), 328–50.   **41** K.T. Hoppen, *Governing Hibernia: British politicians and Ireland, 1800–1921* (Oxford, 2016).   **42** French revolutionary wars (1792–1802) and Napoleonic Wars (1803–15).   **43** S.J. Connolly, 'The Catholic question, 1801–12' in W.E. Vaughan (ed.), *A new history of Ireland*, v: *Ireland under the Union, I, 1801–70* (Oxford, 1989), pp 33–5.

after 1807.[44] But, wherever Richmond's personal politics lay, it was cabinet policy to express neutrality.

The tour then was a way of positioning the viceregal government with regard to contemporary challenges. The duke hoped to achieve a number of potentially conflicting purposes: present a spectacle of military strength; express support for Protestant interests to cement his relationship with the elite; and demonstrate impartiality by making gestures towards Catholics. Using the tour to express these ambitions, Richmond put culture, in a broad sense, at the service of politics.

Military strength was manifest in the ubiquity of the British army during the tour which was both highly visible and audible. The viceroy, a military man (lieutenant-general of the 35th foot), was received with military honours as he passed down the parade in Waterford.[45] On arrival and departure at Cobh, the harbour resounded to the roar of cannon followed by a royal salute: 21 guns fired from each naval vessel.[46] In the garrison at Limerick the duke performed the duties of a commanding officer by putting the resident troops – Royal Artillery, 1st German Dragoons, North Cork and Waterford Militia – through their paces.[47] Little was said about the underlying reasons for such displays, except at Tralee Castle, where Judge Robert Day, flanked by the provost and corporation, expounded on the lawlessness of Kerry and referred to recent government measures to control the population; a veiled reference to the Insurrection Act of 1807, and the new barracks built 'upon a respectable scale'.[48]

Detachments of yeomanry lined the tour: the viceregal entourage rode through Colonel Prendergast Smyth's corps on the avenues to the Bishop's Palace in Limerick; Captain Locke's Newcastle corps proceeded the carriages to the bounds of the county.[49] Although funded and controlled by the government, these amateur militias were raised and officered by local gentlemen. Allan Blackstock has argued that in the immediate post-Union years, when Protestants feared that government would enact further Catholic relief measures, many Protestants valued the yeomanry as a symbol of the survival of their social and political position.[50] The parading of yeomanry in front of the viceroy was no doubt interpreted as a demonstration of mutual support between the Protestant interest and the viceroy. Connections between the Protestant elite and viceregal administration were further cemented by the entertainments in private houses where hostesses drew on their local networks. The countess of Clare in Mount Shannon, Co. Limerick, received particular praise from the *Freeman's Journal* for 'judiciously inviting different guests for each day, there-by giving the principal gentry of the country the honour of being presented to their Graces, and giving the Viceroy an opportunity of knowing the subjects of his Sovereign, which certainly is not the least considerable advantage to be derived from such a tour.'[51]

---

44 Ibid., p. 36.   45 *Freeman's Journal*, 6 Sept. 1809.   46 Ibid., 26 Sept. 1809.   47 Ibid., 6 Oct. 1809.
48 Ibid., 2 Oct. 1809.   49 Ibid., 6 Oct. 1809; 4 Oct. 1809.   50 A. Blackstock, 'A forgotten army; the Irish yeomanry', *History Ireland*, 4:4 (Winter, 1996), 28–33.   51 *Freeman's Journal*, 13 Oct. 1809.

Viceregal demonstrations of impartiality were rare and a little clumsy. Having congratulated the Catholic bishop of Waterford on his support for the government during the recent 'disturbances', the duke of Richmond spelt out that the terms of his appointment as Lord Lieutenant included the injunction to make no distinction, 'as far as the existing laws would permit', between Protestants and Catholics.[52] At the conclusion of a dinner in the recently completed commercial buildings in Limerick, where Britain and the empire had been celebrated in song, the viceroy addressed the wealthy Catholic banker, William Roche, who had earlier refused a knighthood: 'Mr Roche, I believe you and I are of different religious persuasions, nevertheless I hope we will meet in Heaven, after passing through life in harmony.'[53]

The image that the viceroy wished to give was probably summed up by one journalist who wrote of his 'good sense and splendor'.[54] This seems paradoxical. On the one hand it was a possible response to the ambiguity of the viceroy's position: he needed to temper pre-Union grandeur with gestures that implicitly acknowledged contemporary challenges in Ireland, and there was a lingering uncertainty about his role.[55] However, tempering aloofness with approachability also gestured towards a change in social tone. Although quasi-monarchical and, as an English duke, of higher social status than anyone he met, the viceroy, and vicereine, could not, in a changing social environment, afford to adopt the traditional distance of their caste. Instead, they had to be engaged. The *Freeman's Journal* frequently commented approvingly on his 'condescension' and her 'mild affability', and how these expressions were met by a 'cordial and affectionate welcome' from the people.[56] There was, however, still a long way to go. Twenty-six years later when the Mulgraves toured to meet the many rather than the few, Lord Mulgrave was praised by journalists for his 'strict impartiality' and Lady Mulgrave for her 'kindliness'.[57] By then the type of entertainment had altered too, with Lady Mulgrave remarking, 'The days are gone by when great dinners, balls and fêtes made a government popular in Ireland.'[58]

The duke of Richmond was more approachable than his predecessors, but he confined this to his encounters with the elite. This tension between a relaxation of the rules of established social intercourse and the retention of older values is not dissimilar to that expressed in the planning and furnishing of Charleville, which embraced modern sociability whilst adhering to a grandeur that was intended to impress, even intimidate.

---

52 *Waterford Chronicle*, 9 Sept. 1809.   **53** *Freeman's Journal*, 6 Oct. 1809; 10 Oct. 1809. William Roche built the celebrated hanging gardens over a store house at the rear of his bank on George's Street (now O'Connell Street), which was visited by the duchess of Richmond.   **54** *Freeman's Journal*, 18 Oct. 1809.   **55** There were those in Westminster who did not consider the viceroy necessary. K.T. Hoppen, 'A question none could answer: "What was the viceroyalty for?" 1800–1921' in P. Gray & O. Purdue (eds), *The Irish lord lieutenancy, c.1541–1922* (Dublin, 2012), pp 132–47.   **56** Marlay papers, My 1130/2, newspaper cutting, 17 Oct. 1809.   **57** M. Campbell, '"A subject for history": Maria, marchioness of Normanby as vicereine of Ireland, 1835–9' in Campbell (ed.), *Vicereines of Ireland*, p. 134.   **58** Ibid.

VISIT

The encounter at Charleville Castle, from Thursday 12 to Monday 16 October, was yet another variation on the theme enacted throughout the tour: in this case, the socially and politically ambitious Charlevilles exhibiting their grandiose and fashionable castle to the popularity-seeking viceroy. Both needed each other. In terms of theatre, each side played the part of both performer and audience. This was true too of other players; the yeomanry, the invited guests, the servants and tenants all had parts in the drama, but were also there to observe and to be impressed.

The Charlevilles were socially connected to the Richmonds, not only as part of the tight Irish elite, but also through their friendship with several Lennox aunts of the duke, including Louisa Conolly of Castletown and her sister Emily FitzGerald, wife of the duke of Leinster of Carton. Their social cachet was enhanced by Catherine Maria's outstanding abilities in her dealings with others. These were outlined by Louisa Conolly's worldly sister, Lady Sarah Napier, in a letter persuading Catherine Maria to attend court: she was, she was told, sufficiently pragmatic to take opportunities when they arose; she was endowed with wit, being a good conversationalist and commanding respect.[59]

The Charlevilles optimized all their assets to ensure that the four-day visit of the viceroy and his entourage played out to perfection in the physical and social setting of Charleville. No expense was spared to make a good impression, as Catherine Maria told her son in one of several surviving letters about the event. She described the food – partridges, snipe, grouse and turbots, much of which had to be re-ordered when the viceregal party arrived three days late – and the new uniforms for the servants: 'Magnificent full dress liveries have been made for the servants, & a uniform of Blue & Scarlet for the upper men'. '[I]n short', she concluded, 'it ought to go off handsome for money has not been spared.'[60]

Good use was made of the yeomanry (Bury was the captain of the Tullamore Cavalry of the King's County Yeomanry), while the castle and demesne were the ultimate stage set. This was evident in the choreography of arrival. The viceregal party was met at the western entrance to the demesne by several hundred tenants who, as tenants had done elsewhere, took the horses and shouldered the viceroy's carriage themselves, carrying it half a mile to the castle (fig. 7.8).[61] It was a traditional gesture of landlord power and authority, and of tenant loyalty. The route through the demesne gave the party a view of the castle from a distance where it would have appeared as a extending series of towers and battlemented walls dominated by the great round tower with its projecting, telescopic tourelle. Approaching slowly, past the lake and the Camden Tower, the wooded river to the left, ancient woodland to the right, their

---

59 Lady Sarah Napier to Catherine Maria Bury, 30 Aug. 1805 in Bond, *The Marlay letters*, p. 84. **60** Marlay papers, My 1127/1–3, C.M. Bury to James Tisdall, 7 Oct. 1809; My 1132, Louisa Tisdall to James Tisdall, 24 Oct. 1809. **61** Marlay papers, My 1127/1–3, C.M. Bury to James Tisdall, 7 Oct. 1809.

7.8 Part of the demesne of Charleville Castle, Co. Offaly, from the Ordnance Survey of King's County, sheets 16 & 17, surveyed 1838, engraved 1840. Reproduced courtesy Trinity College Dublin.

guests would have experienced the full force of the castle's romantic setting and all its suggested ancestral overtones (fig. 7.9).

When the carriages arrived at the castle entrance, set at the base of a great battered wall, they were met by the Tullamore Yeomen, 'ranged in order at each side of the hall door', and peremptory shouts of 'huzza'.[62] In the distance they could see the light from the bonfires and illuminations that the inhabitants of Tullamore had lit; more evidence of Charleville's reach and power.[63] The next day the duke of Richmond reviewed the Tullamore Cavalry on the lawn watched by a large crowd of

[62] Marlay papers, My 1132, Louisa Tisdall to James Tisdall, 24 Oct. 1809.   [63] *Freeman's Journal*, 18 Oct. 1809.

Entertaining royalty after the Union 163

CHARLEVILLE CASTLE FROM S.E. ANGLE
From a Drawing by LADY BEAUJOLOIS BURY, MAY, 1843

7.9 Charleville Castle, Co. Offaly, from a drawing from the southeast by Lady Beaujolois Bury, May 1848. Courtesy of the Irish Architectural Archive.

spectators.[64] These displays by the tenants and amateur officers were not without dangers, as Louisa Tisdall, Catherine Maria's daughter, reported to her brother: 'an unfortunate shoemaker in drawing the duke's carriage fell down and the wheel went over his leg. He was immediately carried to the infirmary, and is now much better'; in another instance, 'a poor officer fell from his horse up on his head and being very much stunned was carried home to his lodgings'.[65]

That evening there was a grand dinner and ball during which the house came alive. Catherine Maria described the adjustments that had to be made in the eating parlour to accommodate 38 people – 18 house guests (viceregal party, relatives and friends of the Richmonds and Charlevilles), nine yeomanry captains, the bishop of Clonfert and county gentry: 18 on the main table and an additional side table for 20.[66]

[64] Marlay papers, My 1132, Louisa Tisdall to James Tisdall, 24 Oct. 1809. [65] Ibid. [66] Marlay papers, My 1127, C.M. Bury to James Tisdall, 7 Oct. 1809.

Music was supplied from the hall below where the band of the 19th Dragoons played. A traditional 'grand Ball and Supper' for about 100 people followed for which we can imagine that the gallery, drawing room, dining room and stair were brought into play: dancing at eleven, two o'clock all sat down to supper, after which, singing: catches and glees.[67] They departed at four o'clock, 'the Company ... highly pleased with the polite attention of the noble Host and Hostess, and the gracious affability of his Grace & and the Duchess of Richmond.'[68]

This was followed by a three-day house party. They were up for breakfast at 10 o'clock to please the duchess and in bed at four in the morning to suit the duke.[69] With the weather too poor for hunting – Catherine Maria was glad of this, for the duke was an enthusiastic sportsman and they were not – the guests, except for a church service in Tullamore on Sunday, would have been largely concentrated in the house. Charleville was not as well provided for this as some contemporary houses; the library was not large and there was no billiard room or music room as we have noted, but Catherine Maria did not report feeling their absence.[70] She has left two vignettes of their activity in the house. Cards dominated after dinner. Every evening Catherine Maria played cassino, a card game popular in England since the early 1790s, with Lady Rossmore and Lady Rosse until the men arrived when 'a whist party could be got up for her [the duchess]'.[71] This probably took place in the gallery. At some time on Sunday, probably in the afternoon and also in the gallery, Catherine Maria described writing her letter in the presence of a large gathering of house guests: 'the party are all here in the room with me 43 persons! (in all)'.[72] Charleville had only recently been completed and this was probably the first time the room had been used for entertaining in this free-ranging, informal manner.

While the modern elements of Charleville would have facilitated the social interactions, the only external appraisal that seems to survive comes from a journalist who was impressed by the grandeur of the castle:

> [The] reception [of the viceroy] at the Castle was truly worthy [of] the Representative of his Majesty, for whether we consider the magnificence of the building, the splendour of the furniture, the number of attendants with the extreme richness of their liveries, seldom have we witnessed as grand a spectacle.[73]

Tensions resulting from social changes discussed above emerge from Catherine Maria's correspondence. The duchess of Richmond persisted in demonstrating her social superiority by not taking the trouble to conceal her emotions. Catherine Maria

---

67 *Freeman's Journal*, 18 Oct. 1809.   68 Ibid.   69 Marlay papers, My 1129/1–3, C.M. Bury to James Tisdall, 19 Oct. 1809.   70 Catherine Maria's bedroom would have become a music room by the early 1840s.   71 Marlay papers, My 1129/1–3, C.M. Bury to James Tisdall, 19 Oct. 1809.   72 Marlay papers, My 1128, C.M. Bury to James Tisdall, 15 Oct. 1809.   73 Marlay papers, My 1130/2, newspaper cutting, 17 Oct. 1809.

commented on her bad temper, writing to her son, 'tho' to me she was very civil, yet I confess her tantrums to him made me think her disagreeable'.[74] The duke, in contrast, made the necessary modern social adjustment: Catherine Maria found him consistently pleasant, and 'condescending & affable with great dignity to all about him'. Older values were also manifest in the clergy. Catherine Maria was horrified by the unctuousness of the bishop of Clonfert, whose sermon in Tullamore consisted of what Catherine Maria described as '*fulsome* verses' on the 'serene charms' of the bad tempered duchess; it was, she told her son, 'a disgrace to the Church'.

CONCLUSION

The Richmonds' 1809 visit to Charleville Castle reveals political responses, couched in cultural terms, to the changed circumstances brought about by the Union. The visit allowed the Charlevilles to combine contemporary sociability with a grandiose insistence on a largely fabricated past, while the viceroy could perform as the representative of the British sovereign, at home with members of the Irish Protestant elite. On both sides, contemporary social changes emanating from England served; but only to a point. The viceroy was, after all, asserting position and power, and the Charlevilles were seeking acceptability within a traditional hierarchical structure, both ambitions calling for more traditional means of expression.

At the centre of this performance was a new species of domestic space, the post-Union Irish castellated house. Its combination of the forward-looking with a pronounced insistence on old fashioned grandeur arguably reflected the Irish elite's anxiety to be an integral part of British culture while asserting caste in Ireland where their authority was threatened by both the Catholic majority and government policy emanating from Westminster.

---

[74] Marlay papers, My 1129/1-3, C.M. Bury to James Tisdall, 19 Oct. 1809.

'A taste for building': domestic space in elite female correspondence

PRISCILLA SONNIER

Between 1773 and 1776, Lady Elizabeth Aymler (neé Cole) was actively involved with the reconstruction and 'finishing' of her husband's ancestral estate, Donadea Castle, Co. Kildare. During these three years, Lady Aylmer strongly relied on the advice of her close friend, Lady Elizabeth Caldwell (neé Hort), who Alymer described to her architect Francis Sandys as an 'esteemed' woman that emphatically shared 'a taste for building.'[1] Lady Caldwell's extensive experience in overseeing improvements to the demesne and domestic spaces of her own home, Castle Caldwell, Co. Fermanagh, made her empathetic to Lady Aylmer's challenges of managing the construction of Donadea Castle while her husband, Sir FitzGerald Aylmer, 7th Baronet, was preoccupied with politics as an MP for Old Leighlin, Co. Carlow.[2] The commission was socially significant for the Aylmer family, as a new structure was to replace the large fourteenth-century castle that had been burned by English forces in 1641 in retribution for Sir Andrew Aylmer's involvement with the Catholic uprising.[3] Neglected for over a century, the home was to recognizably become the prominent seat of the Aylmer family from 1776, when Sir FitzGerald Aylmer was made MP for County Kildare.[4] The improvements made to Donadea in the late eighteenth and early nineteenth-centuries reestablished the family's prominence in Kildare, and by 1851, they were described in J.B. Burke's *Visitations of seats and arms* as being 'truly resident landlords.'[5] Now in ruins, Donadea Castle owes much of its known history to women, as Lady Ellen Aylmer (neé Butler, sister of James, 1st duke of Ormonde) defended the Castle and its demesne in 1641, and Lady Caroline Maria Aylmer contributed articles to local journals in the early twentieth century about the history

---

1 John Rylands Library, Manchester, Bagshawe Muniments (hereafter Bagshawe Muniments), MS 3/30/8, Lady Elizabeth Aylmer to Lady Elizabeth Caldwell, 8 May 1773. 2 For a detailed discussion of Lady Caldwell and in particular, her husband, Sir James Caldwell's improvements to Castle Caldwell, see T. Barnard, 'The artistic and cultural activities of the Caldwells of Castle Caldwell, 1750–1783', *IADS*, 10 (2007), 91–107. Additionally, Lady Caldwell's frustration of often managing the estate with her husband away is also reflected in her correspondence with Lady Arbella Denny throughout the period. Denny's letters to Lady Caldwell from 1754 to 1757 have been transcribed and thoughtfully introduced in R. Raughter, '"My Dear Lady C": Letters of Lady Arbella Denny to Lady Elizabeth Caldwell, 1754–1757', *Analecta Hibernica*, 41 (2009), 135–200. See also E.M. Johnston-Liik, *MPs in Dublin: companion to the history of Irish parliament, 1692–1800* (Belfast, 2006), p. 68. 3 J.B. Burke, *Visitation of seats and arms* (London, 1855), p. 81. 4 The family's main residence in the first half of the century was on Jervis Street. W. Sherlock, 'Donadea and the Aylmer family', *Journal of the County Kildare Archaeological Society and Surrounding Districts*, 3 (1900), 175. 5 Burke, *Visitation of seats and arms*, pp 80–1.

'A taste for building': domestic space in elite female correspondence 167

DONADEA CASTLE.
From a drawing by Miss Sherlock.

8.1 Drawing of Donadea Castle in the *Journal of the Kildare Archaeological Society*, 3 (1900). Courtesy of the Irish Architectural Archive.

of the family and the estate, which she had inherited in 1886.[6] Additionally, as the original plans and documents from the eighteenth-century rebuild of Donadea Castle have largely been lost or destroyed, correspondence between Lady Aylmer and Lady Caldwell is one of the only surviving sources which describes the architectural process and design of the domestic space before it underwent a series of Gothic additions in the nineteenth century, including the Elizabethan gate and tower (fig. 8.1).[7] Despite the current condition of Donadea Castle, Lady Aylmer and Lady Caldwell's letters thoughtfully reveal gendered perspectives and influences on shaping the 'poetics of space' within the home, as well as reflecting the social significance of elite female networks in Ireland throughout the period. By considering how women visualized the aesthetics and experiences within their domestic spaces, the 'lost' homes in this chapter, like Donadea Castle and Castle Caldwell, can once again be visualized and experienced through the conceptualizations expressed within female correspondence (figs 8.2 and 8.3).

[6] In 1935, Donadea Castle was donated to the Church of Ireland by Lady Caroline Maria Aylmer. It was shortly thereafter the building fell into ruin and the home was stripped of its interior furnishings. *Irish Times*, 5 Sept. 1992. Burke, *Visitation of seats and arms*, pp 80–1.   [7] Ibid.

8.2 Photograph of Castle Caldwell, *c.*1865–1914. Lawrence Photograph Collection, L ROY 01580. © National Library of Ireland.

8.3 Photograph of Donadea Castle, 1958. O'Dea Photograph Collection, ODEA 3/80. © National Library of Ireland.

While prominent women's involvement with designing grand homes, follies and *cottages ornées*, and interior furnishings and decorations in eighteenth- and early nineteenth-century Ireland is well-established in works by Finola O'Kane, Judith Hill and Ruth Thorpe, among others, further insights into women's social networks during this period can be enriched by female designs for functional elements of the home such as staircases and chimneypieces.[8] These 'finishing' features of the home and the spaces they functioned within intimately expressed gendered practices of domestic improvement and women's roles in shaping cultural taste through their choices of architects, merchants and aesthetics.[9] O'Kane's thoughtful research has also emphasized how elite women in Ireland suggestively had more freedom in 'creating their own distinct environments' than their English counterparts, as the 'divisions within the Ascendancy … may have created a more cohesive cultural environment' in the country.[10] Recent socio-cultural scholarship by Rachel Wilson, Toby Barnard and Amy Prendergast has also demonstrated how female networks, as well as their public, charitable and domestic roles, were crucial to disseminating and shaping polite culture in Ireland throughout the eighteenth century.[11] However, the broader theme of this chapter is to provoke insight and imagination into how polite and gendered culture was experienced within these domestic spaces, which were thoughtfully designed by women with assistance from their social networks. Building upon prior scholarship, this chapter addresses the social and spatial impact of elite women like Lady Alymer, whose days consisted of 'mornings with Company like upholders, painters, paper men, carpenters etc. and the evenings with other *Fine Ladies* at card parties'.[12] Letters between Lady Alymer, Lady Caldwell and Lady Arbella Denny (neé Fitzmaurice) in the late 1760s and early 1770s actively constitute what Gaston Bachelard describes as 'a community of memory and image' as they shared architectural drawings, plans and advice with one another.[13] When described

---

[8] For a comprehensive gender-based history of Irish women's architectural practices and their roles in shaping the designs of their estates and demesnes throughout the eighteenth century, see J. Hill, 'Catherine Maria Bury of Charleville Castle, Co. Offaly, and the design of the country house, 1800–1812' in T. Dooley et al. (eds), *Women and the country house in Ireland and Britain* (Dublin, 2018), pp 116–38; F. O'Kane, 'Design and rule in the Irish countryside 1715–1831', *Eighteenth-Century Ireland*, 19 (2004), 56–74; F. O'Kane, *Landscape design in eighteenth-century Ireland: mixing foreign trees with the natives* (Cork, 2004), pp 99–129; R. Thorpe, *Women, architecture and building in the east of Ireland, c.1790–1840* (Dublin, 2013); R. Johnstone, 'Lady Louisa Conolly's print room at Castletown House, in E. Mayes (ed.), *Castletown: decorative arts* (Dublin, 2011), pp 67–77.   [9] Scholarship by Amanda Vickery has meticulously acknowledged the significance of female 'taste' and women's influence on design, decoration, and decorum in the process of finishing the home in the British Isles. See A. Vickery, *Behind closed doors: at home in Georgian England* (London, 2009), and idem, *The gentleman's daughter: women's lives in Georgian England* (London, 1998).   [10] O'Kane, 'Design and rule', 74.   [11] Discussion throughout their works strongly emphasizes the unique and gendered influences of women in Ascendancy visual and material culture. T. Barnard, *Making the grand figure: lives and possessions in Ireland, 1661–1770* (London, 2004); idem, *A new anatomy of Ireland: the Irish Protestants, 1649–1770* (London, 2004), pp 63–79; A. Prendergast, *Literary salons across Britain and Ireland in the long eighteenth century* (London, 2015); R. Wilson, *Elite women in Ascendancy Ireland, 1690–1745: imitation and innovation* (Woodbridge, 2015). [12] Bagshawe Muniments, MS 3/30/23, Lady Caroline Aylmer to Lady Elizabeth Caldwell, 4 Apr. 1776. [13] G. Bachelard, *The poetics of space* ([1958] Boston, 1994), p. 5.

8.4 Author's photograph of Donadea Castle, 2020.

in correspondence, functional elements of the home, like staircases, furnishings and chimneypieces, can enrich our understanding of how women significantly influenced comfortable and maternal experiences within their domestic spaces.[14]

The correspondence between Lady Aylmer and Lady Caldwell not only reflects the domestic visions for Donadea Castle but can also provide a phenomenological exercise in visualizing how an 'inhabited space [can] transcend [a] geometrical space' through contextualized and gendered experiences.[15] Women's meticulous, emphatic and (sometimes) cynical descriptions of the building process and the features of their country estates lends itself to an imaginatory and poetic process. Bachelard noted that literary experiences of domestic space 'forcefully prove to us that the houses that were lost forever continue to live on in us; that they insist in us in order to live again … [by] assembling exact recollections, bit by bit, the house that was lost in the mists of

14 In the process of designing the home, Ruth Thorpe has noted that women considered their drawings as 'visions'. Thorpe, *Women, architecture and building*, p. 18. 15 Bachelard, *Poetics of space*, p. 47.

time will appear from out of the shadow'.[16] Considering that Donadea Castle and Castle Caldwell are both in ruins, it is important to readdress how these 'lost' spaces can once again be experienced from women's descriptions. The following elements to be discussed, which are now missing or overgrown with lush foliage, ivy and trees, tantalizingly provoke 'images [of spaces] to be lived directly' through the lives of women, whose 'narratives ... retain the treasures of former days.'[17] When viewed for the first time, Aylmer, Caldwell and Denny's letters replicate a poetic process shared with the original intended recipient, as one is left to 'dream' and constitute a body of images 'in uncompleted (and now ruined) homes.'[18] By phenomenologically reconsidering these letters, the spaces described within Donadea Castle and Castle Caldwell allow for them to be 'lived directly', in spite of their current condition (fig. 8.4).[19]

When Lady Aylmer wrote to Lady Caldwell in May 1773, the reconstruction of Donadea Castle had just begun.[20] She was faced with unique challenges regarding its design, as she charged her architect, Francis Sandys, with building on the site of the original mediaeval castle. She was particularly concerned about the staircases, which had to be repositioned on account of the drawing room, as the underlying foundation frustratingly forced Lady Aylmer to 'make our entrance into [the] drawing room backwards'; an observation which acknowledges the difficulties of fashionably updating a older structure for modern domestic life and Alymer's appreciation for design in the process.[21] Her lengthy descriptions, as well as plans for new staircases and gallery railings drawn by Sandys (now lost), were conscientiously sent to Lady Caldwell to inform her of the conceptual 'vision' for the space. This allowed for Caldwell to thoughtfully provide Aylmer with advice, as Aylmer excitedly sought 'her honest opinion as to both plans' and asked her to 'bring them back,' presumably with Caldwell's thoughts or designs appended to Sandys' sketches.[22] Her home and the letter, both of which revolve around a staircase, presents further insights into the question central to George Perec's suggestion that 'We should learn to live more on staircases. But how?'[23] Although each answer to this question will be subjective to experience, it can also enrich our understanding of how women conscientiously approached functional domestic elements like staircases when designing and 'finishing' their estates (fig. 8.5). The notion of 'living' on and around the staircase was crucial to Aylmer's design, as the visual impact of her home was to be affected by its placement, and she thoughtfully considered the height of the banisters for the safety of her young children. Although the original drawings by Sandys are missing from the letter, her description poetically visualizes the space, its functionality and how she crucially relied on Caldwell's advice to inform her decisions.

16 Ibid., pp 56–7. 17 Ibid., p. 56. 18 Ibid., p. 17. 19 Ibid., p. 47. 20 Burke, *Visitations of seats and arms*, p. 80. 21 Bagshawe Muniments, MS 3/30/8, Lady Elizabeth Aylmer to Lady Elizabeth Caldwell, 8 May 1773. 22 Ibid. 23 G. Perec, *Species of spaces and other pieces* ([1974] London, 1997), p. 38.

8.5 Cantilevered staircase, Florence Court, Co. Fermanagh, *c.*1760–70. Courtesy of the Irish Architectural Archive.

Lady Alymer's letter of 8 May 1773 to Caldwell topically concerns the designs for her new staircase and how she was 'so very busy Building and Planning' at Donadea Castle (fig. 8.6). It reveals that she had reached out to Caldwell as she was 'in some doubts to the staircase' and described her previous evening 'after supper' as having been spent with Sandys, so she could 'express my wishes [to] him that I could

8.6 Lady Elizabeth Aylmer to Lady Elizabeth Caldwell, letter of 5 May 1773.
© The University of Manchester.

by any description convey to you an Idea of our design.'[24] Her wishes were for two sketches of the staircase, but her architect reminded her that despite 'try[ing] to give a sketch as well as he could express it … he said it was very hard to make a stair case understood without your being on the spot.'[25] The 'spot' of the staircase at Donadea Castle may be comfortably imagined from its ruin by glancing through the Elizabethan-style portico, which reveals a large wall with two flanking doors leading into the lower hall. Considering that Caldwell was in no position to survey the property, Sandys' plans are complemented by Aylmer's descriptive account, which essentially 'guides' the reader through her conceptualizations for the family home. Both plans, being on the site of a mediaeval castle, acknowledge her unique challenges in creating a functional and fashionable space. Her first, and preferred plan, had the stairs taking 'in much more ground to the hall than first intended', with her 'greatest objection [being] the first assent [sic] of the stairs being too near the front of the lower Hall' on account of the position of the drawing room.[26] Alymer's concerns for the hall

24 Bagshawe Muniments, MS 3/30/8, Lady Elizabeth Aylmer to Lady Elizabeth Caldwell, 8 May 1773.
25 Ibid.   26 Ibid.

were valid, as 'the size of the hall and often how well it was lit provided the overall impression for visitors'.[27] The depth of the staircase into the lower hall would have diminished visual impact between transitioning from outdoors to indoors, but she was willing to compromise on account of the drawing room, which was typically regarded as a 'feminine' space, where one 'spared no expense'.[28] Considering its 'backwards' positioning and that the ascent to the principal storey came from a shortened lower hall, Aylmer may have compensated for these 'unfashionable' inconveniences through the acquistion and display of fine furniture and works of art. In this capacity, she actively managed and concerned herself with the final decoration and furnishing of her home, and was keenly aware of its appearance to others before the rebuild was complete. In fact, in the process of 'finishing' the home, Aylmer describes herself as 'being ten times busier than I have been yet.'[29] However, despite her days being consumed in 'preparing to make the house someway comfortable', she 'truthfully' admitted to Caldwell that the house was 'not [comfortable] at present' and had been sending excuses to other women so she 'could stay at home and write letters'.[30] This honest acknowledgment not only reflects the tiresome process of furnishing the home, but also demonstrates the cultural and social significance that women attached to good taste and domestic comfort.[31] Her thoughtful emphasis in this first design, which focuses on the formal relationship between hall, staircase and drawing room, reflects how she was astutely aware of the symbiotic relationship between rooms and circulation spaces, and how the transition between them would perceivably impact both friends and family.

Lady Aylmer's second proposed design for the staircase is seemingly grander in its ambitions, with the ascent 'beginning to the left of the street door' which would lead up to a 'Gallery at the new Parlor door'.[32] The gallery was to be quite large, as it was 'to be carried around like the Attick storey is, [being] open from bottom to top'.[33] Unlike the first plan, this staircase was to lead into an impressive open space, but Sandys' design raised a different set of problems and she 'objected to [it] on account of the Children'.[34] In this instance her concerns were maternal and gendered in nature, being focused on the wellbeing of her three sons, Fenton, John and Arthur; her objections to the openness and height of the stairs were in fact due to the 'passions boys have for sliding down banisters'.[35] She was fearful that one of them would fall and become seriously injured, and was feeling especially protective after one of her sons had been experiencing an infectious and reoccurring fever, while another had become ill with smallpox.[36] Describing herself as being 'in more fears about them even in their present situation [with illness]', she decided to make the rails of the

---

27 P. McCarthy, *Life in the country house in Georgian Ireland* (London, 2019), p. 44. **28** C. Lucey, 'Keeping up appearances: redecorating the domestic interior in late eighteenth-century Ireland', *PRIA*, 111C (2011), 174–5. **29** Bagshawe Muniments, MS 3/30/23, Lady Caroline Aylmer to Lady Elizabeth Caldwell 4 Apr. 1776. **30** Ibid. **31** Ibid. **32** Bagshawe Muniments, MS 3/30/8, Lady Elizabeth Aylmer to Lady Elizabeth Caldwell, 8 May 1773. **33** Ibid. **34** Ibid. **35** Ibid. Her daughter Margaret evidently did not represent a similar potential problem. **36** Throughout her previous correspondence with Caldwell in 1771 and 1772, Aylmer frequently mentions her boys being ill. JRL, Bagshawe

gallery 'four foot high' to prevent the boys from *living* too much on the staircases.[37] Aylmer's description of the staircase and gallery, in addition to the thought of three lively boys sliding down banisters, captures the nuanced and maternal 'poetics of space' within the domestic ambit of Donadea Castle. She arguably relied on evocative imagery to provoke Caldwell's insights, not only as a woman who shared her 'taste for building', but also as a mother who could empathize with her concerns for the children. Furthermore, Caldwell's previous experience with designing staircases at Castle Caldwell, with the assistance of her close friend Lady Arbella Denny, provided Caldwell with unique knowledge and perspectives into the building and finishing process, which she could disseminate to Lady Aylmer. In this capacity, Aylmer's thoughtful approach to her staircases and sharing her plans with her female network, provides measurable insights into the gendered and maternal influences on functional elements of the home in the eighteenth century. Alymer's correspondence not only reflects what the interior of Donadea Castle may have looked like, but also uniquely complements Bachelard's imaginatory and 'dream-like' process in 'visualizing' the nuances of the 'old house' through memory and subjectivity.[38] Women's narratives contribute to this process of imagining and evoking lost spaces, with Bachelard suggesting that 'the old house, for those who know how to listen, is a sort of geometry of echoes. The voices of the past do not sound the same in the big room as in the little bed chamber, and the calls on the stairs have yet another sound.'[39]

Like staircases, chimneypieces can also thoughtfully contribute to our understanding of experienced and lived spaces within 'old homes'. The functionality of the chimneypiece and how they 'revolve[d] around the notion of reception' in the eighteenth century enriches gendered insights and experiences within the domestic realm.[40] While the chimneypieces at Castle Caldwell are no longer in situ, correspondence between Lady Arbella Denny and Lady Caldwell reveals how they were intended to correspond to life in the drawing room and parlour in terms of comfort and aesthetics. The chimneypieces at Castle Caldwell, and the feminine spaces in which they were installed, can be visualized through Denny's descriptions of glimmering firelight on the walls and chairs placed beside the fire.[41] Emphasis on a 'well-appointed' chimney for the wealthy and middling-sorts, in addition to the works of art hung above them, is evident in Dublin by mid-century: in 1747, for example, Samuel Dixon advertised 'Landscapes in Oyl for Chimneys' at his 'picture shop' in Capel Street.[42] Additionally, Lady Caldwell's own 'taste for building' may be partially traced to her 'fixing up and changing [the] Chimney Pieces' at her childhood home on Dawson Street at the age of 19 in 1748.[43] Caldwell's early efforts were fondly

Muniments 3/30/5-8. **37** Bagshawe Muniments, MS 3/30/8, Lady Elizabeth Aylmer to Lady Elizabeth Caldwell, 8 May 1773. **38** Bachelard, *Poetics of space*, pp 60–1. **39** Ibid. **40** Perec, *Species of spaces*, p. 31; M. Craske, 'Conversations and chimneypieces: the imagery of the hearth in eighteenth-century English family portraiture', *British Art Studies*, 2 (2016): https://doi.org/10.17658/issn.2058-5462/issue-02/mcraske. **41** Bagshawe Muniments, MS 3/30/87, 3/30/89, Lady Arbella Denny to Lady Elizabeth Caldwell, 28 Mar. 1770 and 27 Sept. 1770. **42** *Dublin Journal*, 12 Mar. 1747. **43** Caldwell inherited the Dawson Street property but had to let the house in 1773 to cover the debts

8.7 Strickland Lowry, *Interior with members of a family*, oil, 1770s.
Photo © National Gallery of Ireland.

recollected by her father, Dr Josiah Hort, who described her as 'tak[ing] much trouble about the house,' while he was away on business.[44] She was particularly interested in the 'fixing up and changing [of] Chimney Pieces' and was, in the absence of her father, advised to meet with his architect who had the 'whole scheme of Directions upon paper' since he '[couldn't] recall every part of it'.[45] Her input for the new

---

accrued on her husband's travels and improvements to the house. She respectively wrote to both Aylmer and Denny in 1772 and 1773 to express her frustrations and gather honest advice. In 1772, Denny suggested she let the house and take her furnishings to Castle Caldwell and by 1773 Caldwell had decided to let it. The landlord was Francis Sandys, Aylmer's architect, who she recommended to Caldwell while finishing her staircase in 1773. Bagshawe Muniments, MS 3/30/90, Lady Arbella Denny to Lady Elizabeth Caldwell, 28 June 1772; 3/30/8, Lady Elizabeth Aylmer to Lady Elizabeth Caldwell, 8 May 1773. See also Barnard, 'Caldwells of Castle Caldwell', 94. **44** Bagshawe Muniments, MS 3/30/105, Dr Josiah Hort to Lady Elizabeth Hort, 12 July 1748. **45** Ibid.

chimneypiece was welcomed by her father, although he discouraged her from 'running over in wet dirty weather to Dawson Street unless it may amuse and divert her'; moreover, the timber wainscotting needed to be completed before it could be installed. Significantly, while Hort was insistent on his choices for the 'stripes of mended Wainscot', he encouraged the advice of his daughter in the decision to 'determine ... what Chimney Piece to put up'.[46] Considering his absence in Dublin, the assistance of Elizabeth was evidently crucial in matters of taste, as she could keep up with the latest designs and fashions in town, and heed the advice of grander relations like Lord and Lady Shelburne. Additionally, Hort may have suggestively relied on the gendered perspectives of his daughter, as the chimney and hearth had strong maternal and domestic associations in eighteenth-century British culture.[47] This gendered process of refurbishing the home throughout the period is one that Amanda Vickery has described as the 'key to a woman's heart', with the hearth becoming 'a metonym for domesticity' with its 'sense of [an] emotional core and life-sustaining warmth.'[48] Just as the socio-cultural significance of the hearth is captured in the correspondence between elite women, as they provided one another with advice on fashionable designs for chimneypieces, so too does it reveal how the fireside was experienced.

Lady Caldwell and Lady Denny's considerations for pleasurable experiences within the drawing room at Castle Caldwell – characterized by Denny as the 'room you'll pass much time in' – can be reimagined from their description for the design of the chimneypiece, and how its warmth would contribute to the comfort of the space.[49] Their recollections of the home and the stone chimneypieces chosen for the drawing room and parlour may be partially realized in Strickland Lowry's *Interior with members of a family* (1770) (fig. 8.7). Lowry's conversation piece, which is recognized for its representation of fashionable Irish interiors in the last quarter of the century, also prominently features a chimney, which emphasizes the domesticity of the space and 'the transition between the indoors and outdoors'.[50] Despite the static and conventional positioning of the sitters, the chimneypiece serves as reminder of how the space was comfortably experienced, both formally and informally, by revolving around the fire in day-to-day life.[51] In public and shared spaces, such as fashionable drawing rooms and parlours, architectural elements such as chimneypieces conveyed status and taste due to their decorative designs, which were frequently copied and disseminated through viewership and patronage in elite circles. In completing Castle Caldwell, Lady Caldwell relied upon Denny, one of Dublin's most influential and wealthy widows, for advice on chimneypieces, fabrics and furnishings to ensure that her home was not only comfortable but also suited to the latest mode. As one of Denny's favourite relations, Caldwell benefitted from Denny's honest perspectives and her working relationships with Dublin's favoured tradesmen

---

46 Ibid.   **47** Vickery, *Behind closed doors*, p. 28.   **48** Ibid.   **49** Bagshawe Muniments, MS 3/30/86, Lady Arbella Denny to Lady Elizabeth Caldwell, 5 July 1769.   **50** McCarthy, *Life in the country house*, p. 44.   **51** Craske, 'Conversations and chimneypieces'.

and builders.[52] Being twenty years Caldwell's senior, Denny's experiences with building her home, Peafield Cliff in Blackrock, Co. Dublin, her oversight of the fundraising and construction of the Magdalen Chapel on Leeson Street, and her commitment to Irish craftsmanship and industry, made her a considerable and respected authority among Ireland's elite women for her architectural knowledge and taste.[53] Denny and Caldwell's choices for local merchants and materials is also noteworthy, as the display of an Irish-made chimneypiece and furnishings also complemented Sir James Caldwell's improvements to the house in the late 1750s, in support of his hopes of being elevated to the Irish peerage.[54] His alignment with Irish patriot party politics in the mid-to-late century was reflected in his choice of local merchants, craftsmen and builders as it acknowledged the family's support of Irish socio-economic development.[55] As Lady Caldwell was primarily managing the estate and its improvements due to her husband's lengthy absences on business, her personal choices for chimneypieces, fabrics and papers would not only have reflected their tastes, but also engaged in an act of political theatre.[56] In visiting the home, Ireland's Protestant elite would have recognized the Caldwell's commitment to promoting Irish industry and manufacture through the materiality of the domestic space. Women's choices within this context were crucial, both aesthetically and culturally. Their shared recommendations for Irish builders and craftsmen through close social networks, not only shaped architectural spaces but also reflected specific gender-based expectations among elite Irishwomen at mid-century. In this capacity, women's display and support of Irish materials and merchants demonstratively communicated their nuanced roles with improving 'the prosperity of their country' through fabrics and designs that were recognized by an elite audience.[57] Caldwell and

---

[52] Denny was Caldwell's cousin once removed, as Caldwell's mother, Elizabeth, was Denny's cousin. For a concise account of Denny's familiar connections see Raughter, '"My Dear Lady C"', 135–8. [53] As the daughter of the earl of Kerry who was left widowed with a large fortune at the age of 35, Denny was well respected among Ireland's male and female elite for her charitable contributions to the Irish textile industry. She was highly involved with the (Royal) Dublin Society and the building and running of the Magdalen Chapel on Lower Leeson Street following its opening in 1768. For more particulars on Denny's life see B. Bayley Butler, 'Lady Arbella Denny, 1702–1792', *Dublin Historical Record*, 9 (1946–47), 1–20; A. Peter, *A brief account of the Magdalen Chapel, Lower Leeson Street* (Dublin, 1907), pp 21–36; K. Sonnelitter, *Charity movements in eighteenth-century Ireland: philanthropy and improvement* (Woodbridge, 2016), pp 122–45. [54] Sir James's life, politics and improvements to the home is discussed in Barnard, 'Caldwells of Castle Caldwell', 90–108. Correspondence with his wife by 1760 reveals Sir James's enthusiasm to be elevated to the peerage. Bagshawe Muniments, MS 3/29/16, Sir James Caldwell to Lady Elizabeth Caldwell, 17 Sept. 1760. [55] This unique socio-cultural and economic movement in Ireland is further discussed in S. Foster, '"An honourable station in respect of commerce, as well as constitutional liberty": retailing, consumption and economic nationalism in Dublin, 1720–85' in G. O'Brien & F. O'Kane (eds), *Georgian Dublin* (Dublin, 2008), pp 30–44, and P. Higgins, 'Consumption, gender and the politics of "Free Trade" in eighteenth-century Ireland', *Eighteenth Century Studies*, 41:1 (2007), 87–105. [56] Barnard notes that in the finishing of the home many choices made between Sir James and Lady Caldwell can be difficult to separate. Barnard, 'Caldwells of Castle Caldwell', 98–9. For more on women's acts of political theatre through the display of Irish-made products, see M. O'Dowd, 'Politics, patriotism, and women in Ireland, Britain and Colonial America, *c*.1700–1800', *Journal of Women's History*, 22:4 (2010), 15–38. [57] Foster, 'An honourable station', 33–43; *Faulkner's Journal*, 20 June 1767.

'A taste for building': domestic space in elite female correspondence 179

8.8 Design for a white statuary chimneypiece, George or Hill Darley, ink on paper, *c.*1770.
By permission of the Royal Irish Academy © RIA.

Denny would have been aware of the social significance of their choices and commissions within Ascendancy culture; especially as Denny and Sir James Caldwell were actively involved with the charitable improvements and encouragements supported by the Dublin Society throughout the period that the parlour and drawing room at Castle Caldwell were being finished.[58]

In completing Castle Caldwell, Denny emphasized to Lady Caldwell the importance of 'agreeable improvement'; a process of domestic finishing which Denny

---

58 Minutes of the Royal Dublin Society, vol. 4 (31 Mar. 1768) and vol. 7 (15 May 1771).

described as being 'accomplish[ed] in one season of doing it by degrees'.[59] Within this context, Denny's influence on Caldwell can be determined from their correspondence of July 1769 to September 1770, which aesthetically reconstructs the firesides of the drawing room and parlour at Castle Caldwell. In 1769, the focus was on the design of two large chimneypieces for the respective rooms:[60] both were the same size, however one lacked the signature 'key stone' of the other, and was instead to be a 'bespoke design of variegated Egyptian marble' by Denny.[61] The drawing room and parlour chimneypieces, along with her choice of furnishings and fabrics, provided Caldwell with spaces that Denny described as 'such good place[s] for the reception of the things you will want'.[62]

Although Denny's designs for the chimneypieces are now lost, a portfolio of designs by her commissioned stonecutters, George, Hill and John Darley of York Street, Dublin, represent a strong visual reference for what she likely intended for Castle Caldwell (fig. 8.8).[63] Together, Denny's textual descriptions and Darley's illustrations can narratively recreate the chimney pieces that complemented life in Caldwell's 'handsome rooms'.[64] A design of c.1770 for a black and white marble chimneypiece is a likely example of the style Denny created for Lady Caldwell, as it was a favoured design of the Darley's clientele in Dublin in that year and was also best suited to her choice of materials.[65] It is also in accordance with English architect Issac Ware's advice about how to aesthetically proportion and design chimney pieces with variegated and coloured marbles: expensive variegated marble was properly suited to simple designs and reserved 'for the best chimneys'.[66] It is within this context that Denny and Caldwell's architectural taste can be measured: similar to the Darley's design, Denny proposed a 'uniform layer' of white marble with contrasting coloured or variegated varieties 'for those parts which are detached and plain'.[67] Despite the lack of ornamentation, their materiality was socially significant; marble was considered the 'luxury of architecture' and 'the material of the ceremonious chimney-piece and hearth'.[68] The elegant design and expensive materials also

59 Bagshawe Muniments, MS 3/30/90, Lady Arbella Denny to Lady Elizabeth Caldwell, 28 June 1772. **60** Bagshawe Muniments, MS 3/30/86, 89, Lady Arbella Denny to Lady Elizabeth Caldwell 15 July 1769 and 27 Sept. 1770. **61** Ibid. **62** Bagshawe Muniments, MS 3/30/86, Lady Arbella Denny to Lady Elizabeth Caldwell, 15 July 1769. **63** Raughter notes that John Darley was 'probably' her stone cutter; however, he was also in practice with his two brothers George and Hill at their premises on York Street from 1768 until 1775. As Lady Denny refers only to 'Mr. Darley', any one of the brothers could have possibly spoken and worked with her to execute the design. The illustrations in the RIA Darley Collection are attributed to George and Hill Darley, and it is highly likely John would have been completing pieces in a similar style. Raughter, '"My Dear Lady C"', 184. For more information on the Darley's see https://www.ria.ie/sites/default/files/special_list_no._a045_darley_collection.pdf. **64** Bagshawe Muniments, MS 3/30/86, Lady Arbella Denny to Lady Elizabeth Caldwell, 15 July 1769. **65** All the designs by the Darley's specifically dated for c.1770 are remarkably similar in style, except for different coloured or variegated marbles. RIA, Darley Collection, 3 C 34/1/1–5. **66** I. Ware, *A complete body of architecture* (London, 1756), pp 557–8. **67** Marble was a commonly used material among the elite in Ireland and Britain for their chimneypieces. C. Lucey, *Building reputations: architecture and the artisan, 1750–1830* (Manchester, 2018), p. 146; Ware, *A complete body of architecture*, p. 567. **68** J. Aiken & A.L. Barbauld, *Evenings at home: or the juvenile budget opened* (Philadelphia, 1851), p. 100; Craske,

complemented the Caldwell's social status as members of the Protestant elite, whose 'highest social expectation was to conduct a display of decency in a room modestly outfitted to receive company'.[69] Denny was astutely aware of the social significance of 'modest' finishing at Castle Caldwell: decorative use of 'flower work or scrolls or any ornaments, if I was Sir James and Lady Caldwell, I would hold in contempt as useless'.[70] Additionally, the strictly classical profile of Darley's design also approximates Caldwell's preference for cornices 'with only dentils', leaving what Denny described as 'straight lines' that would fashionably suit and 'be quite enough for your two [best] rooms'.[71] Following the completion of the parlour and drawing room chimneypieces, Denny also intended to 'bespeak two small [chimneys]' for other rooms in Castle Caldwell, once she received the dimensions: she 'wish[ed] you would tell me how wide you would have them from jamb to jamb, at the inside of the jambs'.[72] Having received the measurements in 1770, she 'insist[ed] on [Darley] making your chimney pieces good if I can', to personally reassure Caldwell of her oversight throughout their construction. These conscientious decisions for simple designs were significant as they not only complemented the aesthetics of Caldwell's best rooms, but the decision to engage local stonecutters and materials uniquely demonstrates Denny and Caldwell's knowledge of architectural practices and an awareness of socio-cultural expectations within the domestic sphere.

The functionality of chimneypieces and their gendered associations for providing domestic warmth and 'comforts' in the eighteenth century can conceptually express how women 'long enjo[yed] the fruits of joint labours' upon completing their rooms, as numerous days were to be spent by 'good fires in the new house'.[73] Denny's frequent letters of support and advice confirm how this gendered aspect of familial life was of particular importance to Lady Caldwell, as methodical consideration was given to the fashionability and felicity of life with 'Sir James and [her] numerous fireside'.[74] Denny's drawings of furniture for the parlour, as well as her description of the drawing room with the chimney in use, contributes to our understanding of how women thoughtfully considered how these spaces were to be occupied throughout the day. The first bespoke chimneypiece designed by Denny was to be placed in Lady Caldwell's drawing room, accompanied by 'furniture of check green and white,' with instructions for the room being of no more than 'four windows for pleasure' and no less than 'three windows for light'.[75] The large size of the

'Conversations and chimneypieces'.   **69** Craske, 'Conversations and chimneypieces'.   **70** Denny felt that these decorative elements were 'useless' although they were also 'things necessary … to aim at'. However, considering the Caldwells' financial difficulties in the early 1770s, of which Denny was well aware, these items would also have represented an added expense. Bagshawe Muniments, MS 3/30/86, Lady Arbella Denny to Lady Elizabeth Caldwell, 15 July 1769.   **71** Bagshawe Muniments, MS 3/30/86, Lady Arbella Denny to Lady Elizabeth Caldwell, 15 July 1769; RIA, Darley Collection, 3 C 34/1/1. **72** Bagshawe Muniments, MS 3/30/86, 89, Lady Arbella Denny to Lady Elizabeth Caldwell, 15 July 1769 and 27 Sept. 1770.   **73** Bagshawe Muniments, MS 3/30/89, Lady Arbella Denny to Lady Elizabeth Caldwell, 27 Sept. 1770.   **74** Bagshawe Muniments, MS 3/30/92, Lady Arbella Denny to Lady Elizabeth Caldwell, 10 Dec. 1773.   **75** Bagshawe Muniments, MS 3/30/86, Lady Arbella Denny

chimneypiece in the drawing room was not only impressive for guests but also functional for how Caldwell intended to spend her days within it. Denny emphasizes in her letter of 5 July 1769 how often Caldwell would likely occupy the room once completed and outfitted to her taste. Denny felt that the drawing room '[would] be very handsome' and hoped that the windows would not be higher than 23 inches from the floor so Caldwell could view the demesne unobscured while seated.[76] The addition of two large bookcases, designed by Caldwell with 'looking-glass doors', which Denny described as being 'commodious and cheerful', was also essential for materially enhancing time spent in this room, which was informally used for reading and relaxation.

Within Perec's conception of domestic space, the 'particular function' of Caldwell's drawing room can further be reconsidered through Denny's descriptions of the Caldwells' familial life, which 'bears the essence of the notion of home'.[77] The drawing room was of particular importance to Denny and Caldwell, not only for its fashionable and comfortable surroundings, but also for its functionality for the family in question. As Lady Caldwell was often in 'a condition that wants rest', and Sir James suffered from gout, Denny strongly emphasized how their furniture should be arranged in relation to the chimneypiece to ease any personal discomforts.[78] Considering their health, Denny suggested 'two ample and easy couches on each side of the drawing-room end window' and 'put[ting] the chairs on each side of the fire'.[79] Visualizations of the couple informally enjoying an evening by the fire, the fine views of their estate, or Lady Caldwell indulging in an afternoon of reading, is further enhanced by Denny's sketch for a parlour sofa in her letter of 28 March 1770 (fig. 8.9).[80] Commissioned from joiner Christopher Hearn on Fishamble Street, Dublin, Denny's design for a 'genteel sofa' with 'the ends scrolling off', measuring 7 ft 10 in, was to be of the latest mode, but also conscientious of the size of Caldwell's rooms.[81] In her accompanying letter, Denny notes how Caldwell's original plan for three chairs would unlikely 'stand in seven feet eleven inches' of functional space comfortably, as taste dictated 'for such a room they can't be less than two feet in front of the seat'.[82] Considering their conceived placement directly beside the chimneypiece, Denny instead recommended 'having three chairs of each side the window, and one sofa of seven feet ten inches on one side of the fire, and two chairs on the other' for comfort and fashionability.[83] For the design of the two corresponding parlour chairs, Denny recommended 'the same pattern as those which Lords Louth and Westmeath have just bespoke for their houses in town', providing a glimpse of the sort of cultural capital concomitant with an active social life among Dublin's fashionable elite.[84] As the drawing room and parlour were most often used by the Caldwell family, Denny's conception of furnishings and chimneypieces

to Lady Elizabeth Caldwell, 15 July 1769. **76** Ibid. **77** Perec, *Species of spaces*, p. 28; Bachelard, *Poetics of space*, p. 5. **78** Bagshawe Muniments, MS 3/30/86, Lady Arbella Denny to Lady Elizabeth Caldwell, 15 July 1769. **79** Ibid. **80** Bagshawe Muniments, MS 3/30/87, Lady Arbella Denny to Lady Elizabeth Caldwell, 28 Mar. 1769. **81** Ibid. **82** Ibid. **83** Ibid. **84** Ibid.

8.9 Lady Arbella Denny to Lady Elizabeth Caldwell, letter of 28 March 1770.
© The University of Manchester.

recreates the everyday intimacy of fireside domesticity in candle-lit rooms. While Caldwell's answers to some questions are now lost, including 'What do you propose to cover your sofa and stuffed-back chairs with?', Denny's descriptions of green and white checked furniture, or the possibility of 'yellow English moreen window curtains' and 'chairs with yellow serge of the same shade', suggestively responds to

Bachelard's process of reimagining 'the house [and] the warm substance of intimacy [to] resume its form'.[85]

By phenomenologically reconsidering lost homes within their nuanced cultural and gendered contexts, the correspondence between Aylmer, Caldwell and Denny intimately reveals the significance of women's influence in shaping and conceptualizing life at Donadea Castle, Co. Kildare, and Castle Caldwell, Co. Fermanagh. Their discussions and visualizations for functional and decorative elements of the home such as staircases, chimneypieces and upholstered furniture, were not only spatial reassurances of taste from elite female networks, but also self-assured and sentimental reflections of social and familial duties, female legacy and the role of 'act[ing] the part of the wife and tender mother' within the Irish social imaginary.[86] In becoming reacquainted with how eighteenth-century women intended to inhabit their rooms, it can recognizably 'recapture the intimacy of the past' within their descriptive experiences and taste for building; for, it is 'in the intimate harmony of walls and furniture, it may be said that we become conscious of a house that is built by women'.[87]

---

[85] Bagshawe Muniments, MS 3/30/87, Lady Arbella Denny to Lady Elizabeth Caldwell, 28 Mar. 1769; Bachelard, *Poetics of space*, p. 48.   [86] Bagshawe Muniments, MS 3/30/91, Lady Arbella Denny to Lady Elizabeth Caldwell, 1 Dec. 1772.   [87] Bachelard, *Poetics of space*, p. 48.

Single lives, single houses

CONOR LUCEY

Though historically neglected in the literature on the eighteenth-century domestic interior, scholarship devoted to the single household, and particularly to the domestic lives of single men, has gathered momentum in recent years.[1] In a pioneering article published in 2009, entitled 'Men making home: masculinity and domesticity in eighteenth-century Britain', Karen Harvey pointed to what she called the 'feminine feel' of much of the literature on British domestic life, suggesting that, if we were to take it at face value, 'the eighteenth-century home appears to be peculiarly women's business'.[2] However, by focusing on the nature of domestic *oeconomy* (defined as 'the ordering of the house'), especially among the burgeoning middling sorts, Harvey discovered men to be 'a (literally) central part of its constitution'.[3] In the same year, Amanda Vickery's study of the domestic circumstances of single men addressed a range of themes from hospitality to housekeeping, although the emphasis here was plainly on those who 'yearned for women's company' and enjoyed varying degrees of access to 'feminised domesticity'.[4] Margaret Ponsonby's account of bachelors from different ends of the social spectrum arrived at similar conclusions, finding little evidence of the type of domestic comforts associated with a married household.[5] But singleness, then and now, connotes multiple lifecycles and lifestyle choices and circumstances. Jon Stobart's recent account of the consumption patterns of Edward, 5th Lord Leigh (1742–86), for example, explored the household of a never-married man in which 'no female hand can be detected'. Though characterized as being of unequivocally conservative taste, with rooms furnished in 'a somewhat dated, masculine style', Stobart argued that Leigh's 'decorative sensitivity' signifies a more complex masculine form of homemaking at odds with what Vickery, Ponsonby and others might have us expect of a bachelor home.[6] More recently, Helen Metcalfe has challenged the view that single men or bachelors (here used interchangeably) 'led solitary and discontented lives', arguing that 'neither bachelor status nor the style and duration of accommodation reduced single men's desire for respectable, comfortable

---

[1] This essay is written partly in response to the suggestion that 'the domestic culture of singles in the past has barely been touched upon'. A. Schmidt, I. Devos & B. Blondé, 'Single and the city: men and women alone in North-Western European towns since the late Middle Ages' in J. De Groot, I. Devos & A. Schmidt (eds), *Single life and the city, 1200–1900* (London, 2015), p. 14.   [2] K. Harvey, 'Men making home: masculinity and domesticity in eighteenth-century Britain', *Gender & History*, 21:3 (2009), 523.   [3] Ibid., p. 527. For this definition of *oeconomy*, Harvey cites N. Chomel, *Dictionaire oeconomique: or, the family dictionary*, revised by R. Bradley (London, 1725).   [4] A. Vickery, *Behind closed doors: at home in Georgian England* (London, 2009), p. 68.   [5] M. Ponsonby, *Stories from home: English domestic interiors, 1750–1850* (Aldershot, 2007), pp 135–7.   [6] J. Stobart, 'Rich, male and single: the consumption practices of Edward Leigh, 1742–86' in De Groot, Devos & Schmidt (eds), *Single life and the city*, pp 225, 228.

and secure surroundings'.[7] Some clearly relished the situation. In September 1817, having moved from lodgings to a suite of rented rooms in Lisson Grove, Paddington, the artist Benjamin Robert Haydon recounted: 'I breakfasted for the first time in my life on my *own* tea cups and saucers. I took up my *own* knife. I sat on my *own* chair. It was a new sensation!'[8] For most men, home was also the premier site for homosocial recreation and entertainment.[9]

Beyond singlehood, studies of family domesticity have yielded similar, more complex interpretations of male patterns of consumption and 'domestic self-fashioning'.[10] In her recent study of 'manliness and the home', Joanne Begiato argues that while men were 'absent from home in the performance of their duties, they were considered to be psychologically and emotionally inseparable from it.'[11] This complements Kate Retford's account of the evolution of the family group portrait which reveals how 'the father took on a new role' as the eighteenth century unfolded, resulting in him being 'increasingly pictured as absorbed and engrossed in the wellbeing of his dependents'.[12] Neither domesticity nor consumption was a female preserve. Jane Whittle's wide-ranging study of the early modern household economy conclusively establishes that 'the purchasing of goods was not an activity that was strongly gendered'.[13] Moreover, the second half of the eighteenth century witnessed the design and marketing of furniture created specifically with intimate masculine ablutions and grooming rituals in mind, from shaving tables to dressing commodes (fig. 9.1).[14]

The Irish context, though less substantively researched, confirms the present view that men's homes presented them with what Metcalfe has described as 'opportunities to practise their domesticity through establishing respectable, sociable and, importantly, comfortable domestic environments.'[15] Toby Barnard's account of Dublin *'rentier* and townee' James Ware notes that this particular (if atypical) bachelor furnished his St Stephen's Green house with all the 'accessories of polite hospitality: coffee-pots and teapots, punchbowls, drinking and jelly glasses and china plates'.[16]

---

[7] H. Metcalfe, 'To let or for lease: "Small, but genteel" lodgings for bachelors in and about the large Georgian town', *Journal for Eighteenth-Century Studies*, 44:1 (2021), 3, 13. On the varied 'pathways to singleness', see D. Hussey & M. Ponsonby, *The single homemaker and material culture in the long eighteenth century* (Oxon., 2012), pp 22–7.   [8] W. Bissell Pope (ed.), *The diary of Robert Haydon* (Cambridge, MA, 1960), p. 130, cited in Hussey & Ponsonby, *The single homemaker*, p. 156.   [9] B. Heller, 'Leisure and the use of domestic space in Georgian London', *The Historical Journal*, 53:3 (2010), 623–45.   [10] M. Finn, 'Men's things: masculine possession in the consumer revolution', *Social History*, 25:2 (2000), 133–55.   [11] J. Begiato, *Manliness in Britain, 1760–1900* (Manchester, 2020), p. 139.   [12] K. Retford, *The art of domestic life: family portraiture in eighteenth-century England* (London, 2006), p. 115.   [13] J. Whittle, 'Gender and consumption in the household economy' in J. Eibach & M. Lanzinger (eds), *The Routledge history of the domestic sphere in Europe, 16th to 19th century* (Abingdon, 2020), p. 208.   [14] C. Edwards, *Eighteenth-century furniture* (Manchester, 1996), p. 188; A. Vickery, 'Fashioning difference in Georgian England: furniture for him and for her' in P. Findlen (ed.), *Early modern things: objects and their histories, 1500–1800* (London, 2013), pp 342–59. For designs of shaving tables, see T. Chippendale, *The gentleman and cabinet-maker's director* (London, 1762), pl. 54; George Hepplewhite, *The cabinet-maker and upholsterer's guide* (London, 1794), pl. 80; T. Sheraton, *The cabinet dictionary* (London, 1803), pl. 69.   [15] Metcalfe, 'To let or for lease', 4.   [16] T. Barnard, *Making the grand figure: lives and possessions in*

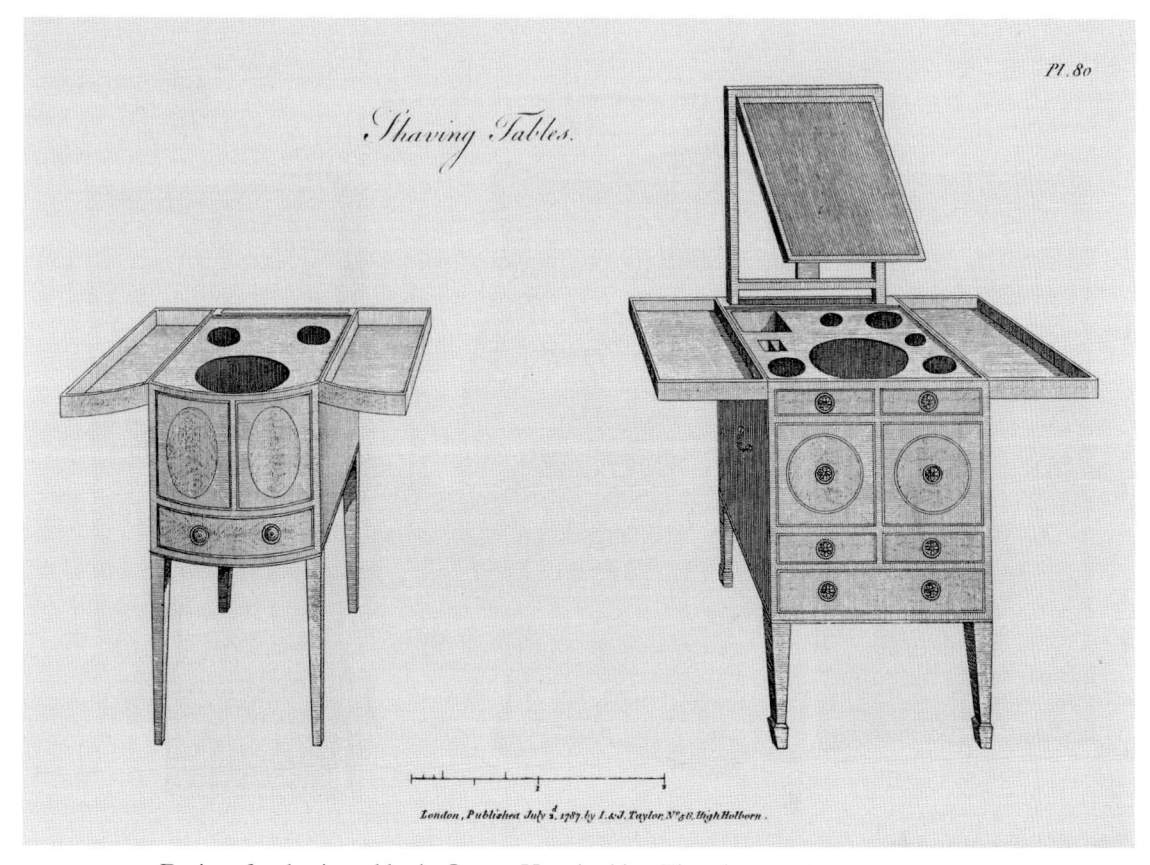

9.1 Designs for shaving tables in George Hepplewhite, *The cabinet-maker and upholsterer's guide* (London, 1794), plate 80.

Manuscript sources provide further tantalizing glimpses of the domestic lives of eighteenth-century Irish men. The account book of Dublin merchant Daniel Geale records, among other things, the various improvements and redecorations made to his Marlborough Street home throughout 1783–5, from painting, wallpapering and the purchase of new furniture for his office, to payments for curtains and upholstered chairs for the bedroom.[17]

Mindful that 'singles are an extraordinarily diverse group, with unique experiences and identities', and that 'classifying and defining singles in a historical context is highly problematic',[18] this chapter explores the intersection between a condition and a typology, neither of which have received sustained attention in the literature on domestic architecture in Georgian Ireland. If Reyner Banham was right and the terraced house was conceived principally as 'a way of stacking people', then

Ireland, 1641–1770 (London, 2004), p. 305. **17** NLI, MS 2286, 'General account book of Daniel Geale of Dublin, 1779–1803', fos 310–11. This included the purchase of a 'writing desk & shaving stand' from Robert Morgan, cabinetmaker of Henry Street, for £18 17s. 9d. **18** Schmidt, Devos & Blondé, 'Single

it is worth considering how Dublin accommodated the lives of those for whom an entire house was neither a necessity nor a practicality, or for some even an aspiration.[19] As Niall McCullough noted in his seminal study of the city, first published in 1989, the terraced house forms 'an adjustable typology capable of bearing immense transformation and adjustment';[20] a view echoed in Peter Guillery's account of non-elite housing in eighteenth-century London, in which he suggests that an 'indeterminate flexibility may have been foremost in the minds of speculating builders'.[21] This chapter explores that quality of adjustability or flexibility by focusing first on the domiciliary needs of single professional gentlemen in Dublin; and secondly, on how a terraced typology of so-called 'two-room' houses was adapted (and in turn evolved) to satisfy the demands of that market.

SINGLE LIVES: LODGERS AND HOUSEHOLDERS

What was considered polite accommodation for a young Irish gentleman in the decades either side of 1800? While rented rooms were the mainstay of most urban dwellers in the Georgian era, histories of lodgings have typically concentrated on the meaner end of the social spectrum, foregrounding issues of trespass and theft, surveillance and security.[22] Writing in 2006, John Styles, reflecting on aspects of choice and agency in the homes of working Londoners, argued that personal options were 'dictated by the workings of the market in furnished rooms and, specifically, by the landladies who provided them'.[23] Since then, a more nuanced literature has emerged. In her comprehensive study of lodging in Georgian London, Gillian Williamson examines the social hierarchy of multiple occupancy houses – what she describes as the 'language of floors' – and makes a distinction between the 'houseful' and the 'household'; the former characterized as 'those who slept under the same roof', but who lacked the bonds of family and kinship associated with the latter.[24] This language of floors confirms the contemporary view regarding 'the dignity of each [storey] being in the inverse ratio of its altitude'.[25] But while it is clear that garrets

and the city', pp 10, 14.   **19** K. Downes, *The Georgian cities of Britain* (Oxford, 1979), p. 13. The source of this comment attributed to Banham is not cited. Sir John Summerson characterized the 'insistent verticality of the London house' as being 'idiomatic'. J. Summerson, *Georgian London* (1945; rev. ed. London, 2003), p. 51.   **20** N. McCullough, *Dublin: an urban history* (Dublin, 1989), p. 98.   **21** P. Guillery, *The small house in eighteenth-century London* (London, 2004), p. 58. See also S. Muthesius, *The English terraced house* (London, 1982), pp 79–88.   **22** J. McEwan, 'The lodging exchange: space, authority and knowledge in eighteenth-century London' in J. McEwan & P. Sharpe (eds), *Accommodating poverty: the housing and living arrangements of the English poor, c.1600–1850* (Houndmills, 2011), pp 50–68. A notable exception, in an Irish context, is R. Musielak, 'Madame da Cunha prefers her own "dunghill" to a palace: city lodging and country visiting in early eighteenth-century London', *IADS*, 14 (2011), 56–77. **23** J. Styles, 'Lodging at the Old Bailey: lodgings and their furnishing in eighteenth-century London' in J. Styles & A. Vickery (eds), *Gender, taste and material culture in Britain and North America, 1700–1830* (New Haven, 2006), p. 63.   **24** G. Williamson, *Lodgers, landlords and landladies in Georgian London* (London, 2021), p. 3.   **25** F. Grose, *The Olio* (1793), cited in D. Cruickshank & N. Burton, *Life in the Georgian city* (London, 1990), p. 62.   **26** Amanda Vickery's account of lodgings similarly confines itself

and back rooms were reserved for those living on reduced incomes,[26] lodgings were perennially attractive to all classes in offering 'convenience, choice and flexibility, in terms of location and budget as well as duration of stay'.[27] More pertinent to this study, Joanne McEwan and Pamela Sharpe have argued that lodgings for young unmarried gentlemen represented 'one exercise in freedom and independence'.[28]

Bachelorhood in the Georgian social imaginary represented 'a temporary and unprestigious state best solved by marriage',[29] and the married household remained the basic (approved) societal unit.[30] Crucially, however, it is clear that lodgings were regarded as both 'a convenient and extended lifestyle choice' for single men,[31] and, more significantly, that the quality of accommodation and furnishing was not determined by marital status.[32] Indeed, a moral dimension to masculine lifestyle choices, and its manifestation in the selection of appropriate domestic quarters, was visualized by London engraver Carington Bowles in an instructive series illustrating 'the contrast between virtue and vice, exhibited in the characters of two brothers', published in 1787. (At least one plate of this series was subsequently pirated by Dublin print-seller William Allen and available from his Dame Street premises.)[33] Here the character of Frederick, 'elegantly furnishing a large house' is contrasted with the figure of Charles, 'at breakfast in a genteel private family' (figs 9.2 and 9.3). Mindful of his prospects and duties, Charles has prudently taken respectable lodgings; the profligate Frederick, on the other hand, squanders his fortune in furnishing and decorating an entire house. The implication here is that Charles manages to live within his means yet also in a manner conducive to his social station as a young single gentleman.[34] While visual representations of domestic interiors are certainly contested forms of documentary evidence, often manifesting particular cultural and ideological systems and moral codes, they nonetheless speak to verifiable social customs and practices:[35] in 1797, for example, the potential lodger of

---

to the lower end of the social spectrum. On the spatial hierarchy of the home she writes: 'Probably the owning family kept the ground floor; the smarter tenant secured the lighter first floor, with the least pretentious lodgers consigned to the higher and nether regions.' Vickery, *Behind closed doors*, p. 34. **27** Metcalfe, 'To let or for lease', 6. **28** J. McEwan & P. Sharpe, '"It buys me freedom": genteel lodging in late-seventeenth- and eighteenth-century London', *Parergon*, 24:2 (2007), 145–6. **29** A. Vickery, 'What did eighteenth-century men want?', Royal Historical Society/Gresham College Annual Lecture 2010, online at www.gresham.ac.uk/lectures-and-events/what-did-eighteenth-century-men-want (accessed 15 Apr. 2021). **30** Schmidt, Devos & Blondé, 'Single and the city', p. 5. **31** McEwan & Sharpe, '"It buys me freedom"', 151. **32** Metcalfe, 'To let or for lease', 11. **33** 'Frederick elegantly furnishing a large house' was printed (in reverse) by William Allen and available from his shop at 32 Dame Street. (This is often, erroneously, assumed to be an original design.) Allen, the leading print-seller in late Georgian Dublin, published many copies of London prints. See M. Pollard, *A dictionary of members of the Dublin book trade, 1550–1800* (London, 2000), pp 6–7. **34** This is borne out in subsequent scenes where Frederick consorts with prostitutes while Charles successfully courts the daughter of a nobleman. **35** Curiously, this image and its obvious moral imperative has been either misunderstood or misrepresented in recent scholarship of the eighteenth-century British interior and its representation: while Hannah Greig simply takes the scene entirely at face value (a couple furnishing their home), Amanda Vickery sees it as evidence of conspicuous male consumption in the pursuit of dynastic continuity. H. Greig, 'Eighteenth-century English interiors in image and text', in C. Grant & J. Aynsley (eds), *Imagined interiors: representing the domestic interior since the Renaissance* (London, 2008), pp 126–7;

9.2 Carington Bowles, 'Frederick elegantly furnishing a large house', engraving, 1787. The Colonial Williamsburg Foundation. Museum purchase.

'apartments' in a 'genteel private house' in Dublin was advised that he 'may breakfast with the family if agreeable to him'.[36]

This parallel of architectural and social decorum loomed large among the professional classes. The 'central, retired, genteel situation' of new built houses in Cope Street, 'being so near my principal connections', was attractive to William Drennan, an *accoucheur*, or male midwife, looking for a Dublin house in the summer of 1796.[37] Economy and convenience were essential requirements in his protracted search for a suitable property, and complementary to the received wisdom in popular

Vickery, *Behind closed doors*, p. 133. Rachel Stewart understands the image in the context of young gentleman making 'a proper figure' and suggests that the seated women represents 'his wife in a modest supporting role'. R. Stewart, *The town house in Georgian London* (London, 2009), p. 111.   **36** *Saunders's News-Letter*, 27 Mar. 1797. In the same year, lodgings in an unspecified part of the city, described as suitable for a lady or gentleman, offered 'a good table, pleasing society, and roomy house, or the lodgings without board, if more agreeable' (*Saunders's News-Letter*, 25 Jan. 1797). This further confirms the suggestion that 'single lodgers of quality could expect some latitude in the use of the wider household infrastructure' and 'experience a level of material comfort normally associated with the family home'. Hussey & Ponsonby, *The single homemaker*, p. 171. On the topic of family dining options for lodgers, see Williamson, *Lodgers, landlords and landladies*, pp 108–10.   **37** W. Drennan to M. McTier, 8 July 1796, in J. Agnew (ed.), *The Drennan-McTier letters, vol. 2: 1794–1801* (Dublin, 1999), p. 249.

9.3 Carington Bowles, 'Charles at breakfast in a genteel private family', engraving, 1787. The Colonial Williamsburg Foundation. Museum purchase.

advice literature aimed at the proper management of the household:[38] in October 1798, a house in Cumberland Street offering the standard 'two-room' accommodation – described by Drennan as 'two parlours, two drawing rooms, finished neatly, etc.' – was deemed by him to be 'very convenient'.[39] But gentility was evidently the determining factor. Having decided that he would not take a house 'unless it is cheaper and more eligible for me in every respect than a lodging' – substantiating the appropriateness of lodgings for single men of his rank and position – Drennan finally acquired the lease of a house in Marlborough Street, on the north side of the city.[40] In response to this news, William's sister Martha counselled that

> I think it is good, and believe it cheap, and it may be difficult to get one more agreeable – yet, as *gentility is for you more eligible than room*, I would like one more modern and even a pleasanter street, and as you are not in a hurry such might be picked up.[41]

38 Harvey, 'Men making home', 533. 39 W. Drennan to M. McTier, 15 Oct. 1798, in Agnew (ed.), *The Drennan–McTier letters*, ii, p. 414. 40 W. Drennan to M. McTier, 26 Aug. 1798, in Agnew (ed.), *The Drennan–McTier letters*, ii, p. 412. 41 M. McTier to W. Drennan, 13 Dec. 1798, in Agnew (ed.),

Although generally acquiescent to Martha's advice on domestic matters, Drennan better understood the social geography of Dublin:

> I believe I shall keep the house, as I am pretty well persuaded it would take some time to suit me as conveniently, and there is not a street on that side of the water less dull, until you come to the neighbourhood of the squares, and out of the professional circuit.[42]

Clearly, the 'neighbourhood of the squares' was not within his budget, a situation likely shared with many of his social class. But not all young gentlemen were so shrewd. An early nineteenth-century cartoon entitled 'A pair of exquisites regaling' satirizes the pursuit of gentility in even very reduced circumstances, illustrated in the marked contrast between the characters' fine clothing and their meagre furnishings (fig. 9.4). A pirated (and modified) version of a popular English print – Isaac Cruickshank's 'Dandies at Tea', published in 1818 – the specific reference to the Carlisle Building at the corner of Burgh Quay and D'Olier Street (glimpsed through the window), and to recognisable luxury brands (Kinahan's and Costigan's), lends this caricature a particularly local resonance.[43] Amanda Vickery interprets their 'ramshackle' surroundings as a sign that 'they lack the wholesome domesticity that women provided', but it seems more likely that this satirizes the perils rather than the condition of bachelorhood.[44] These dandies are clearly a pair of Fredericks.

If we accept that 'lodging was a convenient and extended lifestyle choice' for single gentlemen, then what did the Dublin market offer?[45] From a review of newspaper advertisements for lodgings and 'apartments', it is clear that the spatial needs of single gentlemen remained largely unchanged across the long eighteenth century and typically comprised one or two reception rooms and a bedroom (often, but not necessarily, located on the same floor). Representative examples include the advertisement, in April 1771, of 'A Dining-room and Bed-chamber, genteely furnished' in a house in an unspecified 'open fine Street';[46] and 'A Middle Floor furnished' in a 'genteel airy part of Marlborough-street', described in 1793 as suitable for 'a single gentleman'.[47]

The Drennan-McTier letters, ii, pp 435–6. Author's emphasis. 42 W. Drennan to M. McTier, 15 Dec. 1798, in Agnew (ed.), *The Drennan-McTier letters*, ii, p. 437. 43 In Cruickshank's 'Dandies at Tea', the conversation ('do you buy it?') mocks the supposed opportunism predicated on a single life. This Dublin version, replacing the view of the dome of St Paul's Cathedral in Cruickshank's design with that of the Carlisle Building, evidently adapted the humour for the purposes of advertising the named brands. Another Dublin edition of the print, published by J. Le Petit in Capel Street, replaces the dome of St Paul's with that of the Four Courts. On the topic of the 'spectrum of invention and imitation' typical of the Irish trade in printed caricature, see S. Beltrametti & W. Laffan, 'William McCleary and the trade in pirated caricatures in early nineteenth-century Dublin: part I – "Unlawfully participating in the profits of their labour"', *IADS*, 23 (2020), 118. 44 Vickery, *Behind closed doors*, p. 81. Elsewhere, Vickery concedes that 'The bachelor householder had a stake in society that the lodger was seen to lack'. Ibid., p. 68. 45 McEwan & Sharpe, '"It Buys Me Freedom"', 151. 46 *Hibernian Journal*, 29 Apr. 1771. 47 *Saunders's News-Letter*, 9 Jan. 1793.

9.4 'A pair of exquisites regaling', hand-coloured etching, Dublin, c.1818.
© Victoria and Albert Museum, London.

Then as now privacy was at a premium. In March 1796, 'a drawing-room and bed-chamber, with the use of another room occasionally', in a house in South Great George's Street, was described as 'very convenient, as no other lodger will be in the house';[48] board and lodging 'in the immediate vicinity' of Mountjoy Square in January 1820, aimed at single gentlemen (or ladies), specified that the number of tenants was 'limited to eight'.[49] Serviced rooms were patently as important as furnished rooms, confirmed by frequent references to houses and lodgings offering 'the attendance of a servant' or 'the use of a servant'.[50] In January 1797, 'a drawing-room, bed-chamber and closet, neatly furnished, in a genteel private house', also included 'so much of the attendance of a man and maid servant as may be agreed on'.[51] In other instances, the living quarters were adapted to accommodate a potential tenant's own personal household. In May 1774, an apartment in Dame Street, consisting of a dining room, drawing room and three bedrooms, also boasted 'a Kitchen and Apartments for Servants';[52] in April 1784, furnished lodgings in York Street comprised 'a handsome First Floor, with a bed for a servant'.[53]

Individuals also sought to have their specific needs addressed. In 1823, a single gentleman 'who boards out', desired a 'private house' in either North Frederick Street, North Great George's Street, Dominick Street, Gardiner Street, 'or in any other respectable private street in their neighbourhood'. Here, the desired apartments were 'a first floor, with a small bedchamber upon the upper story'.[54] In other instances, the nature of the accommodation and its suitability for a certain type of tenant was emphasized. Indeed, while 'single gentleman' was frequently used to delimit potential enquiries, in one instance the proprietor of lodgings in Dorset Street advised that 'None need apply but those whose Character will bear the strictest Scrutiny'.[55] And although the quantity, character and condition of rooms was foremost in advertising lodgings and houses to let, a pragmatic location was a relatively common selling point, not least when aimed at the highly stratified middling sorts: in November 1775, a first floor in a 'genteel part of the town' was 'contiguous to the Four-Courts, Castle, and Parliament House', making it 'convenient for a lawyer';[56] in February 1790, furnished lodgings in Ross Lane, off Bride Street, were 'well adapted for a Gentleman at the Bar, who does not keep House in Town'.[57] In other instances the accommodation itself might be adapted to serve professional demands: in 1793, an advertisement for a first floor in a 'private family', comprising a drawing room and two bedrooms 'with or without board', boasted that 'a gentleman in the law line can be accommodated with an office'.[58]

Another form of gentleman lodger was the university undergraduate. Given the turnover of students in each academic year, renovation and refurbishment was a

---

48 *Saunders's News-Letter*, 26 Mar. 1796.   49 *Saunders's News-Letter*, 22 Jan. 1820.   50 *Freeman's Journal*, 18 May 1809; *Saunders's News-Letter*, 4 Nov. 1818.   51 *Saunders's News-Letter*, 3 Jan. 1797.   52 *Hibernian Journal*, 11 May 1774.   53 *Dublin Evening Post*, 3 Apr. 1784.   54 *Freeman's Journal*, 1 Mar. 1823.   55 *Hibernian Journal*, 17 Apr. 1775.   56 *Hibernian Journal*, 3 Nov. 1775.   57 *Hibernian Journal*, 12 Feb. 1790.   58 *Saunders's News-Letter*, 23 Feb. 1793.

perennial activity. In 1761, preparations for Richard Lovell Edgeworth's accommodation at Trinity College Dublin involved the negotiation of the sale of the 'chambers' and furniture (at a valuation) from its previous occupant, and payments to carpenters, painters and wallpaper hangers; new luxury accoutrements extended to silver teaspoons and tongs, 'green ivory handled' knives and forks, a decanter, glasses and cruets, and 'confectionary ware'. As well as coal, candles, keys and padlocks for security, and clothes and bedding for his servant, the more quotidian items underwritten by his father included a payment of 19s. to Margaret Moore, 'the College Laundress', for attending his rooms for a period of five months.[59] First-floor rooms at the college for Ralph Howard, later 1st Viscount Wicklow, cost the princely sum of £55 in 1743. Entertaining in his digs was evidently of some importance: in February and March of that year, cabinetmaker and joiner Abraham Walker supplied a tea table and a pair of card tables, as well as 'two new joynts to a dinening table'.[60]

THE URBAN HOUSE AS MULTIPLE OCCUPANCY DWELLING

Central to our understanding of elite urban accommodation was the nature of house building as an enterprise and the markets for real estate. Throughout the eighteenth century, legal conveyances customarily described a property as being intended for a house, a messuage ('a dwelling house together with its outbuildings and the adjacent land assigned to its use') or a tenement ('a portion of a house, tenanted as a separate dwelling; a flat; a suite of apartments, or even a single room so let or occupied'), hinting at the flexible use of the completed dwelling.[61] A deed of lease and release made in August 1755, for example, concerning ground that had been let in Kildare Street in 1751, records that the 'new dwelling house or tenement' at the corner with Nassau Street was then in the possession of the countess of Drogheda.[62] Similar examples may be found in memorials describing properties in elite neighbourhoods across the city. In 1748, the carpenter Benjamin Rudd, for the sum of £300 and a yearly rent of £29, conveyed the lease of a 'new dwelling house or tenement' on the east side of St Stephen's Green to Bysshe Molesworth, seventh son of Robert, 1st Viscount Molesworth (the present number 42).[63] This was one of a pair of houses built by Rudd in 1745–6, evidently as a speculative investment.[64] Even at Henrietta Street, customarily regarded as the paragon of polite living in early eighteenth-century Dublin, a form of adaptable living was if not anticipated then at least permitted within the terms of the contract. A lease made in August 1743, concerning 5 and 6 Henrietta Street, built as a single house in 1739–41, recites that the interest

59 NLI, MS 1527, Personal accounts of Richard Edgeworth of Edgeworthstown, fos 67–70, 104, 126. **60** NLI, Wicklow papers, MS 38,602/2 (1–3). I am grateful to Toby Barnard for these references. **61** 'messuage, n.'. OED Online. June 2021. Oxford University Press. www.oed.com/view/Entry/117128?redirectedFrom=messuage; 'tenement, n.'. OED Online. June 2021. Oxford University Press. www.oed.com/view/Entry/199111?redirectedFrom=tenement (accessed 12 Aug. 2021). **62** RD, 179/17/118399; *GSR*, iv, p. 91. **63** RD, 130/360/89426. **64** C. Casey, *Dublin* (London, 2005), p. 541.

in the 'messuage or tenement built and erected for use of Henry Late Earl of Thomond deceased' had been conveyed to Brabazon Ponsonby, 1st earl of Bessborough.[65] Although it is clear that this language was part and parcel of the customary terminology used in property law, routinely transcribed and replicated by attorneys, land agents and their clerks, the question of adaptability was unambiguously introduced; this stands in marked contrast to the prohibitions against the use of the property for anything other than a domestic residence, and to building lines, materials, parapet heights and other restrictions on the form that the house might take. Indeed, from Henrietta Street in the 1730s to Mountjoy Square in the 1790s, the Gardiner Estate clearly anticipated that multiple occupancy dwellings would be accommodated within the compass of polite living. Toby Barnard's vivid account of consumer life in Dublin for the period 1641–1770 notes that 'grandees from the provinces' often took lodgings rather than investing in a permanent town residence.[66] Use evolved and houses in once fashionable districts might be repurposed as tenements in response to new prestige developments. Dawson Street, laid out as an exclusive residential suburb in 1707, boasted two lodging houses by the end of the century, run by a Miss Connolly and Mrs Whiteside respectively; a further six were recorded in the adjacent Molesworth Street in 1798.[67]

Commercial buildings in busy thoroughfares also provided opportunities for enterprising landlords and landladies. In 1765, Hannah, widow of Thomas Wood, wig maker, advertised 'genteel lodgings' at her house in Castle Street;[68] in 1791, two new houses at the corner of Cavendish Row, described as 'the first Situation in Dublin for genteel Business', were 'likewise well adapted for Lodgings'.[69] In such situations the character of the property was important, where the nature of ingress and egress denoted degrees of gentility and respectability. In 1774, furnished lodgings in Dame Street boasted a 'convenient Hall-Door, unconnected with the Shop'.[70] Later commercial developments created under the imprimatur of the Wide Streets Commissioners, the city's planning authority, customarily provided separate trade doors and private doors in city centre retail premises: this served to underscore the importance of lodgings for the success of smart shopping districts, and was clearly intended to attract a particular social demographic of merchants, shopkeepers and their families. In 1820, furnished lodgings in D'Olier Street comprised two drawing rooms and 'one, two, or three bed-rooms, and sitting-room, as required'; a single gentleman, or a 'small family with no children', was 'preferred'.[71]

This approach to domestic accommodation manifested itself in the formal subdivision of the typical terraced house. While architect Isaac Ware had suggested

---

65 RD, 116/16/79251. **66** Barnard, *Making the grand figure*, pp 282–7. Conversely, maintaining a permanent Dublin residence became steadily more popular among the peerage during the course of the century. See D. Dickson, 'Capital and country, 1600–1800', in A. Cosgrove (ed.), *Dublin through the ages* (1988), p. 71. **67** *GSR*, iv, pp 99–101, 112. Robin Usher has suggested that 'social zoning was rarely absolute' in Dublin. R. Usher, *Dawson Street, Molesworth Street & Kildare Street* (Dublin, 2009), p. 8. **68** *Freeman's Journal*, 15 Oct. 1765. **69** *Dublin Chronicle*, 20 Jan. 1791. **70** *Hibernian Journal*, 12 Oct. 1774. **71** *Saunders's News-Letter*, 22 Jan. 1820.

9.5 12 Gardiner Place (centre), Dublin, built 1790–2. Photograph by the author.

that the common form of four-storeys over basement was suitable 'for the reception of a family of two or three people with three or four servants',[72] it is clear that houses in London, Dublin and other cities were 'commonly occupied by several independent tenants'.[73] The early history of 12 Gardiner Place, formerly part of the Gardiner Estate, confirms McCullough's intuition that the terraced house was inherently a versatile typology – no doubt one of the reasons why it remained a staple of the Dublin builder's portfolio well into the nineteenth century (fig. 9.5). The ground on which this house was built was originally leased in August 1790 to John Manent, described as a 'Gentleman' of Crossboyne, County Mayo; this was one of five houses (now 10–14 Gardiner Place) built 'at the joint expence' of Manent, Leopold Ferry, a perfumer of Marlborough Street, and William Burke, a bricklayer and house-builder of Dominick Street.[74] (As leaseholder of the site, Manent was responsible for its

---

[72] I. Ware, *A complete body of architecture* (London, 1756), p. 347.   [73] Cruickshank & Burton, *Life in the Georgian city*, p. 60.   [74] RD, 462/90/294484. This deed of assignment recites the original 'articles of agreement', dated 26 Dec. 1790, wherein 'there had been five Dwelling Houses built in Gardiners Place

improvement within a specified period of time, although Burke was evidently the builder/contractor of all five properties.[75]) In April 1792, Manent in turn leased the ground, 'together with the dwelling house, stable etc. erected thereon', to Denis Bingham, esq., a title that signified either a gentry or professional identity. Regardless of his occupation, Bingham evidently did not require an entire four-storey house for his purposes: in September of the same year he entered into an agreement with Richard Cox, gentleman (and Maria, his wife), and with Zachariah Fox, an upholder (or upholsterer), in which

> it was covenanted and agreed by and between the Parties thereto, that the said Denis Bingham Should Immediately have, occupy, possess & Enjoy for the Sole and Exclusive use of himself and [his] Servants the after mentioned Apartments. Viz. a Street Parlour, a first floor Consisting of a Dining Room & Bed Chamber, a Three pair Upper Room Backwards, and a Back Servants Room Below Stairs, and Cellar with the Stable and Coach House thereto belonging.

This was acknowledged as 'part or parcell of that new Dwelling House lately erected'.[76]

In a typical 'two-room' house in Dublin – a contemporary reference to the standard urban form of two rooms on both the ground and first floors – the ground floor, or 'parlour storey', was reserved for a street parlour at the front of the house, immediately adjacent to the entrance hall (and facing the street or square), and a dining parlour to the rear, facing the garden. Above this, on the first floor, was the 'drawing room storey', comprised of a front and rear drawing room: these reception rooms, following a system of proportional (and hierarchical) distribution, were the largest and airiest (up to fifteen feet tall by the end of the century), confirming their desirability as genteel lodgings (noted above). The upper floors consisted of the 'attic storey', which housed the principal bedrooms, and finally the garret, reserved for children and retainers or servants (as required).[77] At 12 Gardiner Place, Bingham reserved the street parlour, likely for an office of some sort, and the entire first floor; but here the front and rear drawing rooms served as a dining room (front) and bedchamber (rear) respectively (fig. 9.6). Two rooms were set aside for servants: one in the garret at the top of the house, indicated by the reference to 'a Three pair Upper Room Backwards' (a reference to the number of staircases involved), and one in the basement, identified as 'a Back Servts. Room Below Stairs'. The cellar, stable and coach house were also reserved for Bingham's exclusive use.

at the Joint Expence of sd. three parties'.   75 For a glimpse of William Burke's career see RIA, Haliday MSS, 4.B.31, 'Report on the Trades and Manufacturers of Dublin *c.*1834', fos 66–74.   76 RD, 416/454/277654; 454/504/293026; 456/364/293162. How the remainder of the accommodation was distributed or inhabited is not recorded.   77 For an account of the standard spatial form of the Dublin house, see C. Lucey, 'Specification for a house to be built in Dominick Street', *IADS*, 21 (2018), 96–107.

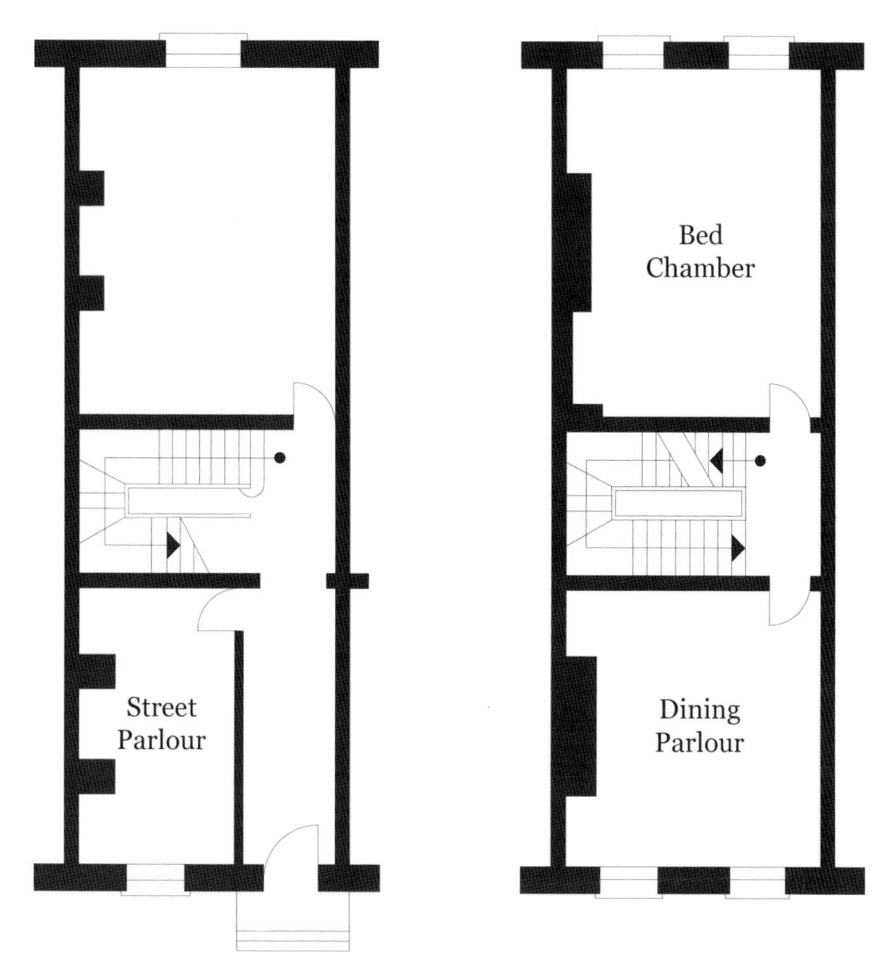

9.6 Ground- (*left*) and first-floor plans of 12 Gardiner Place, built 1790–2. The front and rear first-floor rooms, typically reserved as the 'drawing room storey', function here as a dining room and bedroom respectively. Drawing by Marcus Lynam.

With this formal division of the house into accommodation for three separate households in mind – Denis Bingham, Richard and Maria Cox, and Zachariah Fox – the popularity of Dublin's 'two-room' typology becomes clear. While the grander form of bespoke and speculatively-built house boasted a formal stair (rising from ground to first floor only) and (concealed) service stair, from mid-century it was more common for the principal staircase in terraced houses to serve three rather than two storeys: a survey of plan types utilized at Parnell (formerly Rutland) Square, built in 1755–85, reveals that of the 55 surviving houses, 47 (85%) were built to this model.[78]

[78] A. Duggan, 'Parnell Square: an analysis of house types', *Bulletin of the Irish Georgian Society*, 37 (1995), 13–30. On the general issue, see Casey, *Dublin*, p. 36; McCullough, *Dublin*, p. 103.

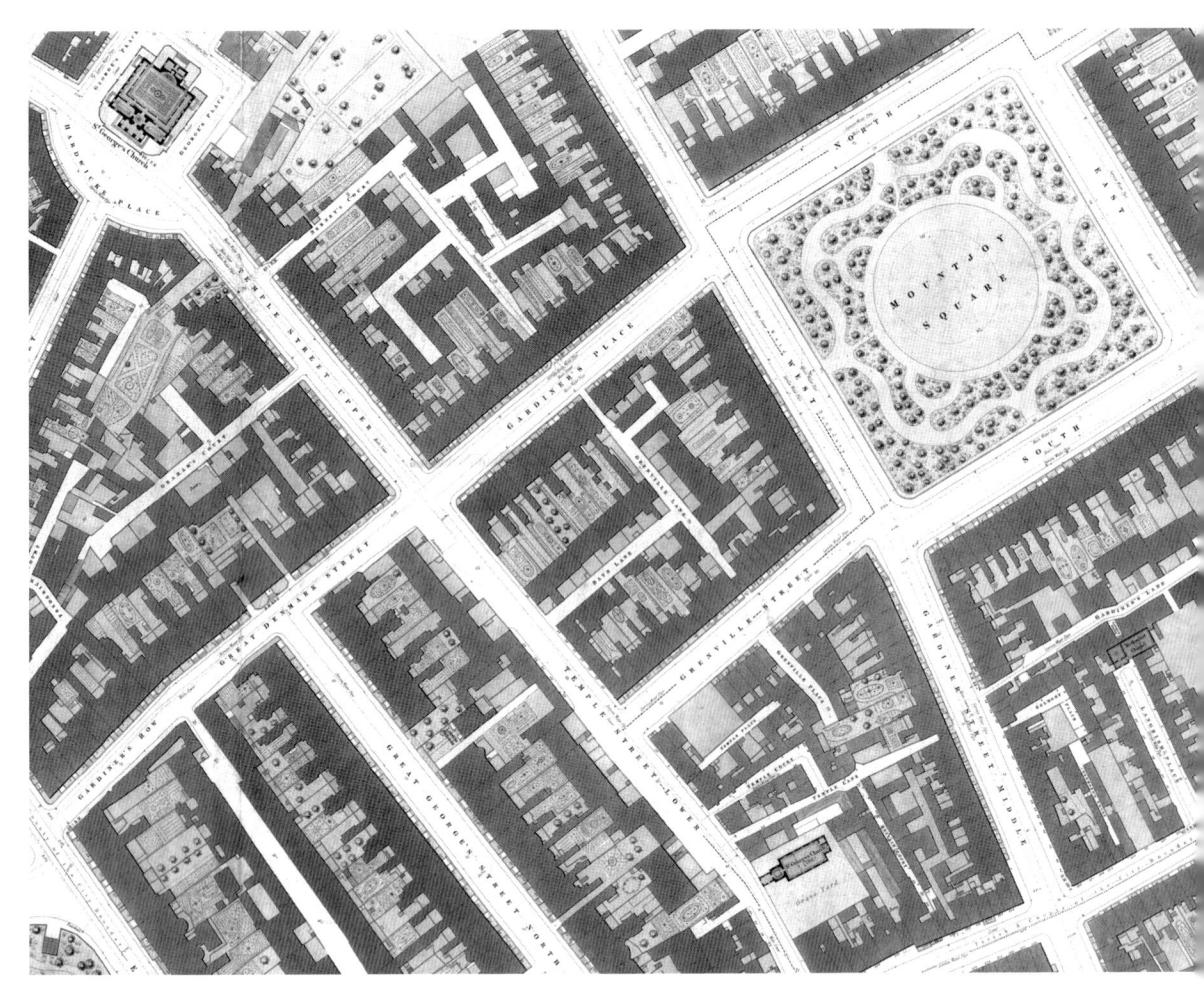

9.7 Location of Gardiner Place relative to Mountjoy Square and environs. Ordnance Survey, City of Dublin, sheet 8 (detail), 1847. Ordnance Survey Ireland (OSi) 19th Century Historical Maps, held by Ordnance Survey Ireland. © Public domain.

This formal development may have evolved in response to demand for different forms of high status living to suit a variety of purses and circumstances: individual apartments, defined by the vertical division of the house into different storeys, were easily serviced by common areas in the form of halls and landings. Indeed, the central location of the staircase in the plan of 12 Gardiner Place, a practical solution for houses built on narrow plots (here, a frontage of a mere 16 feet 9 inches), was more readily adapted to multiple occupancy living: it combined the ubiquitous three storey formal staircase (rising from the ground floor to the attic or bedroom floor) with the single-storey service staircases to basement and garret respectively.

Peter Guillery, writing on the London house, has argued that the verticality common to the urban domestic typology 'could derive from a general awareness that nearly all houses in London were provisional divided housing'.[79] This in fact echoes Isaac Ware's assumption that most speculative housing 'in great towns' was built 'for the chance of letting', and, in such cases, should be related 'to the place where it stands'.[80] Significantly, the spatial organization of Bingham's apartment at 12 Gardiner Place – with the dining room (front) and bedroom (rear) on the first floor – satisfied Ware's description of a 'common house' in London, and was, as noted above, identical to the better sort of lodgings demanded by single gentlemen, representing 'one of many clues to the status of the inhabitant' and conveying his 'respectability and taste'.[81] Bingham also acquired a fashionable address by a commonly understood financing strategy – securing the rent with paying tenants.[82]

With Ware's recommendations in mind, it is also worth considering the location of Gardiner Place relative to Mountjoy Square and its environs, and the juxtaposition of social classes, albeit confined to the upper and middle registers, that determined which streets might be designated as suitable for single or multiple occupancy dwellings (fig. 9.7).[83] It is noteworthy too that building contracts for less prestigious locations elsewhere within the Gardiner Estate, such as at Gloucester Place, issued in 1791, were less prescriptive about the form and character of the property intended for the site.[84]

SINGLE HOUSES

Although the vertical division of the typical 'two-room' house was readily adaptable to serve a range of domestic circumstances and economies, the urban terrace is an inherently two-dimensional form, and corner sites presented 'an opportunity for some, for others a difficulty'.[85] While the houses of prestigious addresses such as Merrion Square prioritized the needs of the individual property facing the central

79 Guillery, *The small house in eighteenth-century London*, p. 60.   80 Ware, *A complete body of architecture*, p. 291.   81 Metcalfe, 'To let or for lease', 10.   82 The terms of Bingham's lease of the property included the annual ground rent of £50 sterling per annum; in turn, Bingham's agreement with Zachariah Fox and Richard and Maria Cox was for ten years at 50 guineas per annum. In her study of London lodgings, Gillian Williamson notes the attraction of 'rent from letting lodgings [that] might fully cover the lease rental'. Williamson, *Lodgers, landlords and landladies*, p. 64.   83 On the topic of social distribution, see E. Sheridan, 'Living in the capital city' in J. Brady & A. Simms (eds), *Dublin through space and time* (Dublin, 2001), pp 136–58. In Edinburgh, in the wake of the Acts of Union of 1707, a burgeoning professional and merchant class fostered 'tall blocks of property' accommodating the different strata of society on the individual storeys of the same building, all served by a common stair. A. Rowan, 'Edinburgh: the town house in the capital of North Britain' in C. Casey (ed.), *The eighteenth-century Dublin town house* (Dublin, 2010), p. 265. By the 1690s, exclusive, purpose-built tenements serving the professional classes and members of the aristocracy were a common feature of Edinburgh's 'dense urban fabric'. C.G. Desmarest, 'Living horizontally: the origin of the tenement in Paris and Edinburgh' in L. Humm, J. Lowrey & A. MacKechnie (eds), *The architecture of Scotland, 1660–1750* (Edinburgh, 2020), p. 480.   84 NLI, Gardiner papers, MS 36,537/1–4. In one instance, on a lease of three adjoining lots of ground forming one side of what would later be known as Gloucester Diamond (a key compositional inflection within the wider design matrix), details of the area width and parapet height have been scratched out; in another, for four lots, these details have been left blank.   85 McCullough, *Dublin*, p. 114.

> TO BE LET,
>
> No. 1. in HARCOURT-STREET,
>
> A SINGLE ROOMED HOUSE, four Stories high, very suitable for a single Lady or Gentleman, or small Family that would not require much Room. As to Air and Situation it is only requisite to view it to pronounce it the First in that desirable Neighbourhood. Apply to Michael Stapleton, No. 80, Marlborough-street.

9.8 Advertisement for 1 Harcourt Street, Dublin, in *Saunders's News-Letter*, 27 April 1789.

figure – with varying degrees of success in articulating the gable wall – elsewhere, corner sites were manipulated to create 'single room' houses which catered to different needs and requirements. In April 1789, the plasterer and house builder Michael Stapleton advertised 1 Harcourt Street as 'a single roomed house, four stories high, very suitable for a single Lady or Gentleman, or small family that would not require much room' (fig. 9.8).[86] Though long since demolished, historic photographs show a one-room deep house at the junction with Cuffe Street.[87]

Prominent examples of this type include the present 11 Fitzwilliam Street Lower and 1 Fitzwilliam Street Upper, situated at the junction with Baggot Street Lower and built after 1791 by William Hendy and David Courtney respectively (fig. 9.9).[88] At 1 Fitzwilliam Street Upper, the stair is situated in a return at the rear, dispensing with the need for windows in the retaining gable wall to Baggot Street (and evidently with no stipulation to render it as a blind elevation); in contrast, at 11 Fitzwilliam Street Lower the staircase compartment takes up fully half of the building's interior volume and is illuminated by windows on the gable end (which in turn form part of an integrated composition with the adjoining 42 Baggot Street Lower).[89] While this discordance between spatial distribution and façade design has been characterized as 'a wafer thin urbanity, an agreed untruth', the single-room house represented an attractive proposition for those desirous of a smaller property in a modish, centralized

---

86 *Saunders's News-Letter*, 27 Apr. 1789. 87 RD, 421/486/275246. Though no boundary details are provided in the memorial, this may be the property leased by Stapleton to George Gray, Esq., on 30 April 1790, described as a dwelling house with a street frontage of 19' 6 and a plot depth, front to rere, of a mere 12' 6. 88 Leases dated 10 and 11 June 1791 recite the grant of these corner sites to David Courtney, esq. and to William Hendy, builder (RD, 436/495/282951, 441/139/284010). Houses on Baggot Street and Fitzwilliam Street Lower were certainly built by 1804, when they formed part of the stock of the partnership between Hendy, John Gibson and John Donnellan (RD, 561/394/377748). The corner site of Baggot Street and Fitzwilliam Street Upper was evidently fully built by 1802, when the ground 'exactly opposite the houses lately built by David Courtney, Esq.' was advertised for sale. *Saunders's News-Letter*, 13 Apr. 1802. 89 This spatial arrangement presents its own aesthetic problems: as the staircase rises through the narrow compartment it cuts across the windows and is visible from the street. A similar issue is encountered at 1 Mount Street Upper, another 'single room' house.

9.9 1 Fitzwilliam Street Upper (*left*) and 11 Fitzwilliam Street Lower.
Photographs by the author.

location.[90] This was certainly the appeal of the present 53 Fitzwilliam Square (formerly 1 Fitzwilliam Square North), advertised as an 'excellent' and 'fashionable' single (or 'single-roomed') house throughout the 1810s.[91] Elsewhere, clever estate agents turned a potential disadvantage (reduced accommodation and likely no coach house or stables) into a selling point: in 1806, a 'neat single house' in Dorset Street Upper was 'perfectly safe, having no rear or back passages'.[92]

This single house typology in turn evolved during the course of the early nineteenth century to attract a broader range of middling sorts. The first houses on Mountpleasant Square (on its South side), built between 1808 and 1811, and those forming Royal Canal Terrace, dated 1825–30, represent such an astute balance between economics and aesthetics: composed of two storeys over basement with a centrally placed stair hall flanked by single (dual aspect) rooms, they are modestly scaled yet in their formal orientation to the street preserve a grandeur of aspect (fig. 9.10). This was likely part of their appeal for the professional classes.[93] Early

90 McCullough, *Dublin*, p. 115. **91** *Saunders's News-letter*, 21 July 1814; 5 Apr. 1815; 8 Apr. 1820.
92 *Saunders's News-letter*, 11 Dec. 1806. The property was further recommended by being 'within one door of Gardiner-street' and 'scarcely 100 yards from Mountjoy-square and the Circular-road'.
93 Other two-storey houses in this square are more typical in their spatial organization, described as 'miniature versions of the city houses with two principal rooms on each floor, one to the front and one

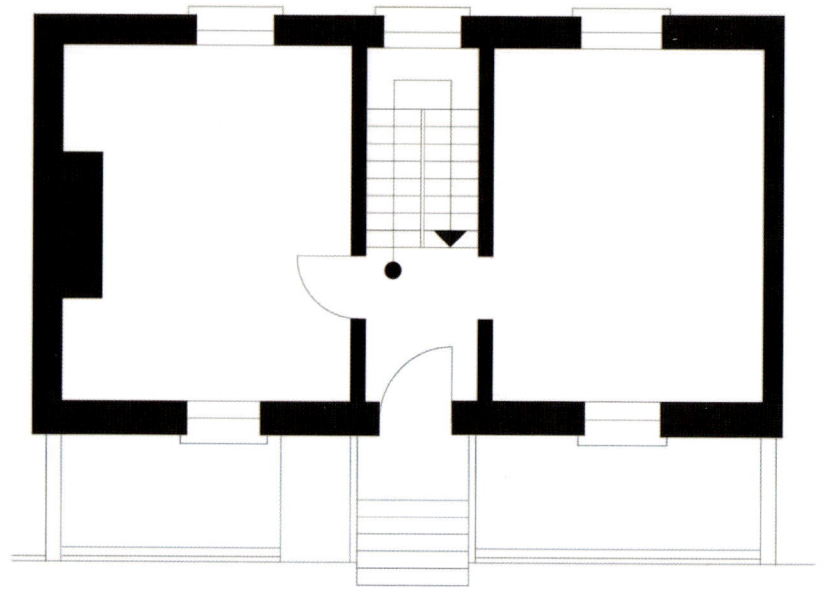

9.10 View of first houses built in Mountpleasant Square, Dublin, *c*.1808–10 with typical ground-floor plan. Photograph by the author. Drawing by Marcus Lynam.

advertisements for Mountpleasant Square note that being 'within 15 to 25 minutes walk of the Castle, Custom-house, Courts of law, all the Banks and Public offices', these 'neat' and 'commodious' houses would 'answer a gentleman in a public office'.[94]

CONCLUSION

In her overview of the relationship between gender and home in the long eighteenth century, Ruth Larsen concludes that 'Masculine identity and the home were closely entwined in this period, although it remains unclear whether the home made men or men made the home; it was probably both.'[95] Focusing on the single male household, this essay represents a preliminary attempt to broaden our understanding of the range of domestic accommodation available in Georgian Dublin, and of the everyday practices and routines that unfolded therein. While the most successful among the professional, merchant and artisan classes rubbed shoulders with their social betters, not least the builders and contractors who raised (and in some cases occupied) houses on exclusive private estates, the intersection between social class, marital status and architectural typology remains largely unexplored.[96] One size did not fit all. The number and type of apartments available to let throughout the eighteenth century, as demonstrated here, coupled with the building of brick houses at different scales and densities in the early decades of the nineteenth century, indicates a diverse real estate market.[97] The scale of urban housing too, in some instances responding to the long gestation of particular districts and to changing social circumstances and demographics (although laid out in 1752, Merrion Square was not fully built until 1818), is suggestive of more complex patterns of ownership and occupancy. With the notion of the city as 'thousands of rooms piled high on one another' foremost in our minds, we might better appreciate how different households and domestic economies were catered for within a flexible and era-defining urban typology.[98]

---

to the rear'. S. Roundtree, 'Mountpleasant Square' in M. Clark & A. Smeaton (eds), *The Georgian squares of Dublin: an architectural history* (Dublin, 2006), p. 135. **94** *Hibernian Journal*, 15 Mar. 1805; *Saunders's News-Letter*, 12 July 1806; *Saunders's News-Letter*, 9 Oct. 1809. **95** R. Larsen, 'Gender and home' in C. Edwards (ed.), *A cultural history of the home in the age of Enlightenment* (New York, 2022), p. 143. **96** For example, plasterer and master-builder Charles Thorp built and variously occupied houses in Hume Street, North Great George's Street, Gardiner Place and Mountjoy Square. C. Lucey, 'The scale of plasterwork production in the metropolitan centres of Britain and Ireland', in C. Casey & C. Lucey (eds), *Decorative plasterwork in Ireland and Europe: ornament and the early modern interior* (Dublin, 2012), p. 214. Architects, too, lived in speculatively-built terraced houses: George Dance the Younger lived at 91 Gower Street, London, from 1790 until his death in 1825; Francis Johnston lived at 64 Eccles Street, Dublin from 1794, one of four houses built by his brother Richard. **97** E. McAulay, 'The origins and development of the Pembroke Estate beyond the Grand Canal, 1816–1880' (PhD, TCD, 2003). **98** N. McCullough, 'The Dublin house' in Casey (ed.), *The eighteenth-century Dublin town house*, p. 14.

Index

Adam, Robert 53, 157
Allen, William 189n33
Ardfert Abbey (Co. Kerry) 108, 157
Ashford, William 147
Austen, Jane 20
Aylmer, Sir Andrew 166
Aylmer, Lady Caroline Maria 166–7
Aylmer, Lady Elizabeth (née Cole) 166–84
Aylmer, Lady Ellen (née Butler) 166–7
Aylmer, Sir FitzGerald 166

Bachelard, Gaston 22, 169–71, 175
Baggot Street (Dublin) 202
Ballyfin (Co. Laois) 49
Barnard, Bishop Thomas 108
Barre, W.J. 91
Barry, Robert 129
Belvedere (Co. Westmeath) 53, 54–5
Berkeley Square (London) 150
Bingham, Denis 198–9, 201n82
Boscawen, Frances 48
Boulter, Archbishop Hugh 100n48
Bowen, Elizabeth 26
Bowles, Carington 189, 190
Bride Street (Dublin) 194
Brown, John 104n3
Burgh Quay (Dublin) 192
Burgh, Thomas 102
Burke, J.B. 166
Burke, William 197–8
Burney, Fanny 150
Bury, Lady Beaujolois 152, 163
Bury, Catherine Maria, *see* Charleville, Lady Catherine Maria
Bury, Charles William, *see* Charleville, Lord Charles William

Caldwell, Arthur 174n35
Caldwell, Lady Elizabeth (née Hort) 166–84
Caldwell, Fenton 174n35
Caldwell, Sir James 55–6, 116, 178, 181, 182
Caldwell, John 174n35

Caldwell, Margaret 174n35
Cantillion, Henrietta (Lady Farnham) 33
Carrick-on-Suir (Co. Tipperary) 116
Carter, Mary 82
Carter, Thomas 82
Carton House (Co. Kildare) 31–2, 33, 49, 53, 142
Castle Blayney (Co. Monaghan) 61
Castle Caldwell (Co. Fermanagh) 55–6, 166–84
Castle Coole (Co. Fermanagh) 60, 149
Castle Street (Dublin) 196
Castletown (Co. Kildare) 49–50, 54, 149, 150, 153, 161
Cavendish Row (Dublin) 55, 94, 196
Charleville Castle (Co. Offaly) 27, 145–65
Charleville, Lady Catherine Maria (née Tisdall) 147, 152–3, 154–5, 163–5
Charleville, Lord Charles William 145–6, 154–5
Chesshire, Edward 94n25
Chichester, Anna May (Lady Donegall) 46, 47
Church Lane (Drogheda) 90, 91, 96, 97, 100
Clayton's house (St. Stephen's Green, Dublin) 74
Clements, Nathaniel 52, 53, 69, 72, 75–6, 83
Cobbe, Thomas 55, 114
Cockburn, George 110–12n47, 120
Coffey, John 105
Coghill, Marmaduke 100–1n50
Connery, James 130, 133, 134
Conolly, Louisa (née Lennox) 31–2, 44, 49–50, 149, 150, 153, 161
Conolly, Thomas 54, 149
Coote Street (later Kildare Street, Dublin) 31
Cope Street (Dublin) 190
Cosby, Pole 55
Courtney, David 202n88
Cox, Maria 198, 199, 201n82
Cox, Richard 198, 199, 201n82

Cramillion, Bartholomew 52, 53
Crofton Croker, Thomas 135
Crossboyne (Co. Mayo) 197
Cuffe Street (Dublin) 202
Culzean Castle (Ayrshire) 157
Cumberland Street (Dublin) 191

Dame Street (Dublin) 194
Darley, George 179–80n63
Darley, Hill 179–180n63
Darley, John 180n63, 181
Day, Judge Robert 159
Delamain, Henry 105
Delany, Mary Pendarves (née Granville) 48, 49, 74, 75, 80, 81–2, 116
Denny, Lady Arbella (née Fitzmaurice) 166–7, 169–78
Dixon, Samuel 175
D'Olier Street (Dublin) 192, 196
Dominick Street (Dublin) 194, 197
Donadea Castle (Co. Kildare) 166–73
Doneraile House (Dublin) 74
Doran, John 155–6
Dorset Street (Dublin) 194, 203
Drennan, Sarah 32, 39, 44–6, 48
Drennan, William 31, 32, 34–5, 38–39, 44, 190–2
Drogheda (Co. Louth) 21, 85–103
Dromoland (Co. Clare) 55
Duke Street (Drogheda) 97n34

Edgeworth, Charlotte 136–9
Edgeworth, Frances 139–40
Edgeworth, Jane 32, 33, 34, 40–1, 46, 48
Edgeworth, Maria 108, 125, 136–7, 139–40, 144
Edgeworth, Richard 31, 32, 33, 40–1, 55, 58–9
Edgeworth, Richard Lovell 119, 195
Edgeworthstown (Co. Longford) 32, 136–7
Elphin (Co. Roscommon) 118
Emo Court (Co. Laois) 49
Evans, Anne 98n41
Evans, Charles William 98n41
Evans, George William 98n41

Fagan, Bryan 16n10–17
Fair Street (Drogheda) 89, 90n13–96, 98–9
Ferry, Leopold 197
Fisher, James Joseph 39

Fisher, Lydia (née Leadbeater) 39
FitzGerald, Emily (née Lennox) 31–35, 40–4, 48, 150, 161
FitzGerald, Henry 41, 44
FitzGerald, James (20th earl of Kildare) 31, 48, 161
FitzGerald, William Robert 55
FitzGibbon, John 104, 114, 119
Fitzwilliam Square (Dublin) 203
Fitzwilliam Street Lower (Dublin) 202–4
Fitzwilliam Street Upper (Dublin) 202–4
Fitzwilliam, William 15–17, 40
Fitzwilliam, Richard (6th Viscount) 15–17, 40
Floyd, Anson 119
Forde, James 96n28
Fota (Co. Cork) 120
Fox, Caroline (née Lennox) 31–2, 33, 41
Fox, Zachariah 198, 199, 201n82
Frederick Street (Dublin) 16
Fyt, Jan 55

Gardiner, Anne (née Stewart) 65–7, 70, 78
Gardiner, Charles 69–70n7, 76, 83
Gardiner, Harriet 77–8
Gardiner, Luke 21, 65–84
Gardiner, Mary 77–8, 83
Gardiner Place (Dublin) 197–9, 200, 205n96
Gardiner, Sackville 69–70n7
Gardiner Street (Dublin) 194, 196
Geale, Daniel 187
Gérard, Marguerite 41
Gernon, Luke 125–6
Gloucester Place (Dublin) 201
Goffman, Erving 24n54, 31, 44
Grosvenor Street (Mayfair) 75
Grubb Family (Clonmel, Co. Tipperary) 41–3

Hagley Hall (Worcestershire) 53–4, 149
Hall, Reverend James 129, 130
Hamilton, Hugh Douglas 127, 128
Harcourt Street (Dublin) 53, 202
Haverty, J.P. 140
Haydon, Benjamin Robert 186
Headfort House (Co. Meath) 51, 53, 57, 63
Hearn, Christopher 182
Hendy, William 202n88
Henrietta Street (Dublin) 65–84, 195–6
Herbert, Dorothea 116

Horner, George 100–1n50
Hort, Dr Josiah 175–7
Howard, Ralph 195
Hume Street (Dublin) 205n96
Hutton, Mrs Mary 39

Ingoldsby, Henry 109–10n38

Jackson, Charles (bishop of Ferns and Leighlin) 16n10–17
Jefferson, Thomas 61–62
Jocelyn, Robert (1st Viscount) 54–5
Johnston, Francis 145, 148, 150, 205n96
Johnston, Richard 205n96

Kenmare, Lady Anne 110
Kenmare, Lord Thomas 110
Kilcorly (Co. Limerick) 32, 33
Kildare House (Leinster House) 31, 33–4
Kildare Street (Dublin) 33, 195
Killeen Castle (Co. Meath) 50

Lacy, Murtagh 16n10–17
Lafranchini, Paolo and Filippo 53
Leadbeater, Mary 39, 125, 126, 133–6
Leeson, Joseph 57
Leggett, Thomas 146–7
Leigh, Lord Edward 185
Leinster House (formerly Kildare House) 31, 33–4
Lennox, Sarah 41
Lissadell (Co. Sligo) 49
Loftus, Lord Adam 59, 60
Longleat (Wiltshire) 81–2
Lowry, Strickland 176, 177
Lowther Castle (Westmoreland) 157
Lying-in Hospital (later known as the Rotunda) 33
Lyttleton, Lord George 53–4

Maclise, Daniel 135
McMahon, Daniel 38–9
McTier, Martha 32, 34, 35, 44, 46, 191–2
Magdalen Chapel (Leeson Street) 178n53
Maistre, Xavier de 20
Manent, John 197–8
Marlborough Street (Dublin) 32, 34, 187, 192, 197
Marsh, Archbishop Narcissus 100–1n48
Marshall, Anthony 94n24
Marshall, John 94n23
Marshall, Rebecca (née Vanhomrigh) 94n24
Mary Street (Dublin) 33
Mass Lane (Drogheda) 97
Merrion Square (Dublin) 94, 201–2, 205
Merrion Street Upper (Dublin) 16–17
Miller, Sanderson 53–54, 149
M'Kenzie, Andrew 128, 142, 143
Molesworth, Bysshe 195
Molesworth Street (Dublin) 96n27, 196
Monck, Charles 16n10
Moore, Charles 145–6
Moore, Margaret 195
Morgan, Richard 100n48
Morris, Robert 78
Mosse, Bartholomew 159
Mountjoy Square (Dublin) 194, 196, 205n96
Mountpleasant Square (Dublin) 203–4
Mullins, George 24

Napier, Lady Sarah 161
Nash, John 50, 145
Nassau Street (Dublin) 195
Newbridge House (Co. Dublin) 55, 114
North Frederick Street (Dublin) 194
North Great George's Street (Dublin) 26–7, 194, 205n96
North Quay (Drogheda) 103

O'Brien, Edward 55–6
Ogborne, William 101
Old Leighlin (Co. Carlow) 105
Otway, Caesar 133

Parnell Square (Dublin) 55, 94, 199
Parsonstown (Co. Offaly) 157
Peacock, Catherine 32, 34, 36–8, 46, 48
Peacock, Nicholas 31, 32, 33, 34, 36–9, 46, 107
Peacock, Pryce 39
Pearce, Sir Edward Lovett 24–5, 68–9
Peel, Robert 147–8
Perec, George 18–19, 171, 182
Peter's Street (Drogheda) 103
Philips, Ambrose 100
Phillips, Robert 81
Phoenix Lodge (now Áras an Uachtaráin) 52, 53
Pilkington, Laetitia 60
Pococke, Richard 144

Ponsonby, Brabazon 196
Ponsonby, Margaret 185
Powerscourt House (Dublin) 75n36, 109
Primatt, Stephen 97n35
Pyne, Benjamin 58

Quilca (Co. Cavan) 51

Rathfarnham Castle (Co. Dublin) 59, 60
Ravell, Joseph 91, 101
Rencher, John 100n48, 102
Repton, Humphrey 148, 149
Ricciardelli, Gabriele 86, 88
Richmond, Charles Lennox (4th Duke) 157–65
Robinson, Sir William 101
Roche, William 160n53
Rockingham (Co. Roscommon) 49, 50
Rouen (France) 112–13
Royal Canal Terrace (Dublin) 203
Royal Hospital (Kilmainham) 101
Rudd, Benjamin 195
Russborough (Co. Wicklow) 57

St James's (London) 15
St Laurence Street (Drogheda) 90, 91, 93, 94, 98, 103
St Peter's Place (Drogheda) 100
St Stephen's Green (Dublin) 195
Sandys, Francis 166, 171, 172–3
Shackleton, Elizabeth (née Carleton) 39
Sheehan, David 74
Sheridan, Richard Brinsley 51
Sheridan, Thomas 51
Singleton, Henry 101
Skinner, Andrew 91–2
Smellie, William 38
Smirke, Robert 157
Smithfield (Dublin) 97
Soane, Sir John 25n56–7
South Great George's Street (Dublin) 194
Stanihurst, Richard 51

Stapleton, Michael 53, 202
Sterne, John 100–1n50
Stradbally (Co. Laois) 55
Suffolk Street (Dublin) 15–17
Sullivan, Daniel 114
Summerson, Sir John 90, 188n19
Swift, Jonathan 59–60, 107
Synge, Edward, bishop of Elphin 112, 114, 118, 119

Taylor, Joseph 91–2
Taylor, Mary Spilsbury 134
Taylor, Theo 43
Taylor, Thomas 57, 63
Thorp, Charles 205n96
Tisdall, Catherine Maria, *see* Charleville, Lady Catherine Maria
Tisdall, Louisa 163
Tomes, Henry 100
Turner, J.W.M. 152–3

Wakefield, Edward 128–30
Walker, Abraham 195
Ware, Isaac 78, 81, 82, 180, 196–7, 201
Ware, James 186
Wellington Quay (Dublin) 119
West Street (Drogheda) 91, 103
Westport House (Co. Sligo) 53
White, Dr Charles 35
Whitworth Hall (Drogheda) 91
William Street (Dublin) 109
Wills, Joseph 135–6
Wills, Michael 101, 102
Wilson, Fanny 139
Wingfield, Edward 75n36, 109, 120
Wyatt, James 53, 60, 145, 148, 154, 155
Wyse, Francis 24
Wyse, John 24
Wyse, Mary Anne 24

York Street (Dublin) 194
Young, Arthur 130, 131, 133